RADICAL REPUBLICANS IN THE NORTH

RADICAL REPUBLICANS IN THE NORTH

STATE POLITICS DURING RECONSTRUCTION

edited by

JAMES C. MOHR

The Johns Hopkins University Press
Baltimore and London

Manufactured in the United States of America

The Johns Hopkins University Press, Baltimore, Maryland 21218
The Johns Hopkins University Press Ltd., London

Library of Congress Catalog Card Number 75-36939

ISBN 0-8018-1774-9

Library of Congress Cataloging in Publication data
will be found on the last printed page of this book.

CONTENTS

v

CONTENTS

CONTRIBUTORS

Richard H. Abbott
is professor of American history at Eastern Michigan
University. He is the author of *Cobbler in Congress:
the Life of Henry Wilson, 1812-1875* (Lexington, Kentucky,
1972) and "Massachusetts and the Negro enlistment law
of July, 1864," *Civil War History* (1968).

George M. Blackburn
is professor of American history and associate dean
of arts and sciences at Central Michigan University.
He is co-author of "A Demographic History of the West:
Manistee County, Michigan, 1860," *Journal of American
History* (1970) and author of "Radical Republican
Motivation. A Case Study,' *Journal of Negro History*
(1969), which deals with Michigan.

Felice A. Bonadio
is associate professor of American history at the University
of California, Santa Barbara. He is the author of
North of Reconstruction, Ohio Politics, 1865-1870 (1970).

Richard N. Current
is distinguished professor of American history at the
University of North Carolina, Greensboro. To his long
list of well-known publications Professor Current will
shortly be adding a volume on the Civil War and
reconstruction era in Wisconsin.

CONTRIBUTORS

Robert R. Dykstra
is professor of American history at the University
of Iowa. Author of *The Cattle Towns* (New York, 1968),
he is currently preparing a book on the black suffrage issue in Iowa
politics during the Civil War era.

James C. Mohr
is associate professor of American history and chairman of
the department at the University of Maryland Baltimore County.
His publications include *The Radical Republicans and
Reform in New York during Reconstruction* (Ithaca, N.Y., 1973).

David Montgomery
is professor of American history and chairman of the
department at the University of Pittsburgh. His publications
include *Beyond Equality: Labor and the Radical Republicans 1862-1872*
(New York, 1967).

John Niven
is professor of American history at the Claremont Graduate
School. He is the author of *Connecticut for the Union* (New
Haven, 1965) and *Gideon Welles: Lincoln's Secretary
of the Navy* (New York, 1973).

Philip D. Swenson
is assistant professor of American history at the
University of Massachusetts, Amherst. In his dissertation
he explored "The Midwest and the Abandonment of Radical
Reconstruction, 1864-1877."

ACKNOWLEDGMENTS

Many obligations are incurred in the long process of seeing a project like this one through to completion. The greatest of those debts, of course, is owed to the contributors themselves, the scholars whose efforts during the last two years have produced the analyses contained in this book. Those historians have already been introduced formally in the preceding pages. During the formative stages of this project I received very helpful advice from Richard O. Curry, David H. Donald, Hugh D. Graham, and J. G. Goellner. Since that time a large number of other individuals interested in the project have kindly offered their assistance and their encouragement; I would like to express my appreciation to them all. Michael F. Holt was a most helpful reader of my own contribution. For patient secretarial help I wish to thank Mary Dietrich. Finally, my acknowledgments could never be complete without mention of my wife, Elizabeth, and my two children, Timothy and Stephanie, all of whom not only put up with the drain of time and energy involved in projects like this, but willingly give me their active support.

Baltimore, Maryland   James C. Mohr
January 1975

INTRODUCTION

During the past three decades historians of the reconstruction period have produced one of the most exciting and remarkable bursts of research and reassessment in the entire record of American historiography. As a consequence of that sustained inquiry we now know a great deal about how the Republican Party in Washington hammered out the nation's reconstruction policies and a great deal about what happened to those policies when their implementation was attempted in the states of the former Confederacy. Much is now known about groups whose fate during the reconstruction era was largely ignored thirty years ago, groups like the freedmen of the South and the workingmen of the North. We have inciteful new biographies of key national figuroo, a oubotantial amount of previously undiscovered evidence, and fresh methodological approaches to many of the perennial problems of reconstruction history. Moreover, we have a much clearer idea of what Radical Republicanism actually was and was not at the national level and in the South than we had thirty years ago.

At least one major area of considerable importance to an understanding of the reconstruction era as a whole, however, has to this point remained relatively underexplored: the question of what was going on at the state level in the North. At a time when Republican Congressmen were debating the possibilities of altering significantly the politcal, social, and economic institutions of the South, what were their political associates back in Des Moines and Springfield, Harrisburg and Hartford, trying to accomplish? What kinds of policies did all of those Republicans sitting in Northern state legislatures fight to enact for themselves and for their neighbors? How successful were they in implementing their policies? In those Northern states where Republicans fell from power during the reconstruction era, when and why did they fall? What was the effect of such shifts of power upon the internal dynamics of the parties involved? Where Republicans managed to maintain control at the state level, what tactics proved most successful? What sorts of policy adjustments became necessary, and how did those adjustments affect the basic nature of the parties specifically and the political system generally?

The essays that follow address these and related questions in an attempt to clarify further our rapidly sharpening image of the reconstruction era. Their basic subject is the history of Radical Republicanism in the North. In an effort to make the volume manageable in size, nine of the twenty Northern states in the Union at the time of Lee's surrender have been singled out for analysis. While no sample adequately represents the whole, and while other scholars might have selected other states, the nine chosen here do have much to recommend them as a representative and significant group. They include two politically different New England states: Massachusetts, the most powerful and influential of the New England bloc and one in which the Republicans seemed invincible, and Connecticut, where spring elections and a strong Democratic Party insured national attention. The four central giants, New York, Pennsylvania, Ohio, and Illinois, are all included. These four states by themselves contained nearly 60 percent of the North's total population and accounted for over half the North's total value of both manufactured goods and agricultural products. And it was in these four crucial states that some of the most dramatic and far-reaching changes in the nature of the Republican Party took place during the late 1860s. Finally, three of the rapidly developing north-central plains states, Michigan, Wisconsin, and Iowa, are also treated in this volume. The sample includes eight of the nine most populous states in 1870, eight of the nine leaders in the value of agricultural production, and seven of the eight Northern leaders in the value of manufactures. Also important to the basic purposes of this project is the fact that each of the nine states selected was controlled at the state level by the reigning Republican Party as the nation began the reconstruction process.

There are several advantages to the state-by-state approach adopted in this volume. First, though much has been made of the alleged centralizing effects of the Civil War, political parties remained during the 1860s and 1870s quite distinctly federated and were themselves run on a state-by-state basis. Indeed, some scholars have argued forcefully that the very concept of a national party is misleading prior to the late nineteenth century, since the machinery necessary for centralized coordination was largely lacking before then. This makes a close examination of policy-making and party reaction at the Northern state level very important during the early postwar years, for it was there that the essential character of parties was formed.

Second, politicians at the state level during the reconstruction era found themselves at the fulcrum of many of the most significant cross pressures of the postwar period. When Andrew Johnson broke with the Congressional

INTRODUCTION

Republicans and tried to form a new political party on the eve of the 1866 elections, individual chieftains at the state level had to decide where to cast their lots. When a party policy was set at the national level, politicians at the state level were the ones who had to make it stick among the Northern people. If the electoral base of a party seemed to be shifting, or if the mood of the rank and file became uneasy, politicians at the state level had to find some method of reconciling the new circumstances to the traditional party lines. When one section of a state clamored for wide open economic incentives and another section favored moves toward corporate control, men at the state capital had to strike some sort of balance. Politicians at the state level, in other words, were power brokers in a very tough position, trying desperately to maintain a number of inherently tenuous reciprocal relationships. The way in which they tried to manage the job on a state-by-state basis reveals a good deal about many of the most significant forces shaping the political fate of reconstruction America and a good deal about the ways in which those forces affected one another.

Third, during the 1860s and 1870s the federal government intervened in the daily lives of American citizens almost not at all. Decisions on a host of crucial issues continued to be made at the state level, rather than at the national level. Politicians in the separate state capitals still decided for themselves what to do about public education, sanitation, safety and public health, the status of public welfare agencies, appropriate standards of public behavior, including the right to drink alcohol, land development, urban growth, economic stimulation, corporate regulation, the length of a working day, and the operational definition of individual civil rights. The political decisions reached on these issues had a lasting impact upon American life after the Civil War, and they can only be explored in detail at the state level where they were made.

Despite the considerable advantages of a state-by-state approach, and there are obviously others in addition to the three just specified, at least one serious disadvantage must also be recognized: the difficulty of keeping broad, generalized, cross-state themes, trends, and political patterns sharply in focus. This is especially the case in a volume like the one at hand, since each author has developed a self-contained essay that stresses the specific themes, trends, and political patterns most prominent in his particular state, with only limited reference to the experience of other states or to the North as a whole. Consequently, it seems appropriate in this introduction to identify explicitly in advance some of the more important themes, trends, and political patterns that run like leitmotifs through the essays as a group in order that readers might be alerted to them from the outset.

The first and one of the most prominent of the larger themes of this volume as a whole is the substantial impact of the issue of race in the Northern states during the reconstruction era. That issue, which emerges as the most difficult one for the Radicals to deal with, generally comes to a head over the suffrage rights of blacks in the separate states. The first case, that of Massachusetts, provides something of a control on this key question, because Massachusetts is the only state of the nine examined here where blacks could already vote without restriction in 1865 and where, as a result, the issue did not have to be faced head-on. The last case, that of Iowa, involves the only Northern state where Republicans were able to persuade a majority of the voters to endorse black suffrage in an unambiguous popular referendum; Robert Dykstra's inciteful essay explores the reasons why. Between these two unique instances unfold seven other fascinating case studies of how postwar Northerners struggled with the issue of race, one of the touchstones of this period of American history, and how those struggles affected political development within the various states.

A second and perhaps equally prominent general theme running through the essays that follow involves the Republicans' attempt to deal with the widespread factionalism which beset their party during the reconstruction era. In state after state internal divisiveness becomes a major factor in Republican policy-making. Some authors trace this remarkable lack of cohesion back to the prewar origins of the party, some to the rise of new leaders after the war, some to ideological cleavages, some to the nature of the issues, and some to the fact that different Republicans within the same state were trying to represent quite disparate sets of interests. In almost every one of the nine cases, however, the ultimate resolution of these internal dissensions produces a significant alteration in the nature of Republicanism itself between 1865 and the middle of the 1870s. Taken together these separate changes comprise one of the significant political transitions in American history; it is a process well worth following in detail.

Governmental activism at the state level provides a third prominent theme to bear in mind when reading the nine essays that follow. Northern Republicans enact during the reconstruction era a large number of educational, economic, charitable, labor-oriented, and health-related laws in the state legislatures they control. This wave of activity seems to move from east to west, affecting Massachusetts even during the war, affecting New York, Pennsylvania, and Illinois all dramatically in the immediate postwar years, and then the north-central plains states somewhat more slowly, diffusely, and unevenly. The emphasis varies from state to state, but the authors of these essays associate this wave of activism and legislation with Radical ideology, with Republican political needs at the state level, and with the developmental imperatives of the states themselves. Where the Republican grasp on power is weak from the outset, as in Connecticut, and where Republicans are too divided internally to cooperate on anything, as in Ohio, little is accomplished. When Radicals fall from power in New York, Pennsylvania, and Illinois, the burst of activity at their state capitals ceases abruptly.

INTRODUCTION

A fourth recurrent pattern in the essays that follow is the emergence, or as some would argue the reemergence, of what are usually labeled ethno-cultural political patterns. As the reconstruction era begins, American political life seems to be dominated by the great questions that arose from the war and its settlement. Republican combinations put together on the basis of those issues hold power in the states examined here. But when race politics, factional dissension, disillusionment with corruption, cross pressures from the local level, and a rebounding Democratic opposition all combine in the North to weaken that power, indeed to overcome it at various points, there seems to occur, following in some cases something of an interregnum, a general retrenchment behind ethno-cultural barricades. Overt nativism reappears across the North from Massachusetts to Wisconsin, and temperance becomes a prime issue at the Northern state level by the late 1860s. Individual authors suggest important variations and exceptions to this basic pattern, but it recurs frequently enough to constitute another of the important trends that readers may wish to trace through the separate essays in this volume.

The relationship between post Civil War politics, especially Radical Republican politics, and economic interests, especially corporate interests, has puzzled and fascinated historians of the reconstruction era for more than three-quarters of a century. Hence it is not surprising that this relationship forms the basis of another of the major themes addressed in most of the analyses that follow. In the East, especially in Massachusetts, Connecticut, and Pennsylvania, economic pressures come to a head over the rise of organized labor, and in those states the Republican Party appears to shift discernibly away from the relatively open and flexible economic policies it espouses immediately after the war toward a more distinctly antilabor and procorporate stance by 1870. Further west, where economic pressures come to a head over land development and railroad regulation, the party's response is much more ambiguous. In states like Illinois, Michigan, Iowa, and Wisconsin intrastate divisions, ideological cleavages, and big business Democrats prevent the emergence of clear-cut partisan positions on many of the important economic issues of the period.

In addition to the five prominent themes already identified, a few less obvious leitmotifs also appear and reappear in several of the essays contained in this volume. The crucial role of courts at the state level, for example, a much understudied subject, merits attention. State courts take Republicans off the hook on black suffrage in Wisconsin, on women and child labor questions in Massachusetts, on state aid to railroads in Michigan, and on the eight-hour day issue in several states. The very considerable impact of governmental corruption and political venality at the state level during the reconstruction era is addressed directly in at least four of the studies and indirectly in others. Scholars interested in the Liberal Republican movement will also find a great deal to interest them in this volume; all of the essays illuminate the political preconditions of Liberalism, and several of the authors address that phenomenon specifically. Finally, notwithstanding the fact that the overall focus of this volume is on the Republican Party as the chief policy-making political organization of the period, the essays shed bright light on the Democrats as well. Though the Democracy is discussed most extensively in the analyses of Connecticut, New York, and Ohio, three states where that party returned to power before 1870, each of these nine studies contains information about political developments among Democrats at the Northern state level during the reconstruction era.

With a single exception, all of the essays that follow were written specifically for this volume and have appeared nowhere else. The exception is David Montgomery's pioneering piece on the era of Radical Republican control in Pennsylvania, which was originally published in 1961 by the *Pennsylvania Magazine of History and Biography*. Montgomery's essay is reprinted here with the permission of the author and of that journal.

RADICAL
REPUBLICANS
IN THE NORTH

1

MASSACHUSETTS

Maintaining Hegemony

Richard H. Abbott

In the 1850s the state of Massachusetts plunged into political chaos as her two national parties, the Whigs and Democrats, began to disintegrate. Antislavery advocates organized a short-lived Free-Soil Party, which in coalition with the Democrats controlled the state during the first years of the decade. Then the coalition gave way, and Massachusetts fell under the momentary sway of the American or Know-Nothing Party. By 1857, however, this nativist organization had also collapsed, and political hegemony in Massachusetts passed to the fledgling Republican Party. By then the Whigs had disappeared, and the Democrats proved unable to muster the leadership and support to mount an effective challenge to the Republicans, who overwhelmingly dominated state elections for the remainder of the century.[1]

The Republican Party that emerged in the 1850s to assume control of the state during the tumultuous years of civil war and reconstruction was a product of both local and national issues and tensions. Its primary focus was opposition to slavery and to Southern political power in the nation. It sought to advance Northern interests, which Republicans identified with the welfare of the independent entrepreneur: the yeoman farmer, the small businessman, and the independent craftsman. Only Northern society, with its emphasis upon the dignity of free labor, availability of public education, and access to cheap land in the West, could provide the opportunity necessary for the individual to achieve economic independence. Republicans warned that this Northern free-labor civilization was engaged in a life-and-death struggle with a Southern civilization based upon slave labor, aristocratic institutions, and a stagnating economy. The whole future of the nation thus hung in the balance.

1. Notes to this chapter are to be found on pp. 22-25.

1

Such a Republican philosophy, which emphasized the importance of maintaining the individual's opportunity to achieve ownership of capital and share equitably in the distribution of wealth, was not designed with the interests of large corporations or permanent working classes in mind. The kind of society envisioned by the Republicans was classless, where the greatest good for the greatest number could be obtained by maintaining open channels for individual advancement. Hence, in Massachusetts the Republicans drew their strongest support from rural areas and small towns, where the ideal of a virtuous, stable, and homogeneous commonwealth, peopled by educated, religious, hard-working farmers, artisans, and small businessmen, still had validity. The Republican ideology had less meaning for city dwellers, and particularly immigrants, who confronted a world of impersonal corporations, factory conditions, poverty, and limited social mobility.[2]

In urban areas Republicans tended to gain the support of native workers, and ultimately of their employers, for many ex-Whig textile magnates and railroad developers found that the Republicans had inherited Whiggish ideas about using the government to promote economic growth, particularly in the form of grants and loans to railroads. But the Whig-Republican philosophy of governmental intervention also embraced the use of state power to attack moral evils, advance the social development of the Commonwealth, and maintain the public welfare. The state of Massachusetts was well known before the Civil War for its system of public education and its institutions of public charity. Reformers eager to extend this tradition of social amelioration flocked to the Republican banner. Prohibitionists, women's rights advocates, and labor reformers all hoped to use the new party to further their goals. Republicans also drew heavily from the ranks of the Know-Nothings, and thus their party also reflected the cultural conciousness of native-born Protestant voters, who feared that waves of immigrants would inundate and destroy their homogeneous Commonwealth.[3]

Because of its wide-ranging constituency, the Republican Party had difficulty in maintaining a consistent and clear-cut position on the multitude of local problems confronting Massachusetts in the mid-nineteenth century. Consequently, party leaders strove to keep national questions foremost in the minds of voters.[4] Even on national issues Massachusetts Republicans differed on details, but they generally approached a position defined at the time as radical. They opposed compromise with the South, favored vigorous prosecution of the Civil War, immediate emancipation of slaves, and Congressional control of the Southern states after the war in order to eradicate rebellious sentiment among the ex-Confederates and insure equal rights for former slaves. Many were ardent nationalists, advocates of vigorous federal action in behalf of the above goals. Massachusetts Radical Republicans, particularly Charles Sumner and Henry Wilson in the Senate, and George S. Boutwell and Benjamin Butler in the House, played an important role in shaping Congressional policies during the years of war and reconstruction.

The state of Massachusetts, which had a long history of antagonism to Southern power and to the institution of slavery, gave overwhelming support to the national policies of the Republicans. Bay State voters gave Republican presidential nominees two to one majorities in the six elections from 1856 to 1876, while Republicans won 105 of the 116 Congressional seats contested during those years. Republicans also controlled the 2 Senate seats from Massachusetts. Republican dominance was equally overwhelming on the local level. Massachusetts held annual elections for state officials and the legislature. In 1856 Republicans secured a control of both houses of the General Court, which they never relinquished through the years of civil war and reconstruction. In the 40-seat state senate, Democrats never held more than 5 seats until 1867, and then the number climbed only to 8; never did the Democrats hold more than 15 senate seats, the number they reached in 1874. In 1867 the Democrats gained control of 62 of the 240 seats in the lower house, but did not reach that level again until 1874, when 79 Democrats were elected to that body.

The state Democratic Party, which rarely had been able to challenge the Whigs for control of the state before the Civil War, never recovered from the bitter internal struggle over the slavery issue which had wracked it in the 1850s. The party emerged from the war years tainted with the odor of Copperheadism, and its opposition to Congressional reconstruction policies continued to deprive it of voting support. Irish Catholics furnished the party its chief source of strength, and this only served to further alienate native voters from the party. Democrats also proved unable to find effective leadership on the state level after the war. Many of their ablest men, like Benjamin Butler and George S. Boutwell, had joined the Republican ranks.[5]

The lack of effective political opposition contributed to the inability of the state Republican organization to define its position on local issues. The men who controlled the state party in 1865 were known primarily for their views on national affairs. These men, who had been active in organizing the Republican Party in the 1850s, also organized the informal "Bird Club," named for Francis W. Bird, a wealthy paper manufacturer from East Walpole. Among the original members of the group were abolitionists and philanthropists like Franklin B. Sanborn, George L. Stearns, and Samuel Gridley Howe; James W. Stone, a Boston Free-Soil ward boss and long-time labor reformer; Senators Wilson and Sumner; William S. Robinson, political correspondent of the *Springfield Republican,* and Charles W. Slack, editor of the Boston *Commonwealth.* These men were instrumental in elevating Radical John A. Andrew to the governorship in 1860, and from that point on exerted commanding control in the Republican Party. They helped secure the reelections of Sumner and Wilson to the Senate, controlled the Republican state committee, and held key positions in the state legislature. In 1865, when Andrew relinquished his position after five terms, the Republicans elected governor Alexander H. Bullock, speaker of the Massachusetts house, who was a close associate of many Bird members; upon his retirement after three years the post went to Lieutenant-Governor William Claflin, Bird Club member, and chairman of the Republican state committee, who in turn served for three years. Thus, from 1860 to 1871 the Bird Club controlled the most important offices in command of the state.[6]

The Bird Club members represented the Radical element in the Republican Party. They had pronounced views on the immorality of slavery; several, including Sanborn, Stearns, Howe, and Andrew, had furnished assistance to John Brown, either before or after his raid on Harper's Ferry. The politicians in the group had all built their careers on opposition to slavery and slavery expansion. Bird Club members were ardent advocates of civil and political equality for blacks and supported Congressional Radicals in their reconstruction efforts to secure the rights of freedmen in the South. On the state level, they shared an interest in achieving some of the goals established by pre-Civil War Massachusetts reformers. In 1867 Radical editor Charles Slack noted that "temperance, equal rights, equal suffrage for women and blacks, the rights of working-men, and the rights of children—all branches of one root—are under brisk discussion, and radical ideas on all these points are pushing on in more vigorous and rapid growth than ever before." Frank Sanborn hoped to use the postwar years to "secure fair wages to every laborer, to discourage monopolies, foster education, and promote temperance."[7]

Yet not all Bird Club members supported all of these goals or agreed on how to obtain them. Almost all were temperance advocates, yet they could not agree on how to limit the consumption of alcohol in the state most effectively. They were, for the most part, advocates of women's rights and suffrage, although they disagreed on what priority to assign to those goals. They had no common position on the need to continue state aid to corporations. A few of the Radicals reflected the nativist views that were more commonly held by the rank and file of their party, and were reluctant to combat the discriminations that immigrants faced in Massachusetts. William S. Robinson, James W. Stone, and William Claflin were advocates of a ten-hour day, but other Radicals, like Charles Slack, questioned the existence of deep-seated injustices facing the working classes, and gave little support to labor reform.

The Radicals' approach to social problems within the state was stongly conditioned by the philosophy that almost all Republicans shared, which emphasized the importance of maintaining opportunity for individuals to move upward through a society based on merit.[8] Such a philosophy emphasized the importance of granting each individual equal rights under the law, the right to vote, to be free from the temptations of liquor, and to have access to public education. Radicals, who earnestly endorsed these goals, believed it was the obligation of the state to ensure that these opportunities were maintained. In such a way the old New England image of a society based upon independent artisans and farmers, with women and children at home and in school, maintaining domestic tranquillity, could somehow still be realized. Hopefully, social abuses could be corrected automatically by free individuals exercising their equal rights to seek self-improvement. If immigration threatened the tranquillity of Massachusetts, then proper liquor laws, literacy tests for voting, and the agency of the public school would somehow maintain the social unity of the Commonwealth.

Massachusetts Republicans found most agreement on the importance of securing civil and political equality for blacks. Republican state legislators gave overwhelming support to the reconstruction amendments. Only a handful of Radicals sought to resist the Fourteenth Amendment, which they claimed compromised the rights of blacks in the South. Democrats joined with Republicans in giving the Thirteenth Amendment, which abolished slavery, unanimous support, but they followed party lines in voting against the Fourteenth and Fifteenth Amendments, which secured black civil and political rights.[9] In Massachusetts, unlike some other Northern states, party polarization on racial issues did not threaten Republican hegemony; Republicans incurred no liabilities in ratifying the last two amendments against Democratic opposition. The black population of Massachusetts was minute; most blacks lived in Boston, where they comprised only 1.2 percent of the city's population in 1865. Before the Civil War the state had extended suffrage to blacks, abolished segregated schools, opened public transportation to both races on an equal basis, permitted interracial marriages, and allowed blacks to serve on juries. In 1865 Republicans extended these principles by securing passage of the nation's first public accommodations law. Under its terms, no licensed inn, place of amusement, public conveyance, or public meeting could refuse admittance to blacks. The law provided a nominal fine of fifty dollars for violators.[10]

In 1867 Frank Bird sought to eliminate discriminations against Indians of the Commonwealth by introducing a bill making them citizens of the state. Failing in that year, Bird, with the support of Governor Claflin, succeeded in 1869 in obtaining legislation that eliminated the civil and political liabilities the state placed on its Indian inhabitants, and granted them citizenship.[11] Bird and his fellow Radicals had less success, however, in removing disabilities that the state had placed on its immigrant populatiom. In 1857 fear of immigrant voting power had led Republicans and Know-Nothings to amend the state constitution to deny the vote to any man who could not read the constitution in English and write his own name. Two years later voters also approved an amendment barring any immigrant from voting or holding office until he had been a naturalized citizen for two years. During the Civil War Governor Andrew continually criticized the two-year amendment, and in 1863 the legislature agreed to remove it from the state constitution. During the reconstruction era, however, when Massachusetts Republicans were demanding the abolition of civil and political discriminations based on race, they could not muster enough votes in the legislature to remove the literacy test for voting. Democrats, who depended heavily upon Irish ballots in Boston, unanimously opposed the test, but Republicans, who feared the same vote, kept it in the constitution.[12]

Most Bird Club members were consistent in their opposition to any discrimination based on race, ethnic background, or degree of literacy. They also attacked discriminations based on sex, but here, as with the literacy test, they were not able to gain their party's full support. Efforts in the state to expand women's rights, as was also the case with black civil rights, ante-dated the Civil War. The Know-Nothing legislature of 1855, which included many men who later became Republicans, enacted a law recognizing a married woman's right to own property. At the end of the Civil War, Governor Andrew recommended liberalizing the state's divorce laws, but the legislature defeated this proposal, as well as others that would have increased the rights of married women. As the issues of war and reconstruction began to recede in the public mind, however, and the pressure for state reforms became more evident, state legislators began to move more willingly to advance women's rights. Beginning in 1869, at the urging of Governor Claflin, the legislature passed bills significantly enlarging the ground upon which either party in a marriage could sue for divorce and giving wives the right to contract for their families' necessities; to serve as executors, guardians, or trustees of estates; to testify in all cases, civil and criminal; and to sue and be sued in actions of tort. In 1874 the legislature summed up many of these advances in a law that placed wives on the same footing as husbands in their right to convey real and other property and to make contracts without their husbands' consent.[13]

Radical Governors Alexander H. Bullock and William Claflin actively espoused the cause of women's rights. Bullock twice urged the legislature, without success, to increase the pay of female teachers, who were compensated at half the rate men received. After stepping down as governor he urged expansion of educational opportunities for women and offered to endow a scholarship for women at Amherst, his alma mater, if the school would admit them. His successor, Claflin, urged that women be placed on school committees and that laws be amended to permit them to serve on the boards of correctional institutions. In 1871 Claflin appointed Julia Ward Howe, an outstanding advocate of women's causes, as a justice of the peace. The state supreme court, however, ruled the appointment unconstitutional. In 1874 the court also refused to compel the School Committee of Boston to seat four women who had been elected to that body; the legislature thereupon enacted a provision that no one could be barred from serving on school committees because of their sex. The same year, at the urging of Governor William B. Washburn and women's rights advocates, the legislature established a separate reformatory school for women, to be staffed by women.[14]

None of the above measures generated much public or party controversy. When the advocates of women's suffrage, however, renewed their pre-Civil War campaign to give females the vote, a great deal of debate and conflict ensued. Beginning in 1867, women's suffrage associations began to send massive petitions to the state legislature in behalf of their cause, and during the next decade legislators voted on the issue in every session. While the matter did not become a party issue, most Democrats opposed extending the suffrage to women. The response of Republican legislators was less decisive. Many party leaders, including most Bird Club members, were sympathetic to women's suffrage, but for several years the party refused to take a public stand in favor of the reform. On four occasions between 1867 and 1870, Republican legislators rejected the plea of the petitioners by large margins.[15]

In 1870 suffragists threatened independent political action if neither party endorsed their reform. They sent representatives to both state conventions that summer; the Democrats turned them down by a large majority, but Republicans, who had just taken an unprecedented step by seating two women as convention delegates, rejected the suffragists by a narrower 193-139 margin. In January 1871, Governor Claflin endorsed women's suffrage, and in May the lower house unexpectedly voted 74-71 in favor of the porposal. A later vote ended in a tie, however, effectively defeating a suffrage amendment, which required a two-thirds vote. That fall the Republicans put a suffrage plank in their platform, and the party and its governors continued to give ritualistic recognition to the reform for several years. At no time, however, did the legislators translate that plank into a constitutional amendment securing women the right to vote.[16]

Nativist sentiment in the Republican Party was at least partly responsible for the failure to secure women's suffrage in Massachusetts. Many Republicans feared that enlarging the electorate would give more political power to the poverty-stricken immigrant masses crowded into the Commonwealth's cities.[17] Nativism also manifested itself in the continued agitation over temperance reform. For years there had been a close identification between the nativist and temperance impulses in the state. For many native Americans, attacking intoxication was a way of dealing with a different culture existing in their midst. They associated the Irish Catholics who congregated in Boston with pauperism, crime, and immoral behavior. Through temperance reform the aliens could be lifted to native standards, and alcohol, the cause of their antisocial activity, would be eliminated. In 1855 the Know-Nothing legislature prohibited the sale of liquor in the state, and the statute was still operative as Massachusetts entered the postwar years.[18]

Prohibition aroused much opposition in the state, particularly in Boston, where it was largely unenforced. As one historian commented, the prohibition issue had been resolved "by letting one side have the law and the other the liquor." Yet this tenuous balance could easily be upset whenever one side or the other pressed for changes in the law or in its enforcement. Prohibitionists, who were well organized, were determined to secure execution of the law. They associated Boston with sin and were determined to redeem the city. During the Civil War they pressed the state legislature to create a metropolitan police force for Boston, controlled by the governor, which would execute the liquor law. In 1865 Governor Andrew, who had little sympathy for the prohibitionists, signed a bill that established a statewide constabulary authorized to enforce all laws, including liquor, gambling, and prostitution legislation. This in effect created the nation's first state police force. The constables proved to be popular in many parts of Massachusetts, where often they were the only peace officers available. But most of their activity in Boston and environs centered on liquor law enforcement and helped set the stage for a bitterly contested debate over liquor legislation that occupied much of the time of the state legislature until 1876.[19]

Although prohibition became the leading political issue in the state, it did not become a clearly partisan matter. The Democratic Party did court antiprohibition votes, and Democratic legislators voted consistently to abolish the state constabulary and replace the prohibition measure with a license law. Republicans, however, refused to be identified with prohibition. William S. Robinson noted that the law would probably become a dead letter, because the majority of the people used liquor, "and, as far as my observation goes, the Republicans drink their share." Yet Republicans feared alienating the prohibitionists, almost all of whom voted the Republican ticket. Consequently, party managers strove to keep the liquor issue out of the annual state campaigns. This proved impossible, however, for Governor Bullock enthusiastically enforced the liquor law, even in Boston. Opponents of prohibition put up a great outcry, and in 1866 and again in 1867 Democrats introduced license bills into the state legislature; in both cases the Republicans voted them down by overwhelming margins.[20]

In 1867 opponents of the liquor law organized an alliance of Republicans and Democrats called the Personal Liberty League and carried the issue into the fall elections. Republican leaders were greatly disturbed. The state elections of 1867 were the first to be held following the adoption by the Republican Congress of a series of reconstruction acts that put the South under military rule and enfranchised the former slaves, and Republicans feared that defeats on the state level would reflect adverse judgments on their national policies. Party leaders urged the Republican state convention to avoid taking a position on prohibition and instead to stress national issues, and the delegates took the advice. Charles Slack, editor of the Boston *Commonwealth*, warned, however, that national issues had very little bearing upon the choice of men for the legislature, and the election bore him out. Two-thirds of the legislators who had voted against licensing in 1867 failed to be reelected, as license advocates swept into control of both houses of the legislature. While

Republicans still controlled the legislature and the governorship, their customarily gigantic majority was greatly reduced. Bullock, who had won 77 percent of the vote in 1866, when national issues of reconstruction were paramount, gained only 58 percent of the vote in 1867, when the license issue dominated the election.[21]

The 1868 legislature proceeded to pass a law abolishing the state constabulary. Governor Bullock, contending that the state police served other important purposes than liquor law enforcement, vetoed the bill, and the senate failed to override. Then the law-makers repealed the prohibition law and passed a liberal license act. This time Bullock, acknowledging that the voters had expressed a clear preference for licensing, permitted the bill to become law without his signature. The new law was poorly drawn and quite liberal, and in 1868 prohibitionists conducted a well-organized campaign against it. This was a national election year, and in the fall Republicans turned out in larger numbers than ever before to elect Ulysses S. Grant President. The Republican vote increased by 30 percent over that of 1867, while the Democratic vote fell by 10 percent. The result gave overwhelming control of the legislature to the Republicans and also to the opponents of licensing. Thus the pendulum of liquor legislation swung back again; the 1869 legislature repealed the license law and reinstated the 1855 prohibitory measure.[22]

For the next three years the state legislature explored various ways to strike a happy mean between unrestricted sale and total prohibition of alcohol. One solution was to permit the consumption of cider, ale, and beer; in 1870, angry at this action of the legislature, prohibitionists executed their threat of abandoning the Republican Party and nominated their own candidate for governor. Their ticket drew only 6,500 votes in the fall elections, thus revealing their impotence as a separate party; after one more futile try in 1871, the prohibitionists abandoned the idea. For the next two years the legislature did not tamper with the temperance question. As one journalist noted, "If anybody is sick of the liquor discussion I think it is the majority of both branches and the reporters."[23]

In 1874 the long controversy over the prohibition law finally reached a conclusion. The issue was forced by the state constabulary, which actively prosecuted violators of the law, and by the prohibitionists, who succeeded in abolishing exemptions for ale and beer. In the fall elections in 1873 the Democrats won 65 seats in the lower house, the largest total they had enjoyed since the Republicans came to power. The following year, joining with antiprohibition Republicans, they abolished the state constabulary and replaced prohibition with a license law. Lieutenant-Governor Thomas Talbot, who had replaced Governor Washburn upon the latter's election to the United States Senate, vetoed both bills, thus handing the Democrats a major issue for the fall election. National issues also entered the campaign and, in a general reaction against Republican leadership that was reflected across the North,

Massachusetts Democrats achieved a momentary interruption in the long period of Republican domination in the state. They elected 5 Congressmen, the governor, and sent 79 Democrats to the lower house and 15 to the upper house of the state legislature, the largest totals they had enjoyed in either chamber since the Republican Party had organized. Republicans, however, still controlled the legislature and all state offices except the governorship. Their gubernatorial candidate, Talbot, was by his vetoes clearly identified with prohibitionism, and the party had courted defeat by nominating him. Once the new legislature had resolved the liquor issue by enacting a new license law and drastically reducing the size of the state constabulary, Republicans resumed their accustomed domination of the state. In the 1875 state elections Democratic seats in the legislature fell by 25 percent, and the Republicans elected A. H. Rice as governor; in the national elections of 1876, Democrats lost 4 of the 5 Congressional seats they had won two years previously, while the Republican presidential nominee easily won the state's electoral vote.[24]

With passage of the 1875 license law, which set high fees for licenses in order to reduce the number of disreputable sellers, the state's citizenry proved willing to abandon further agitation of an issue that had disrupted the state for almost a quarter of a century. Continual discussion of prohibition in the state legislature had consumed much time of the law-makers in the 1860s. Among the neglected issues was the pressing matter of railroad reform. Republican legislators had proved more than willing to continue the state's prewar policy of granting aid to railroads, particularly those that would tie Boston with the trade and population of the western states.[25] Postwar grants, however, began to expand an already immense state debt, and by the end of the 1860s pressures were mounting to reduce such expenditures and to exert some public control over the power wielded by the railroads.

In 1868 Republican legislators first questioned the advisability of continuing state aid to railroads, when they debated a bill which would have committed five million dollars to the completion of a railroad tunnel through the Hoosac mountain in western Massachusetts. In 1854 the state had made its first grant of two million dollars for the Hoosac tunnel, and from 1865 through 1867, the legislature appropriated an additional total of two million dollars to complete the project. Tunnel construction, however, was marked by inertia, mistakes, and general engineering incompetence. Consequently, in 1868 Frank Bird, who was sensitive to the political implications of a Republican legislature granting further state funds in an important election year, took the lead in opposing the five million dollar bill, arguing that the tunnel was a demonstrable failure and that nothing could justify further expenditure of state funds on it.[26]

While Bird was able to organize considerable opposition to the Hoosac bill, particularly from legislators representing constituents on competing railroad lines, the Hoosac tunnel lobby was able to force the bill through the house by promising various other interests votes for their projects if they supported the tunnel. The vote was fairly close, the tunnel gaining approval by a 115-91 margin. Although the Democrats in their 1868 platform did condemn the "lavish and reckless extravagance" of the Republican legislature, both parties were responsible for the approval of the grant. Democrats supported the bill by a vote of 23-21, while Republicans voted 92-70 in its favor.[27]

The tunnel's opponents charged that the lobby had gained approval of its project by corrupting the legislature, not only with log-rolling techniques but with outright purchase of votes. William A. Robinson charged that the lobby had plied legislators with liquor at its "assignation-house." In 1869 a legislative committee investigated the charges and contended that no member was improperly influenced by lobby activity.[28] The committee report did not, however, remove suspicions about the corrupting influence of railroad interests, especially as the legislature considered the Boston, Hartford, and Erie railroad project. This road first applied for state aid in 1867, when it requested a loan of three million dollars. The legislature proved very willing to encourage railroad development; 13 percent of the acts passed that year involved special benefits to the railroads of the state. After only perfunctory debate, the legislature authorized the loan; Republicans like Richard Henry Dana, Jr., and Frank Bird, who had opposed granting aid to the Hoosac tunnel, willingly cast their votes in favor of the Hartford and Erie. Bird shipped products over the road and was a friend of its officers; Dana's business constituents in Boston had investments in the road.[29]

In 1869 the Hartford and Erie asked for additional funds from the state, and by an overwhelming 124-17 vote the legislature complied. A year later, although the railroad was heavily in debt, it brazenly asked the legislature for yet another loan to improve its financial status and complete construction. The majority report of a legislative committee, contending that a new loan could contain provisions giving the state control of funds expended on the road, urged approval of the Hartford and Erie request. Opponents of the new loan, now led by Frank Bird, who admitted his earlier votes for the railroad were in error, argued that the state had been swindled enough. Investigations had demonstrated that the railroad's directors had manipulated the company's resources for private gain. The *Springfield Republican*, representing a section of the state that could not benefit from the road, launched blistering attacks on the loan proposal. W. W. Robinson complained that "since the war closed the whole community has been on a grand financial and business 'drunk' " and would have to come to its senses, for the state debt had increased by 33 percent since 1865. Despite these objections, the railroad lobby, with liberal offers of campaign money to hesitant legislators, obtained passage of a compromise bill that authorized a new commitment of public funds, while simultaneously increasing state control over the road. To the relief of the bill's opponents, Governor Claflin then vetoed the measure and effectively ended further state involvement in the Hartford and Erie project.[30]

The legislatures from 1866 to 1868 that eagerly granted aid to railroads defeated proposals to establish a permanent railroad commission to supervise their operation and protect the public interest. In 1869, however, with only perfunctory debate and without a roll call, legislators agreed to create a three-man railroad commission. Charles Francis Adams, Jr. became its leading member. Under his guidance the commission proceeded to investigate the physical and financial status of Massachusetts railroads. It made recommendations to the legislature concerning railroad repairs, safety requirements, stock issues, and rate levels. The commission depended upon the publicity accorded to its reports to enforce its findings, as it had no independent regulatory power. The legislature supported the recommendations of the commission by passing a general incorporation act to end the granting of special railroad charters and bring system into the launching of future roads; reformed the system railroads used to report information to the commission; and imposed a standard system of accounting on the roads, to facilitate a comparative study of their costs and rates. In this manner, the state was able to exercise some uniform control over its rail system and reduce lobby pressure on the legislature. The success of the Massachusetts railroad commission was revealed by the prestige it exercised in other states, which copied its organization and quoted its reports. Within Massachusetts, the pressure exerted by the commission probably was one of the several factors bringing a downward adjustment of railroad rates in the 1870s.[31]

With the ending of railroad grants and the establishment of the railroad commission, Massachusetts legislators found more time to debate the condition of laboring classes within the state. The Republican Party split wide open on the question of labor reform, and throughout the reconstruction years the organization never defined its position on the matter. A number of Bird Club members, including Robinson, Claflin, and Stone, had supported worker demands for a ten-hour day back in the 1850s and willingly endorsed the proposal when it was revived after the Civil War. They were less inclined, however, to support the more radical proposal of a new Eight-Hour League which petitioned the legislature to institute an even shorter work day. Other Radicals, like Frank Bird, viewed the rising class consciousness of workers with alarm. Bird, noting the increase of day-laborers and mechanics crowded into Boston, warned that "the great danger of the future to Boston is in the aggregation of those classes." No Republican leader condoned strikes. Not only did class consciousness and class action run against the Radical philosophy that stressed social unity and the general welfare, Republican leaders were also sensitive to the fact that the many ex-Whig commercial and industrial leaders who had joined the party after 1860 opposed state interference with labor conditions.[32]

There were nativist overtones in the long debate over factory legislation; the Boston *Advertiser* noted that "the native workers of Massachusetts, the intelligent operatives who have an ambition for the future" had not asked for restrictions on the hours they could contract to work. On the other hand, Republicans were dismayed about the socially destructive consequences of permitting large numbers of foreign-born workers to labor long hours in the mills without relief. Two legislative committees established in 1865 and 1866 to inquire into labor conditions in the state reported widespread violations of state statutes that required mill children to attend school for at least part of each year. As Governor William Washburn noted, if the immigrants had no opportunity to attend public school, "how are we to educate them into unity of aspiration and purpose with native-born citizens?" For Washburn the lesson was clear: "If we are to have in the future a healthy growth of the body politic, all these different elements of population must be blended into one harmonious whole."[33]

Disagree as they might over the propriety of other measures affecting the working classes, Republican legislators proved quite willing to enact and amend labor laws to increase the amount of time children of laboring families had to attend school and thus "be blended into one harmonious whole." Pre-Civil War statutes had limited the hours of work for children under twelve to ten hours a day and required that no child under fourteen could be employed unless he or she had gone to school for at least three months of the year. In 1866 the legislature passed a new child labor law, making it illegal to employ a child under the age of ten, or to employ a child under fourteen for more than ten hours a day. In addition, no child between the ages of ten and fourteen could be employed unless he or she attended school six months a year. The following year, due to protests from both mill-owners and workers' families that family income was not sufficient without the labor of children, the legislature reduced the school requirement to three months and provided that penalties would be invoked only when mill owners "knowingly" violated the law. The legislature also created the office of deputy constable, who was authorized to inspect factories and bring violators to court. Although the laws did mark the beginnings of the first factory inspection system in the nation, the immediate result was minimal. The deputy constable, Henry K. Oliver, noted that the laws were poorly drawn and impossible to enforce, since immigrant families needed the income and would not follow the law. In 1869 he resigned his job in disgust, having failed to secure a single conviction in the courts under the new law.[34]

The same legislators who enacted the child labor laws turned a deaf ear to pleas for establishing an eight-hour day for all workers. For a time the eight-hour movement commanded great attention not only in Massachusetts but elsewhere across the North. In 1867 six states enacted eight-hour laws, and Pennsylvania passed a similar measure in 1868. These victories for labor reformers were only symbolic, since the laws were not enforced. But even a symbolic victory could not be won in Massachusetts, where mill owners maintained the lobbying power they had demonstrated before the Civil War to defeat labor reform measures. In 1866 the house defeated an eight-hour law by a two-to-one margin and also refused to urge Massachusetts Congressmen to seek an eight-hour day for federal employees. In two succeeding years eight-hour bills failed to gain legislative approval, and the number of petitions advocating the reform began to diminish.[35]

The limited response of state legislators to issues raised by labor reformers caused the latter to contemplate independent action. For several years after the Civil War neither political party took a position in favor of labor reform, nor did Republican governors call for action on the matter. In 1869 matters came to a head. Shoemakers in the state organized the Knights of St. Crispin and appealed to the legislature for a charter that would permit them to establish marketing and producing cooperatives. The lower house, under pressure from shoe manufacturers, voted the Crispins down by a margin of 82-121. The handful of Democratic legislators voted by two to one in favor of the petition and blamed Republicans for its defeat. William S. Robinson, noting that the legislature was always ready to grant charters to business corporations, feared that the Republicans were making a record on the labor question that would "be even harder to explain than its position on the liquor law." Two days before the 1869 legislature adjourned, as if to answer Robinson and make a concession to the labor reformers, the lawmakers created a Bureau of Statistics of Labor to collect and publicize data on the conditions of labor within the state.[36]

Most labor leaders were suspicious of the bureau, fearing it would postpone action on labor demands. Its first head, however, H. K. Oliver, formerly in charge of enforcing child labor laws, and his deputy, George McNeill, who was president of the Boston Eight-Hour League, did issue reports calling for a new factory inspection act, a ten-hour day, a half-time system of schooling for factory children, and inspection of tenements. Their reports and the information they gathered regarding the plight of workers in the Commonwealth made the bureau a center of controversy. Many middle-class citizens of Massachusetts were embarrassed at its findings and joined with employers in demanding it be abolished. Newspapers in other states, however, praised the bureau for publishing such information, and its reports were quoted from Maine to Oregon.[37]

Angry Crispins, disdainful of the legislature's last-minute creation of the bureau, did not wait to see if it could be made an instrument to advance labor reform. In the summer of 1869 they joined with the ten-hour advocates to organize a Labor Reform Party, which got 10 percent of the votes that fall with an unknown slate. They also elected twenty-two men to the lower house of the state legislature. In January 1870, perhaps as a result of the organization of independent political pressure, Governor Claflin in his annual message to the legislature called for consideration of the "labor question." The law-makers did respond by chartering the Crispins, but despite receiving over a hundred petitions for a ten-hour day for women and children, the senate defeated a house-approved measure that would have instituted the reform. The senate did approve an eight hour law for state employees, but the house defeated that. During the legislative session, the Knights of St. Crispin struck a shoe factory in North Adams, and employers brought in Chinese coolies to replace the strikers. The state legislature overwhelmingly defeated a resolution condemning the use of Chinese labor in the state and also refused to pass a bill that would have abolished contract labor in Massachusetts.[38]

Democratic legislators sought to capitalize on the labor issue by giving strong support to the anti-contract and anti-coolie proposals, and by backing the ten-hour bill more strongly than the Republicans. But the Democrats were not in control of the state, and labor reformers hoped in the 1870 elections to capitalize upon the failure of the legislature to act. They selected abolitionist Wendell Phillips to run for governor, and Phillips also received the support of hard-line prohibitionists who nominated him separately. Phillips, however, garnered only 13 percent of the vote, and the number of reformers elected to the legislature was halved. Governor Claflin, who was reelected, had a reputation as a ten-hour man that antedated the Civil War, and most workers apparently still hoped that the Republicans would respond to their needs; 1870 was also a Congressional election year, when national issues tended to dominate platforms and campaigning, and Republican voters turned out in large numbers. The political fortunes of labor continued to decline from that point; Labor Reformers made one more attempt in 1871 to run independent candidates, and then their movement collapsed. The Crispins dissolved in 1872 when a major strike failed. By 1874 Wendell Phillips had conceded the failure of the labor movement.[39]

Yet as independent political pressure for labor reform faded, sensitivity of the major parties to the issue increased, and had probably helped bring the downfall of the Labor Reform Party. After 1869 the Democrats annually chastised the Republicans for pampering capital and degrading labor. Republicans likewise began to incorporate pro-labor planks in their state platforms, and, beginning with Claflin, Republican governors began to refer to labor issues in their annual legislative messages. From 1871 through 1873, the lower house of the state legislature easily passed ten-hour laws for women and children, but in each case the senate withheld its approval. In every case, the Republicans furnished the preponderance of votes against the law, while Democrats increasingly gave it their support. The house votes revealed, however, that most Republicans did favor the law.[40]

In 1874 the General Court finally resolved the ten-hour issue by establishing the maximum hours of labor at sixty per week for women and for children under the age of eighteen. The law was considerably weakened, however, by providing for assessment of penalties only if offenders had "knowingly" violated the law. Five years later, the legislature struck this clause and thus paved the way for more effective enforcement of the statute. The achievement of the ten-hour day for women and children, who comprised a large proportion of the operatives in mills, relieved much of the pressure for labor reform.[41]

The action of the Massachusetts legislature regarding labor issues during the reconstruction years had been anticipated by a legislative commission in 1866, whose report urged the state to "give every child *a fair chance* for the good outfit of a healthy body, and an educated mind, and then, if at his majority, with no special misfortune intervening, he can not get his own living, let him take his place without a murmur in some asylum for the unfortunate, or school for the 'feeble-minded'." Laboring classes could expect no special protection from the legislature, other than legislation protecting the health and educational opportunity of women and children, and caring for those who, through infirmity, sickness, or misfortune, could not care for themselves.[42] It was in keeping with this philosophy that the 1869 legislature created a State Board of Health. The board was authorized to investigate sanitary conditions in the state and disseminate the information gathered to the legislature and to the public. In particular, the board was authorized to investigate the causes of diseases and to prevent their organization and spread. As with the Bureau of Statistics of Labor, the work of the Board of Health became somewhat controversial, as it explored health conditions in tenement houses in Boston and in schools and shops around the state. Despite periodic efforts to undermine the board, it survived for ten years, when it was merged with the Boards of Lunacy and Charity. Its reports were respected in other states, several of which created similar boards in emulation of Massachusetts.[43]

The State Board of Charity, with which the Board of Health was merged in 1879, had been created in 1863 by the legislature, also in keeping with the state's tradition of assuming responsibility for those unable to care for themselves. The Board of Charity was responsible for supervising the whole welfare system in Massachusetts. By the time of the Civil War the state had three lunatic hospitals, a reform school for boys, three almshouses, a hospital for sick and disabled aliens, and an industrial school for girls. It also subsidized institutions providing for deaf, dumb, and blind children. Most of these institutions were recently created, and their emergence was accompanied by a rapid rise in welfare costs. There was no system in the state's approach to the problems of dependency, and the various institutions operated under a variety of means of control and definition of responsibilities. The new Board of Charity, like the other boards and bureaus created after the war, had wide investigative and supervisory powers. It quickly became a body of great influence and, like the Board of Health, the Labor Bureau, and the Railroad Commission, its prestige spread to other states.[44]

Two members of the Bird Club, Frank Sanborn and Samuel Gridley Howe, were among the first commissioners of the Board of Charity and dominated its reports, which sought not only to make recommendations to the legislature, but to "kindle the social conscience" of the state. Howe, who wrote the board's influential second report, issued in 1866, did contend that heredity was quite important in the creation of dependent classes of people, but continued to insist, in keeping with the antebellum spirit of optimistic reform, that by improving the environment, breeding could be improved. Hence Howe and the board urged the limitation of hours of work, improvement of dwellings, prohibition of alcohol, and greater availability of clothing and wholesome food.[45]

The board's public reports and recommendations did lead to greater efficiency and economy in the operation of the state's charitable system. It also encouraged the legislature to authorize capital expenditures for additional prisons and hospitals and to establish a school for deaf mutes. The board was also able to encourage the various charitable institutions to institute some reforms in operational care of inmates. Howe's reports, however, by tending to blame the individual's own failings for his indigent or dependent condition, and associating insanity with characteristics found particularly among lower-class groups, tended to support middle-class disdain for immigrants. The resulting pessimism about the efficacy of individual therapy increased the post-Civil War tendency to turn the state's insane asylums into custodial institutions for lower-class patients.[46]

The postwar deterioration of the reform impulse, evident in the reports of the State Board of Charity, was reflected elsewhere in the Commonwealth. Even before the war, as the state struggled with the problems caused by urbanization, industrialization, and immigration, reformers had sought to use the government to create a network of institutions capable of maintaining social order and stability. But in the postwar era, these institutions demonstrated their failure to stem the tide of social dislocation and disruption: the reform school did not reverse the rate of urban juvenile crime; the insane asylums became custodial rather than therapeutic; and, perhaps most importantly, the public school system, in which many reformers had placed their ultimate faith, showed signs of bureaucratic stagnation. The wave of educational reform, led by Morace Mann, that had swept the state in the 1840s slowed or stopped after the war. The decade of the 1870s marked a time of adjustment in the public school system, as school reformers sought new direction. They did manage to obtain increased appropriations for the school system; from 1870 to 1890 Massachusetts was the only eastern state to increase its expenditures per pupil. Educators, however, still were frustrated at their efforts to get immigrant mill children into schools; in 1870 some 25 percent of children ages five to fifteen were not in regular school attendance, and five years later statistics revealed that 91 percent of the 77,550 illiterates in the state were immigrants. As the legislature increased compulsory attendance requirements and sought to enforce them, truancy did begin to drop. But the great emphasis placed on education in Massachusetts as the key to social salvation probably reduced efforts to design other strategies of social reform.[47]

The restlessness and anxiety felt by native middle-class citizens of Massachusetts concerning the growth of the immigrant working-classes and dependent populations of the Commonwealth's burgeoning cities was heightened by the pressure of rising tax rates. The total burden of state taxation in Massachusetts tripled from 1860 to 1870; its per capita expenditures rose four times during that period. While some taxpayers associated the rising expenditures with profligate spending on railroad development, others were convinced that much of this money was being spent on social services for the undeserving and evaded their tax-paying obligations. The legislature did manage to institute some reforms in tax assessment and collection, but the structure remained inequitable and unwieldly. The hardpressed middle class viewed with alarm the growing political sophistication of the immigrants, who were now pressing the state government to address itself to their needs.[48]

Perhaps the resulting pressures and conflicts were beyond the capacity of governing institutions and political leadership to control. The Democratic party was inert during the postwar period; it won its only victory in 1874 by exploiting the liquor issue. Republicans, on the other hand, were unable to formulate programs satisfactory to all of their varied constituencies, and hence tended to take no position at all on the questions of the day. The frustrations of the voting population found expression in occasional fringe party movements organized by labor reformers and prohibitionists, but these efforts soon failed. It was not a third party movement, but rather the efforts of Benjamin Butler to wrest control of the Republican Party from the Bird Club, that most clearly focussed the tensions and conflicts stirring the Bay State.

Butler, who had been an active Democrat in Massachusetts as late as 1860, achieved considerable prominence during the war due to his military service. At the end of the conflict he was elected to Congress as a Radical Republican and assumed an important role in designing reconstruction policies. An extremely ambitious man, he assembled a patronage machine in his district and began to establish "Butler Clubs" in other parts of the state. Since he was not a member of the Bird Club, he was viewed as a potential threat to the established party leadership, and many watched his career with suspicion. While Butler's war record, and his staunchly Radical course on reconstruction, made him very popular with voters of the state, conservative Republican businessmen were horrified when in 1866 he began advocating paying the interest on the national debt in greenbacks and taxing national bonds. In 1868 some of Butler's critics made an effort to oust him from Congress by running the more conservative Richard Henry Dana, Jr. against him.[49]

The Butler-Dana canvass symbolized the growing divisions in the state, both within and without the Republican Party. Dana represented the blue-stocking element in the party; he was cool to Negro suffrage, opposed the eight-hour day, was instrumental in getting the legislature to repeal the state's usury laws, and was an advocate of hard money. For Dana, payment of the national debt in gold was "not even a moral question, but a question of religion." In general, he represented the ideal of patrician leadership, a man supposedly above ambition, who would strive for dignity and honesty in politics. Bank officers, lawyers, and wealthy businessmen contributed money to his campaign. Thus the forces of respectability were marshaled against Butler. On his side, Butler had the support of war veterans, Republican party loyalists, who recognized that he was the regular nominee of the party, Irish Catholics who remembered his opposition to the Know-Nothings before the war, and mill-hands who recalled his championing the ten-hour day in the 1850s.[50]

In the election, Butler easily defeated both Dana and his Democratic opponent. Voting patterns revealed that class lines had been drawn; Dana's votes came from small farming communities with few immigrants. He received almost no votes in working-class communities with large foreign-born populations. State party leaders, who had refused to become involved in the canvass, did not interpret Butler's victory as a defeat for the state machine. As Charles Slack noted, Butler could be overbearing and even unscrupulous in his divisive campaign tactics and appeals to voter interest and prejudice, but he was clearly in touch with the common man. Although Frank Bird and other members of the Bird Club feared the increase of Butler's power, they knew that his defeat would be an adverse reflection upon the Radical position Butler had taken on national issues pertaining to reconstruction. While some Radicals were dismayed at Butler's financial heresies, others, like Bird himself, Slack, Stone, and Robinson, were inclined to support his inflationary proposals.[51]

Conservative Republicans nursed their wounds. One complained that the 1868 election revealed "how much scallawags preponderate over decent men in this world"; another moaned that Butler, "a liar, thief, a slanderer . . . guilty of acts impossible to a man of any honor or conscience," could only misrepresent Massachusetts, "the home of religion, education, and their results, intelligence and honesty." Butler's course after 1868 only intensified their hatred of the man and what he represented. He pursued his inflationary policies, advocated an eight-hour day for government employees, and supported women's suffrage. As he solidified his position with President Grant, Butler was able to exercise increasing influence over political appointments in Massachusetts, and to the horror of Massachusetts conservatives who hoped for civil service reform, Butler brazenly championed the system of spoils politics that had built up his Massachusetts machine.[52]

Despite his growing influence, as long as Butler remained in Congress he could not directly menace the power of the state Republican machine. In 1871, however, he launched a frontal attack on that political machinery by seeking the party's nomination for governor. To do this, Butler had to go outside organizational channels, which were blocked to him, and seek popular support to influence caucus selections of delegates to the state Republican convention. Hence, not only did Butler challenge the established party leadership, which had controlled the dispensation of the governor's chair for over a decade, he also openly sought the office, which was a display of personal ambition that the Republican establishment could not tolerate. The office must seek the man, not the man the office.[53]

Behind the animosity to Butler aroused by his personal ambition and spoilsmanship lay a fear among respectable Republicans that, through his political manipulations, he was organizing the masses of immigrants and workers into a force that would dominate the state. Butler's main line of argument was that the Republican "state-house ring" had neglected the needs of the masses and that the time had come for new leaders, more responsive to popular needs, to come to power. To gain this power, Butler sought to exploit existing class and economic tensions. He charged that Republican-dominated legislatures had operated in the interests of capital, passing hundreds of acts of incorporation for business, while ignoring the needs of farmers and workers. He argued that the legislature had spent money irresponsibly, and had thus created heavy tax burdens that bore more heavily on the working man than on the employer. He particularly took the Republican law-makers to task for creating so many bureaus and boards, which Butler charged were totally unresponsive to popular control. He contended that the expenses of such governmental agencies had increased five times since 1860, and that their benefits went mainly to the commissioners who earned substantial salaries.[54]

Alarmed by what Senator Henry Wilson described as "an upheaval of the scum of various parties" that supported Butler, the Republican organization brought its full power into play to defeat his ambitions. The Bird Club, no longer the powerful influence it once was in Massachusetts politics, gathered its waning membership to combat Butler; major newspapers in Boston attacked his positions; Senators Wilson and Sumner publicly condemned his campaign; and the party machinery went to work to gain control of the local caucuses. Opponents of Butler united behind William B. Washburn, and party management prevailed in the convention; Washburn was nominated over Butler by a vote of 543 to 464. Two years later the same anti-Butler coalition assembled again to deny him the gubernatorial nomination, and he abandoned his efforts to win control of the state party.[55]

In 1872, the year after Butler first attempted to gain the state governorship, the Massachusetts Republican organization faced another dissident movement, this time led by none other than Frank Bird, whose Bird Club had virtually disbanded. Bird, along with a handful of other important Massachusetts Republicans, was disenchanted with the policies of the Grant administration in Washington and hoped for civil service reform, an end to corruption in Washington and in the South, and a return to low tariff policies. Bird, Sanborn, and Robinson were among those from Massachusetts who attended a convention in Cincinnati to nominate Horace Greeley to run against Grant on a Liberal Republican platform. On the state level, Massachusetts Democrats, who had previously indicated their willingness to accept the reconstruction amendments and thus eliminate a roadblock to fusion with discontented Republicans, courted the Liberals and actually made Bird their nominee for governor. In the fall elections, however, Massachusetts voters overwhelmingly cast their ballots for Grant and the regular Republican ticket.[56]

Neither Butler, the Liberals, nor the Democrats offered a serious challenge to the state Republican organization. Butler's movement was one basically engineered to fit his personal ambition. His positions on leading questions were often as compromising and ambiguous as those of the party organization he attacked. When he did win the governorship in the 1880s, running as a Democrat, he did not embark upon any significant new programs.[57] The Liberal Republicans had no position on local issues to offer the voters of the state; they were not concerned with labor, city slums, or farm mortgages. And throughout the decade after the Civil War, the Democrats failed to show any capacity to develop the leadership or program necessary to challenge successfully Republican hegemony. The Republican organization, while reluctant to confront controversial problems, had not abused its mandate from the voters. Republican administrations had given the state honest, efficient government, untainted by major scandal. The state's war-time debt was being retired, and her credit was maintained at the high level Massachusetts citizens were accustomed to. Although extravagance marked several postwar legislatures, the state's rail system was completed and more effectively organized. While the legislature did prove reluctant to confront more directly the pressing questions of railroad regulation, labor reform, public health, and welfare reform, it did establish a variety of boards and commissions to deal with these problems, and other states hastened to create similar agencies of their own.

Throughout the period from 1865 to 1875, Massachusetts Republicans enacted programs that were consistent with their history. A marked continuity existed in terms of the issues posed and the solutions provided in the state from the pre- to post-Civil War years. Long before the war, Massachusetts citizens had accepted the idea that the government should participate in the economic and social progress of society and commit itself to maintenance of the public welfare. Republican lawmakers in the postwar era refused to abandon this tradition and instead expanded it into new areas. Much of the

Republican achievement, however, had been carried out in a paternalistic spirit, and the Republican machine took on more and more the aspect of a closed corporation.

Thus the Republicans, while they could defeat Butler, could not avoid the challenge he presented. To some degree he had pried open that closed political corporation, and made it more susceptible to influence from hitherto apathetic or inactive classes of voters. He had drawn immigrant votes from those offended by the nativist attitude of the Republican leadership; he obtained the support of younger voters who were no longer interested in the issues of the Civil War and reconstruction that had for years provided the staple for Republican platforms; he attracted votes from the mill-workers, who doubted the willingness of Republican administrations to deal with their problems. The Butler and Liberal Republican movements, if they achieved nothing else, did encourage voters to exercise more independence in casting their ballot.[58] If the Republicans were to control the state in the future, they would have to prove willing to confront new issues and seek the support of an increasingly sophisticated, complex, and diverse electorate. The homogeneous commonwealth of the Puritan fathers had long since disappeared.

NOTES

1. The most complete study of Massachusetts politics in the 1850s is William G. Bean, "Party Transformation in Massachusetts with Special Reference to the Antecedents of Republicanism, 1848-1860" (doctoral dissertation, Harvard University, 1922).

2. My discussion of the Republican party's ideology is drawn from Eric Foner's excellent book, *Free Soil, Free Labor, Free Men: The Ideology of the Republican Party before the Civil War* (New York, 1970), esp. pp. 11-40.

3. See the discussion in Foner of the relationship between antislavery, temperance, and nativism, in *Free Soil, Free Labor, Free Men*, pp. 226-60.

4. See, for example, the addresses of the Republican state committee to the citizens of Massachusetts, in the Boston *Commonwealth*, September 9, 1865, September 22, 1866, November 2, 1867, and July 18, 1868.

5. Geoffrey Blodgett, *The Gentle Reformers: Massachusetts Democrats in the Cleveland Era* (Cambridge, Mass., 1966), pp. 10-12.

6. Mrs. William S. Robinson, ed., *Warrington Pen-Portraits* (Boston, 1877), pp. x, 152, 304-05; Henry G. Pearson, *The Life of John A. Andrew* (2 vols., Boston, 1904), I:58-60, 120; David Donald, *Charles Sumner and the Coming of the Civil War* (New York, 1960), pp. 321; *Francis William Bird, A Biographical Sketch, by His Children* (Boston, 1897), pp. 32-35; Frank P. Stearns, *Cambridge Sketches* (Philadelphia, 1905), pp. 164-78; F.W. Bird to John Andrew, September 30, 1865, Andrew MSS, Massachusetts Historical Society, Boston, Massachusetts; Martin Duberman, *Charles Francis Adams, 1807-1888* (Boston, 1961), pp. 334-35; Fred H. Harrington, *Fighting Politician: Major General N. P. Banks* (Philadelphia, 1948), p. 170.

7. Boston *Commonwealth*, March 23, 1867; Sanborn quoted in Michael B. Katz, *The Irony of Early School Reform: Educational Innovation in Mid-Nineteenth Century Massachusetts* (Cambridge, Mass., 1968), p. 196.

8. My discussion of Republican ideology in regard to labor issues is drawn from David Montgomery, *Beyond Equality: Labor and the Radical Republicans, 1862-1872* (New York, 1967), pp. 202-05, 230-33, 295, 304-05; and James Leiby, *Carroll Wright and Labor Reform: The Origin of Labor Statistics* (Cambridge, Mass., 1960), pp. 41-45.

9. Boston *Commonwealth*, March 9, 16, 1867; *Massachusetts House Journal, 1869*, p. 226; *Massachusetts Senate Journal, 1869*, p. 172; Edith Allen Ware, *Political Opinion in Massachusetts during the Civil War and Reconstruction* (Columbia University Studies in History, Economics, and Public Law, Vol. LXXIV, No. 175, New York, 1916), pp. 179-80.

10. In 1866 the legislature weakened the law by forbidding the exclusion of people from such public facilities "except for good cause." In subsequent court rulings, state judges held that unlicensed facilities and municipal skating rinks were not covered by the two laws. See John Daniels, *In Freedom's Birthplace* (Boston, 1914), pp. 94-95, 139; *Massachusetts Senate Documents, 1866*, Nos. 264, 271; *Acts and Resolves Passed by the General Court of Massachusetts, 1865*, p. 650; Boston *Commonwealth*, April 21, 1866.

11. *Massachusetts House Journal, 1867*, pp. 42, 189; *1869*, pp. 542, 565, 654; *Acts and Resolves, 1869*, pp. 780-82, 843.

12. Bean, "Party Transformation in Massachusetts", 330, 365-72; Oscar Handlin, *Boston's Immigrants, 1790-1880* (rev. ed., New York, 1972), p. 215; *Massachusetts House Journal, 1867*, pp. 26, 250, 424; *1870*, pp. 130, 331, 363-65, 403-07; *1871*, p. 415; *1873*, pp. 133-36; *Massachusetts Senate Journal, 1868*, pp. 35, 65; *1871*, pp. 183, 188, 204; Boston *Commonwealth*, April 30, May 7, 1870.

13. Bean, "Party Transformation in Massachusetts," p. 286; *Acts and Resolves, 1865*, p. 734; *1869*, pp. 621, 703; *1870*, p. 308; *1871*, p. 655; *Massachusetts House Journal, 1865*, pp. 114, 149, 203, 337, 370; *1866*, pp. 77, 99, 386; *1868*, pp. 235, 306, 351, 414, 475, 489; *1869*, pp. 181, 376, 377, 414, 546; *1870*, p. 282; *1871*, pp. 360, 413; Boston *Commonwealth*, May 16, 1874.

14. *Acts and Resolves, 1867*, pp. 793-94; *1869*, pp. 831-32; *1870*, p. 361; *1871*, p. 824; *1873*, p. 949; *1874*, pp. 432, 443; William H. Ladd to Alexander H. Bullock, October 4, 1871, Julia Ward Howe to Bullock, June 17, 1874, Alexander H. Bullock MSS, American Antiquarian Society, Worcester, Mass.; *Appleton's Annual Cyclopedia, 1874*, p. 523; Boston *Commonwealth*, July 8, 1871, July 4, 1874.

15. Lois Bannister Merk, "Massachusetts and the Woman-Suffrage Movement" (doctoral dissertation, Radcliffe, 1956), pp. 5-43; *Massachusetts House Journal, 1867*, pp. 221-22; *1868*, p. 422; *1870*, p. 382; *Massachusetts Senate Journal, 1869*, pp. 434, 462; Robinson, ed., *Warrington*, pp. 116-17.

16. *Appleton's Annual Cyclopedia, 1870*, pp. 476-77; Boston *Commonwealth*, October 8, 1879, January 14, 21, 1871, August 31, 1872, February 27, 1875; *Massachusetts House Journal, 1871*, p. 450.

17. James J. Kenneally, "The Opposition to Woman Suffrage in Massachusetts, 1868-1920" (doctoral dissertation, Boston College, 1963), pp. 1-5, 33 ff.

18. Joseph R. Gusfield, *Symbolic Crusade: Status Politics and the American Temperance Movement* (Urbana, Illinois, 1966), pp. 55-57; Samuel Shapiro, *Richard Henry Dana, Jr.* (East Lansing, Mich., 1961), p. 135; Boston *Commonwealth*, March 30, 1867, August 15, 1874; George F. Clark, *History of the Temperance Reform in Massachusetts, 1813-1883* (Boston, 1888), pp. 89-92.

19. Clark, *History of Temperance*, 93; Roger Lane, *Policing the City: Boston, 1822-1885* (Cambridge, Mass., 1967), pp. 122-23, 128, 134-38.

20. Clark, *History of Temperance*, pp. 93-94; Lane, *Policing the City*, pp. 138-39; Robinson, ed., *Warrington*, p. 334; *Massachusetts House Journal, 1866*, p. 401; *1867*, p. 436.

21. Boston *Commonwealth*, August 10, 24, September 14, October 19, 26, November 2, 1867; Boston *Evening Traveller*, April 22, July 3, 1867; Clark, *History of Temperance*, p. 94; *Appleton's Annual Cyclopedia, 1867*, pp. 481, 483; Shapiro, *Dana*, p. 135.

22. Lane, *Policing the City*, pp. 140-41; *Massachusetts House Journal, 1868*, pp. 35, 141-44, 252, 290, 467-70, 477, 721-22; *1869*, pp. 354, 587, 593; *Massachusetts Senate Journal, 1868*, pp. 71, 233, 253, 257; *1869*, p. 469; Boston *Commonwealth*, February 22, April 18, 1868, July 17, 1869.

23. *Appleton's Annual Cyclopedia, 1870*, pp. 468, 473; *1871*, pp. 491, 494; Boston *Commonwealth*, May 8, 1869.

24. Boston *Commonwealth*, February 22, 1873, June 6, 1874, February 13, April 3, 1875; Clark, *History of Temperance*, pp. 94-95, 148-53; Lane, *Policing the City*, pp. 162-63; *Appleton's Annual Cyclopedia, 1874*, pp. 519-20, 522-23; *1875*, p. 480; *1876*, pp. 514-15.

25. Boston *Commonwealth*, March 23, 1867; Edward C. Kirkland, *Men, Cities, and Transportation: A Study in New England History, 1820-1900* (2 vols., Cambridge, Mass., 1948), I:388-408.

26. Kirkland, *Men, Cities, and Transportation*, I:409-14; Boston *Commonwealth*, May 11, 1867, June 13, 1868; F. W. Bird to W. W. Clapp, [1868], Bird MSS, Houghton Library, Harvard University.

27. *Massachusetts House Journal, 1868*, pp. 648-50; Boston *Commonwealth*, June 13, 1868; *Appleton's Annual Cyclopedia, 1868*, p. 454.

28. Robinson, ed., *Warrington*, 326-27, 329; Boston *Commonwealth*, June 27, July 20, 1868, June 12, 1869.

29. Kirkland, *Men, Cities, and Transportation*, II:37-38; Shapiro, *Dana*, 134.

30. Kirkland, *Men, Cities, and Transportation*, II:38-43; *Massachusetts House Journal, 1869*, p. 630; *1870*, pp. 560-62, 664-66; George S. Merriam, *Life and Times of Samuel Bowles* (2 vols., New York, 1885), II:104-05; Samuel Bowles to Alexander H. Bullock, July 1, 1870, Bullock MSS; Boston *Commonwealth*, April 16, May 14, 21, 28, June 25, 1870; John K. Tarbox to Francis W. Bird, October 21, 1870, Bird MSS.

31. *Massachusetts House Journal, 1867*, pp. 372, 391, 398, 459; *1868* pp. 573, 613; *1869*, pp. 516, 540, 567, 597; Edward C. Kirkland, *Charles Francis Adams, Jr., 1835-1915* (Cambridge, Mass., 1966), pp. 46-50; *Men, Cities, and Transportation*, II:230-32, 237-40, 248, 250, 293-96, 304.

32. Charles Persons, "The Early History of Factory Legislation in Massachusetts," in Susan Kingsbury, ed., *Labor Laws and Their Enforcement* (New York, 1911), pp. 59-69; Charles Felton Pidgin, *History of the Bureau of Statistics of Labor in Massachusetts* (Boston, 1876), pp. 11-12; F.W. Bird to W.W. Clapp, [n.d.], Bird MSS; Montgomery, *Beyond Equality*, pp. 230-33; Harrington, *Banks*, p. 197.

33. Boston *Daily Advertiser*, August 25, 1971; Pidgin, *Bureau of Statistics of Labor*, pp. 17-20, 34-36.

34. Persons, "Early History of Factory Legislation," pp. 95-97; Leiby, *Wright*, pp. 49-50; Pidgin, *Bureau of Statistics of Labor*, pp. 14, 24; Montgomery, *Beyond Equality*, pp. 293-95; *Massachusetts House Journal, 1866*, pp. 431-32; *1867*, p. 247.

35. Montgomery, *Beyond Equality*, 262, 203-03; Persons, "Early History of Factory Legislation," pp. 99-101; *Massachusetts House Journal, 1866*, pp. 324, 348; *1867*, pp. 325, 581; *1868*, p. 408; *1870*, p. 679.

36. *Massachusetts House Journal, 1869*, pp. 206, 246, 607, 639; *Massachusetts Senate Journal, 1869*, pp. 140, 507; Boston *Commonwealth*, April 3, 1869; Leiby, *Wright*, pp. 51, 54; Pidgin, *Bureau of Statistics of Labor*, pp. 22-24; Montgomery, *Beyond Equality*, p. 369.

37. Leiby, *Wright*, pp. 29, 55-61; Pidgin, *Bureau of Statistics of Labor*, pp. 40-44, 52, 68-80.

38. Montgomery, *Beyond Equality*, pp. 369-70; Pidgin, *Bureau of Statistics of Labor*, pp. 25-26; *Massachusetts House Journal, 1870*, pp. 402, 473, 615-17, 643-45; Boston *Commonwealth*, June 25, 1870; Boston *Daily Advertiser*, June 16, 1870.

39. Leiby, *Wright*, p. 61; *Appleton's Annual Cyclopedia, 1870*, pp. 473-74, 477.

40. *Massachusetts House Journal, 1871*, pp. 393-95; *1872*, pp. 363-64; *1873*, pp. 401-03.

41. Persons, "History of Factory Legislation," pp. 123-25; *Massachusetts House Journal, 1874*, pp. 231-32.

42. *Massachusetts Legislative Documents, House, 1866*, No. 98, pp. 17, 46.

43. *Massachusetts House Journal, 1869*, pp. 250, 545, 598; *1870*, p. 342; Boston *Commonwealth*, May 14, 21, 1870; Vincent Yardley Bowditch, *Life and Correspondence of Henry Ingersoll Bowditch* (2 vols., Boston, 1902), II:218-30.

44. Robert W. Kelso, *The History of Public Poor Relief in Massachusetts, 1620-1920* (Boston, 1922), pp. 136-50; Gerald N. Grob, *The State and the Mentally Ill: A History*

of Worcester State Hospital in Massachusetts, 1830-1920 (Chapel Hill, N.C., 1966), pp. 180-186.

45. Grob, *State and the Mentally Ill*, pp. 189-92; Harold Schwartz, *Samuel Gridley Howe, Social Reformer, 1801-1876* (Cambridge, Mass., 1956), pp. 275-76; Katz, *Irony of School Reform*, pp. 184-89, 195-96.

46. Katz, *Irony of School Reform*, pp. 180-81; Grob, *State and the Mentally Ill*, pp. 178, 192-203, 227-29, 256-59; Boston *Commonwealth*, January 22, 1876.

47. Katz, *Irony of School Reform*, pp. 164-65, 206-211, 216-17; Marvin Lazerson, *Origins of the Urban School: Public Education in Massachusetts, 1870-1915* (Cambridge, Mass., 1971), pp. 8, 12, 16, 85-92; Boston *Commonwealth*, January 16, 1875; Handlin, *Boston's Immigrants*, pp. 215-16.

48. C.K. Yearley, *The Money Machine: The Breakdown and Reform of Government and Party Finance in the North, 1860-1920* (Albany, N.Y., 1970), pp. xv, 9-12, 18-27, 48-49, 81; Handlin, *Boston's Immigrants*, pp. 219-27.

49. Hans L. Trefousse, *Ben Butler: The South Called Him Beast* (New York, 1957), pp. 193-94, 207-08, 217-18; William D. Mallam, "Butlerism in Massachusetts," *New England Quarterly* 33 (1960): 186-206.

50. Samuel Shapiro, "The Butler-Dana Campaign in Essex County in 1868," *New England Quarterly* 31 (1958): 340-60; Trefousse, *Butler* p. 208; Mallam, "Butlerism," pp. 200-04; Leiby, *Wright*, pp. 52-53.

51. Shapiro, "Butler-Dana," pp. 358-59; Merriam, *Bowles*, II:93; Boston *Commonwealth*, September 19, 29, October 10, 13, 1868; William S. Robinson to Franklin B. Sanborn, August 10, 1868, Houghton Library, Harvard University; E.J. Sherman to Butler, September 9, December 6, 9, 1867, Charles Winslow to Butler, September 17, 1868, William E. Chandler to Butler, October 21, 1868, Butler MSS, Library of Congress.

52. Samuel Hoar to my Dear Uncle, November 5, 1868, George F. Hoar MSS, Massachusetts Historical Society, Boston, Massachusetts; Henry Lee to Frank Bird, November 28, 1868, Bird MSS; Trefousse, *Butler*, pp. 218-20; Mallam, "Butlerism," 193-99.

53. Boston *Daily Advertiser*, August 5, 21, 1871; Boston *Commonwealth*, August 30, 1873.

54. Trefousse, *Butler*, pp. 222-23; Boston *Commonwealth*, October 2, 9, 1869; Boston *Daily Advertiser*, August 21, 25, 31, September 9, 18, 22, 25, 1871.

55. Trefousse, *Butler*, pp. 224-27; Robinson, ed., *Warrington*, pp. 131-34; Merriam, *Bowles*, II:108; Boston *Commonwealth*, September 30, 1871 August 30, September 13, 1873; W. B. Washburn to George F. Hoar, September 29, 1871, Waldo Higginson to Hoar, September 29, 1871, George F. Hoar MSS; E.R. Hoar to U.S. Grant, September 13, 1873, Norcross MSS, Massachusetts Historical Society; N. E. Green to Butler, October 2, 1871, Henry Wilson to Butler, October 7, 1871, Butler MSS.

56. Richard E. Welch, Jr., *George Frisbie Hoar and the Half-Breed Republicans* (Cambridge, Mass., 1971), pp. 40-44; Harrington, *Banks*, 201-03; Merriam, *Bowles*, II:179, 206; Boston *Commonwealth*, April 20, September 14, 1872; *Appleton's Annual Cyclopedia, 1872*, p. 503.

57. Richard Harmond, " 'The Beast' in Boston: Benjamin F. Butler as Governor of Massachusetts," *Journal of American History* 55 (1968): 266-80.

58. Mallam, "Butlerism," p. 206; Merriam, *Bowles*, II:215, 272; Robinson, *Warrington*, p. 390; J. F. Aspen to William Atkinson, October 1, 1871, Atkinson MSS, Massachusetts Historical Society; E. J. Sherman to Butler, June 15, 1867, T. J. Hastings to G. F. Sargent, August 18, 1871, Walter Scott to Butler, September 11, 1871, Alfred Puffer to Butler, September 29, 1871, John Pope Hodnett to Butler, September 16, 1873, all in Butler MSS.

2

CONNECTICUT

Poor Progress in the Land of Steady Habits

John Niven

The end of hostilities in the spring of 1865 found Connecticut as unprepared for peace as it had been for war. Economically, the industries of the state had been more involved with the Union war effort than those of any other state in the North. Connecticut's highly diversified industrial plants had become a veritable arsenal for war production to the immense profit of its manufacturers, few of whom had the foresight or the inclination during times of high labor costs and higher material costs to make any significant conversion to the unknown demands and dimensions of a peace-time market. Notable exceptions were the heavy investments made during the war in the machine tool industry of Hartford, a lucrative spin-off from small arms manufacture, the construction of cotton mills to capitalize on the renewal of the plantation trade, and a resumption of railroad expansion.

But for most enterprises in the state, the transition from an expanding war-time market to a diminishing, harshly competitive peace-time economy was difficult and hedged about with uncertainty. Sudden and drastic retrenchment became general. Most of the new war-time factories and many established plants had closed their doors before Appomattox. Everywhere the labor force was cut back and, more frequently than not, wages reduced, just when 35,000 discharged veterans were seeking employment and immigration was on the upswing.[1] Despite the widespread unemployment, the cost of living for the average family remained at or near inflated war-time levels, only beginning to decline six months after the collapse of the Confederacy. It was not surprising then that these conditions resulted in a good deal of popular unrest, nor that there was a dramatic rise of drunkenness and crime. There

1. Notes to this chapter are to be found on pp. 46-49.

was an equally dramatic rise in agitation for social reform, which found outlets in the temperance movement and, to a lesser degree, in the eight-hour day movement to improve working conditions.[2] These problems of adjustment claimed the attention of politicians, even though the leadership of both parties would probably have preferred to concentrate exclusively on national concerns.

The war had made a profound impression on the public mind, and as the people of Connecticut had been unprepared economically to deal with the problems of peace, so they were confused about the problems of reconstruction. Almost from the outset of the war the Republican Party had been divided between a state faction and a Congressional faction. The state faction, headed by Governor William A. Buckingham, was closer to the grass roots of Republican power in the countryside and the rural mill towns. Its stance on war aims, as expressed in its most persuasive newspaper, the Hartford *Evening Press,* was consistently more Radical than that of the Congressional faction, whose sentiments were echoed in the venerable *Hartford Courant.* James Dixon, who had been a United States Senator since 1856, was the controlling influence of the Congressional faction and through federal office-holders made his power felt in party councils. An inveterate conservative, he had for a time backed McClellan against Lincoln in the presidential campaign of 1864.[3]

Timid and irresolute as a public man, Dixon was a skillful operator in local politics, a dangerous adversary who blocked Radicals and moderates and blurred the party's image in the public mind. His conservative attitude on emancipation, and on other war-time measures, was consistent with his views on reconstruction.[4] He had backed Lincoln's 10 percent plan for the readmission of Southern states, and he wholeheartedly endorsed Andrew Johnson's program of reconstruction. Though Dixon had been a Whig and a Know-Nothing before he became a Republican, he was as devoted to states rights and to white supremacy as the most confirmed peace Democrat. To members of the state faction Dixon was the enemy. His deviousness, his opportunism, his very real personal power, his seemingly callous disregard for everything they thought worthy and moral and true, made him not only hated and feared but disruptive.[5]

Worried lest trimmers like Dixon confuse the electorate and permit the defeated Confederacy to win through political maneuver what it had lost on the battlefield, Radicals and moderates alike saw a conspiracy hatched by President Andrew Johnson that would restore the prewar coalition of Southern and Northern Democrats. Men like Buckingham, Charles Dudley Warner, editor of the *Press*, and ex-Congressman Orris S. Ferry, envisaged a nation turned over to its recent enemies. Southern response to Johnsonian reconstruction was seen as proof of their intentions with the enactment of "Black Codes," which Warner declared flatly in the *Press* to be a first step in the repeal of the Thirteenth Amendment.[6] The election of many former

Confederate leaders to Congress under the Johnsonian program seemed further evidence of the coming political takeover.

Closer to home the Republicans had already received a jolt that confirmed some of their deepest forebodings about the future. In May 1865, the General Assembly ratified the Thirteenth Amendment without a dissenting vote. But heavy opposition suddenly developed when the exultant Radicals then moved an amendment to the state constitution that would have granted suffrage to some 2,000 Connecticut blacks. The proposed amendment as originally drawn would have simply striken the word "white" from the qualifications prescribed for a voter. But the issue of whether blacks were citizens was unclear. Had the Thirteenth Amendment superseded the Dred Scott decision on the question of citizenship? In a resolution passed along strict party lines the General Assembly asked the state supreme court to rule on the subject. The court rendered its verdict on June 27, 1865; "A free colored person born in this state,"said the court, "is a citizen of this state and of the United States within the meaning of the Amendment referred to." Radical leaders now felt secure; they had no difficulty in securing a two-thirds majority for their amendment in the General Assembly. But they were staggered when the people rejected it in seven of the state's eight counties by a resounding popular majority of 6,173 votes. That leaders of the state faction blamed Dixon for this mighty rebuff as much as they blamed the Democrats is readily apparent from many sources.[7] On the eve of the referendum a worried Warner had beseeched Secretary of the Navy Gideon Welles for public endorsement of the suffrage amendment to counter Dixon's influence. Welles was reluctant because he felt whatever he said would be misinterpreted. But he finally let the Republican papers in the state print that he believed education not race should determine whether a man was competent to exercise the suffrage intelligently.[8] His statement was of little help to the state faction, or to more conservative Republicans for that matter. Charging Dixon and his lieutenants with major responsibility, the New Haven Palladium blamed those "treacherous Republicans, who, in city and county struck hands with the Copperheads to perpetuate the mean prejudices of race and caste."[9]

However much they may have raged in their prints and in their private correspondence, proponents of black suffrage could not ignore the overwhelming defeat of their suffrage amendment. With a state ticket and a United States senator to be chosen in 1866, common prudence suggested that they bide their time. But what formula could they devise for a delaying action? The campaign and election came too early for any positive indication of the relative strength of the President or of his opponents in Congress. Connecticut Radicals and moderates decided to shelve their principles for the time being, straddle the issue of reconstruction, and rely on placing their men in strategic positions.

Governor Buckingham, one of the Union's great war governors, had refused to be a candidate for reelection. He had his eye on a Senate seat, and so did Joseph R. Hawley, a founder of the Republican Party in the state, former abolitionist, political general of some distinction, and part owner of the *Evening Press*. Hawley had begun his career as a protégé of Gideon Welles, but his recent course had been sufficiently Radical to alarm Dixon. Hawley in the Senate could be a dangerous opponent as well as a supporter of Congressional reconstruction. Although Hawley's friends, notably Warner, were pushing him for the Senate, they feared he might lose in a three-cornered contest with the incumbent conservative, L. S. Foster, and the openly Radical, Buckingham. When Dixon suggested Hawley for the governorship, they accepted his proposition, albeit reluctantly, rather than risk the enmities that the senatorial contest would surely stir up.

With the surface appearance of a united party, the Republicans enthusiastically nominated Hawley for governor,[10] and their platform tried to suggest a spirit of harmony by ignoring the struggle between President and Congress.[11] The Democrats, sensing victory after more than seven years of defeat, chose for their standard bearer James E. English, a highly respected New Haven businessman, who had served in Congress during the war and had supported most of Lincoln's war measures. Unlike the ambiguous Republican platform, Democrats came out four-square behind Johnson and presidential reconstruction.[12]

During the campaign both sides sought presidential support and both claimed to have received Johnson's blessing.[13] But the issues were so unclear that the election could not be considered a mandate for either the President or his critics.[14] Hawley beat English by 541 votes and the Republicans carried the General Assembly by reduced margins. A change of from 35 to 55 votes in three districts would have given the Democrats the upper house and hence a decisive say in who should be the next United States Senator.[15] Even as it was, had Gideon Welles or the incumbent Lafayette Foster, both conservatives, made a vigorous effort for the seat, either could probably have won. But neither Welles nor Foster would make the fight and a moderate, Orris S. Ferry of Fairfield County, prevailed over the more radical Buckingham, though for regional rather than ideological reasons. This closely divided legislature did approve the Fourteenth Amendment, but only near the end of the session and only after sharp and extended debate over whether or not suffrage would remain a state right.[16]

The Republican Party in Connecticut, and more particularly its Radical wing, gained strength and confidence when the Democrats and their allies among the Johnson-sponsored National Union movement were heavily defeated in the fall elections of 1866. Clearly, it was reasoned in party circles, forthright support for Congressional reconstruction in the spring election of 1867 was what the public wanted. Accordingly, Republican managers drew up a Radical platform, renominated Hawley, and dropped all conservatives from the state ticket. In an excess of foolhardy enthusiasm, they also purged Dixon's principal officeholder in the state, the astute politician Nehemiah D.

Sperry, postmaster of New Haven and a member of the Republican National Committee.[17]

The Democrats renominated James E. English for governor and added to their slate a leading conservative Republican. Their platform, however, was far from the moderate document they had framed a year earlier. Its resolutions dealing with national affairs were written as if no war had been fought, no victory won. An extreme expression of states rights led to a bitter arraignment of Congress and a pledge to resist "centralism" in every aspect. These points were cleverly interlarded with fulsome praise for Johnson's policy on reconstruction, as if to imply that the Democratic platform was also the President's platform. Conservatives who had sponsored the Philadelphia National Union Convention were outraged. As Henry J. Raymond wrote in the *New York Times* on February 14, 1867: "the Democrats propose to recognize elements with which the country will have nothing to do under the management of men in whom the country has no confidence. Aptly illustrated by Connecticut . . . it would have the country governed as if no war had been waged and won."[18]

These state tickets and platforms, then, presented a relatively clear political choice on national issues. The Congressional conventions and candidates, on the other hand, though decidedly more important in deciding actual issues, permitted no choice at all. The candidates especially were more concerned with their own personal ambitions than with reconstruction. Typical of the Congressional races was one in the Fourth District where two millionaires had not only bought their nominations but waged their campaigns on a dollar-for-dollar basis. Even the easy going political morals of the late 1860s could not accept the Republican candidate, Phineas T. Barnum. Even with powerful support from Hawley and Ferry, eleven ballots had been required before Barnum wrung his nomination from the reluctant convention. This evidence of strong distaste from members of his own party was ominous. Too many sober and industrious citizens in the land of steady habits did not care to be represented in Congress by "Joyce Heth," "The Wooly Horse," or "The Cardiff Giant." His Democratic opponent, William H. Barnum, was a wealthy ironmaster from Lime Rock. Like his more notorious namesake, the Democratic Barnum was primarily interested in the personal prestige of public office, although he had an economic motive in raising the tariff on iron, and his political views were notably conservative.

President Johnson was concerned about the outcome of the Connecticut election, but beyond a wavering pressure on federal officeholders, his interference was slight. The Republicans had little cause for worry from bolting Conservatives, whose numbers had dwindled for want of strong leadership. But Republicans were vulnerable in other areas. The party had a poor record on labor reform, a vocal issue that could mean the loss of several hundred votes in some closely contested key districts; the postwar industrial recession still lingered; and New Haven Republicans were jealous of the pretensions and the power of their Hartford associates. P. T. Barnum was an awesome handicap.

Nor were the issues of reconstruction important enough to keep many of the publications influential in Connecticut, including the *New York Tribune* and the *Nation*, in line. The *Nation* supported the entire Republican ticket except Barnum, regretting that "General Hawley should be saddled with him," and urging every Connecticut Republican to scratch his name as a "religious duty." James Gordon Bennett, however, a bitter personal enemy of the great showman, furnished the most effective attacks, sparing not an arrow in his editorial quiver of abuse. Scarcely a day went by that the *New York Herald* did not feature some unsavory bit from Barnum's past, some allusion to his complete unfitness for public office.[19]

More menacing than the onslaught against P. T. Barnum or the clamor of the workingmen's movement in New Haven was the depth of the resentment that Nehemiah Sperry exhibited toward the Hartford Radicals. Sperry had announced to New Haven Republicans after the Republican convention that he would support all of the Republican candidates except Hawley. Sperry had early seen in Hawley a menace to his own control and resolved to destroy the latter's growing power. Although several New Haven Radicals, including O. H. Platt, who was then a rising Republican politician, hoped for a reconciliation, Sperry began to refer to Hawley as "a drunkard and a black hearted wretch." When Sperry openly consulted with English, he left no doubt in the Governor's mind where he and his friends stood. The prospects for an increased Hawley vote in New Haven, never bright, dimmed perceptibly when the New Haven postmaster swung his very real influence over to the Democrats.

Few Republicans were hopeful when they went to the polls on rainy April 2, and their gloomy prognosis was confirmed by a 987 vote majority for the Democratic state ticket. In addition, the Republicans were defeated in three of the four Congressional districts, though they managed to cling to their control of the state legislature. The Democrats, elated at their first victory in a decade, read into it a complete repudiation of Radicalism.[20] But the scantiness of their margin in all contests was, as in the case of the previous spring's result, still insufficient to determine a clear verdict on anything. In fact, the Democratic margin may well have hinged upon their skillful handling in Connecticut of the eight-hour day movement.

Radicals were deeply chagrined at their defeat and painfully aware that winning command of the Republican Party was not the same as winning a majority of the Connecticut electorate. Should the Sperry-Hawley feud continue indefinitely, the Republican position might well become hopeless. So prudence dictated a gesture of conciliation to New Haven, as well as to all conservatives who still remained in the party. Other Radicals were intrigued by tactics that seemed to be proving successful elsewhere, especially the effort to attract rural factory workers in the textile manufacturing regions of New England. "We must secure the cooperation of business men in our mechanical and manufacturing establishments," wrote Congressman H. H. Starkweather of Norwich to Governor Hawley in April 1867. "The Copperheads have possession of the *grog shops*. We must take possession of the workshops of this state."[21] The fact that the Democrats had apparently won the election with workingmen votes lent a sense of urgency to this proposal. Unless more labor votes went to Republicans, or at least were kept from the opponent, an expanding labor population might eventually doom the party to minority status. Hence Radicals moved to control the votes of workers. In their quest they were able to make common cause with uneasy industrialists.

Almost one-fifth of Connecticut's total population was foreign-born in 1870, and 50 percent of the foreign-born lived in Hartford and New Haven. Yet it was not in the areas of greatest population growth that political coercion of workingmen was first employed, but rather in the near feudal mill towns, where employers were accustomed to regulating the habits of their employees. Immigrant and native workers in these towns were wholly dependent on the local owner. The matter of controlling their politics seemed simple and logical, especially now that the new industrial society seemed jeopardized by defeat at the polls. Many Connecticut mill owners had experienced a thrill of fear at the apparent strength of the Democratic-workingmen alliance and were ready to adopt punitive measures against what they regarded as a menacing labor movement. The owners found it easy to work in close harmony with those Republican politicians who also wanted to break the labor-Democratic alliance, and they struck a union that was destined to hold the Democrats in check for seven years and all but obliterate labor as a political force in Connecticut.

The earliest incident of political coercion in the postwar period occurred at the Portland quarries in 1866, but not until after the hotly contested campaign of 1867 did such an approach emerge as a definite instrument of political policy. Political coercion, when it became general, was practiced to its greatest extent in those areas where eight-hour agitation had been most intense, at the textile towns of Rockville, Vernon, Sprague, and Hannover and, of course, at the Portland quarries. Republican mill owners of Rockville lost no time in a frontal assault upon the local eight-hour organization. One day after the election of 1867 they discharged forty spinners and weavers and at the same time posted notices that all members of the Workingmen's Union Eight-Hour League would, if discovered, suffer immediate dismissal. Employers also announced an increase of one hour in working time and a 10 percent reduction of wages as a blanket penalty for the prevalence of labor agitation. In neighboring Vernon, Edward Senior, an eight-hour leader, reported that between 150 and 200 workmen had remained away from the polls because of intimidation. Even so, he boasted, the normal Republican majority had been cut in half. Again, retaliation was swift. Vernon woolen manufacturers locked out a number of suspected employees and notified the rest that the mills would be run twelve hours a day with a 10 percent reduction of wages.

At Portland, already the scene of flagrant employee coercion, a large number of workmen were discharged for voting the Democratic ticket. But F. W. Russell and his quarry-owner colleagues apparently overreached themselves. Their summary action precipitated a grave strike in the area. Republican workmen, with their Democratic brethren, to the number of over 1,000, left their jobs, bringing the industrial life of that busy little city to a complete standstill. Following the advice of labor leaders, representatives of the striking workmen called upon Democratic Congressmen-elect Julius Hotchkiss of Middletown and Richard D. Hubbard of Hartford to arbitrate their case with the quarry owners. Hubbard and Hotchkiss accepted the arbitration proposal and, together with Samuel Babcock and Edward Strauss, representing the strikers, met with the quarry owners on Saturday evening, April 6. What followed was a display of intransigence, insolence, and tactlessness on the part of the quarry owners, which was as insulting to the well-meaning Hubbard and Hotchkiss as it was overbearing to the workers' representatives. The owners brusquely told the arbitrators that when the advice of outside parties was needed in quarry management, they would be informed; that they, as owners, should hire whom they pleased without dictation from anyone.

Stung by this peremptory rebuff, James Gallagher, a New Haven cigarmaker and an ambitious Democratic politician, resolved to see what he could accomplish in his dual capacity as chairman of the Democratic state committee and state senator. He prepared a legislative program that would correct obvious mistreatment of laboring men and called a meeting of the state committee to convene at the Tontine Hotel in New Haven on the 18th of April to discuss: "such measures as may be necessary to protect the workingmen of Rockville, Vernon, and Portland against the infamous course pursued by their employers in depriving them of their employment, or forcing them to vote contrary to their oaths and the dictates of their own consciences and to consider whether the laboring classes can be protected by that provision of our Constitution which requires the General Assembly to pass laws to protect the free ballot, by prohibiting bribery and all undue influence."

Minutes of the meeting were not made public, but the Democrat press cautiously discussed various reforms in labor-management relations. The *Norwich Advertiser* thought the state ought to compel corporations to pay their employees money instead of orders on the company stores, and weekly rather than monthly or quarterly. On the overall picture, the *Advertiser* was more forthright. An editorial, entitled "The Tyranny of the Factories," stated that what "Connecticut wants is an Emancipation Act," and Editor Stedman gave notice that the *Advertiser* and its weekly edition, the *Aurora*, would battle for the abolition of "factory slavery of Eastern Connecticut, and if we should happen to tread on the toes of some arrogant mill owner he had better . . . thank his stars that he got off so easily. We have less respect for the man who attempts to coerce free white men to vote against their wishes than for any slave driver who ever trod an Alabama plantation." Regardless of editorial activity and Democratic threats, however, the quarry owners in Portland and the textile manufacturers of Vernon and Rockville abated not one jot in their accustomed dealings with their employees. The Portland strike was a failure after four weeks, the Eight-Hour Leagues of Vernon and Rockville were smashed, and the extra hours for less pay continued as before.[22]

The Democratic-workingmen alliance countered by securing the passage of a law in the 1867 legislative session that forbade political coercion, but it was general in nature and contained no provision for enforcement. Throughout the fall of 1867 and the spring of 1868, numerous manufacturers continued to demand the political allegiance of their workers. In his eagerness for a successful campaign, O. H. Platt, newly appointed chairman of the Republican state central committee, was reported to have urged every manufacturer in the state to influence as many of his employees as possible. No direct evidence exists that Platt entered actively into a political combination with the mill owners, but when the manufacturers of his home town, Meriden, employed political coercion openly and successfully for the party in 1868, it seemed more than merely coincidental.

About a month before the election Meriden manufacturers and local Radical leaders became uneasy at very definite signs of political independence and a smoldering eight-hour sentiment among the mill-workers. Resolved to instill discipline at all costs, they formed a Manufacturers' League, made a general reduction of wages, notified all employees that they would be blacklisted if they attempted to resist, and purchased the Meriden *Visitor*, renamed the *Republican*, to defend their course in print.[23] Heedless of the warning, many workers in the Meriden vicinity formed a Workingmen's Union, which promptly went out on strike over a reduction in wages when living costs remained so high. The usual retaliatory devices, however, such as loss of credit at company-owned stores and the daily threat of eviction from company-owned tenements, soon broke the Union's spirit. After enduring ten days of privation, the workmen were more than ready to meet with representatives of the Manufacturers' League, where they agreed to disband their union and pledge support to the Republican ticket in return for some trifling wage concessions. On election day, the entire Meriden area returned one of the largest Republican majorities in the history of the party.[24]

Manufacturers in other cities and towns took advantage of the dull 1868 market to wring political advantage from wage cuts. A cold winter and low prices for cotton cloth had fallen with crushing severity upon the mill-workers of eastern Connecticut. The Sprague mills of Baltic had been operated only part time during the winter months, and wages had been reduced 20 percent under the previous summer rates. In March the Sprague managers resumed full-time work without an increase of wages. Despite this loss of worker purchasing power, prices of most necessities at the company store rose to higher levels until the operatives were driven to the breaking point. When their demand for a 20 percent increase in wages was peremptorily rejected, 1,500 of them left their jobs on the same day as the Meriden strike, bringing operations in Sprague to an abrupt halt. Although the Sprague strikers paraded the streets and kept the village at a fever pitch of excitement, the managers made no move except to close the mills and the company store. They had decided to wait until the day before the election, promise a wage increase, and let hunger chasten their working force. On March 28, 1868 this decision was made known to the strikers, together with certain hints regarding the imminent election. On April 2 the township of Sprague turned in its usual Republican majority. As an example of how political intimidation was probably practiced in Sprague, and with all due allowance to its partisanship, the *New Haven Register* had this to say: "A. and W. Sprague, the wealthy cotton manufacturers, own a granite quarry at Oneco, in the town of Sterling, in which a considerable number of men are employed. Of course the cotton lords cannot personally superintend the business and they have intrusted it to Isaac M. Sweet . . . . He has been in the habit of standing guard over the ballot box to "spot" his workmen when they vote, and he has given them to understand that continued employment depended upon following his wishes politically. At the presidential election four men braved his displeasure and were discharged."[25]

The Meriden and Sprague settlements were only the most notable of the many examples of political coercion that, once established, became a customary expedient until the panic and depression of 1873. Originally directed against the eight-hour movement, and having achieved its purpose in smashing that organization, it became an invaluable method of ensuring Republican control in the mill towns.[26]

Since the Democrats saw little possibility of gaining votes in the mill towns, and since the Workingmen's Union, now seemingly wrecked beyond repair, was neither a benefit nor a menace, the Democratic Party and press became largely indifferent to labor problems. Abandoned by the Democrats, practically harried out of the state by the Republicans, their economic existence threatened by imported cheap labor, workingmen leaders became convinced that only a radical change of some recognized institutions would improve the lowly estate of the worker. But with this change in policy, which became evident after 1868, what support they had received from liberal-minded men of both parties melted away. By 1871 the cause of labor reform itself was largely discredited in the public mind.

Political coercion might bring in the votes, but it was of no avail in dampening the factionalism that continued to beset the Republican Party in

Connecticut at the state level. A Senatorial seat was to be filled in 1868 and that was sure to renew personal quarrels and regional rivalries. Hawley was again a candidate, and former Governor Buckingham was campaigning for the nomination too. Forces were set in motion, both in Hartford and New Haven, to check Hawley and prevent, if possible, the almost certain rupture of the Republican Party into opposing camps. An alliance was entered into between the Norwich adherents of Buckingham, Sperry, and the peppery Isaac "Ike" Bromley, who had recently assumed the editorship of the *Hartford Post.* United by common opposition to Hawley and a desire to modify the extreme Radicalism of the Hartford set for the good of the party, these men of dissimilar outlooks were engineering the first practical attempt to block a mass withdrawal of Republican moderates and conservatives. As a reaction to ultra Radicalism, it would prove eminently stronger than the handful of Johnson Republicans who were working with the Democrats.[27]

The coalition needed a Hartford moderate as candidate for governor. Marshall Jewell, a rich leather manufacturer, seemed the ideal man, and he was nominated at the Republican convention on January 16, 1868. As the guiding force of the Jewell Leather company of Hartford, he had made a fortune in harnesses and machine belting during the Civil War. In common with other successful men of his generation, the portly Jewell developed a fondness for art treasures, European trips, and the luxury of politics. He had opened his purse wide to the party in 1867 and had been nominated for state senator, only to be defeated badly by his Democratic opponent. Discounting the obvious reasons that made Jewell the candidate of New Haven and Norwich, it would seem remarkable that a man with such an undistinguished political career should be selected to lead the state ticket.[28]

But there were other factors that combined to assist Jewell. He was an affable representative of the new industrialism, unsullied by any contact with competing railroad interests, and he was very acceptable to moderates and conservatives. His views on reconstruction, it was assumed, would be much more businesslike than those of the Radical doctrinaires. Besides, the depression, which still hung over Connecticut's economic life, had spread the Southern market heresy among Republican businessmen. Jewell was a prominent heretic.[29] As if to emphasize this aspect, the managers concocted a platform on national affairs, stating boldly that the South must be made safe for blacks and loyalists.

Undeclared in the platform but clearly on the minds of most delegates, and especially the rural mill owners, was the fate of black labor in the South. For many of them prosperity was utterly dependent on supplies of cheap raw cotton, cotton that black labor produced. They opposed mass migration of blacks to the North or the West, not for any particularly racist reasons but squarely on the grounds of their own particular economic interests. Protection of the blacks, education to a point, civil rights, and wages, were looked upon as incentives to keep the labor force where it was and to keep the bales of cotton rolling North. As William W. Ellsworth, the state's most respected jurist and spokesman for the moderate Republicans, had said during the war: "These laborers are wanted, every man of them where they now are—where they were born and have lived . . . fully acclimated and taught the labors of the Plantation. . . . Once freed, enjoying the benefits of free labor and secure in their property and rights, they would," Ellsworth asserted, "assume a new character at once."[30] Ellsworth's stand, while not entirely devoid of humanitarian impulses, was with rare exception the view shared by the rural mill owners, local autocrats, who brooked no interference in the management of their factories and the regulation of their villages. They would resort to any tactic, including political coercion, to support moderate but not Radical measures and candidates on the issue of reconstruction.

An instant chorus of denunciation arose from the Radicals, to whom Jewell's nomination had come as a surprise. The *Meriden Republican* saw in it an alignment of forces against Hawley and detected the sinister hand of Postmaster Sperry. Another Radical paper, the *Litchfield Enquirer,* opposed Jewell on political principles as a compromiser—whose nomination was the result of "timid and corrupt leaders who are willing that the party do right . . . provided it does it softly and in the dark."[31]

No such vocal disputation appeared to disturb Democratic harmony. Irish workingmen and states rights groups were silent, and to all outward appearances the Democracy would again represent an unbroken phalanx. The appearance of a considerable number of Johnson Republicans lent an air of nonpartisanship, which was dramatized when the state central committee took the unusual step of dropping the word "Democrat" and substituting "Conservative" in its convention notice. The previous year's ticket was renominated by acclamation, and the delegates approved a platform devoted in the main to national affairs which breathed confidence in the President's policies.

The two parties entered into a desperate struggle, both knowing full well the effect a resounding victory might have in national politics. For looming over the political battle was the great impeachment trial in Washington and the Presidential election in November. But neither side won a clear-cut victory on election day. English doubled his 1867 majority to defeat Jewell by 1,772 votes, while the Democrats failed to gain in the legislature. In the house the Republicans held a 22-seat majority and they picked up 2 senate seats. Once again a Connecticut election had failed to produce a distinct victory for either side.[32]

The *Courant*, which had been purchased and merged with the *Press*, called the election "an ineffaceable and eternal blot upon the record of the Commonwealth." But Hawley could not have been too chagrined at the defeat of Jewell, which seemed at the time to have disposed of a major hindrance in his campaign for the United States Senate. The election result had certainly improved the position of the Hartford Radicals. Apparently ignoring the enmity of New Haven, Hawley forged ahead in his canvass of Republican assemblymen until H. H. Starkweather, the Republican Congressman who represented the New London-Windham district, suddenly arrived to conduct Buckingham's campaign. The brisk trading of the persuasive Starkweather, assisted by Sperry and the *New York Tribune,* which had been induced to support Buckingham, soon narrowed the margin. It took only two ballots at the Republican caucus on May 10 to finish Hawley off, and a third to nominate Buckingham, so smoothly functioning was the Norwich-New Haven arrangement. On May 14, 1868 the Republican legislature elected Buckingham to the Senate by a strict party vote.[33]

The ill will between New Haven and Hartford, which had been intensified by the election of Buckingham, remained, but like many factional arguments, hot words quickly ran their course. The greater needs of the party demanded unified action. The Republican Party had suffered two defeats in three years; Negro suffrage, an objective which promised political supremacy, had been scorned both by the electorate and by the legislature. With their minority position amply demonstrated by two state elections and by the increasing popular vote of the Democrats, some means other than the apparently unobtainable Negro vote had to be found. In the recent state campaign and election. Republican leaders had become uncomfortably aware of the wholesale Democratic registration of immigrant voters, a process which, if allowed to continue unchecked, might cost them the governance of the state indefinitely. Republicans were quick to see that if it were made difficult for immigrants to vote, a power clearly within the province of the legislature, the Democrats would be severely weakened not merely for one or two elections but possibly for a decade.[34]

To a certain extent, the Democrats were to blame for this kindling of interest among Republicans in the political consequences of immigration. Had they conducted themselves with more discretion; had they not been quite so zealous in garnering immigrant votes for the election of 1868, the Republicans might not have been impelled to take drastic action. But the Democrats had openly flaunted all precepts of good citizenship, evidently caring little whether their new voters understood the American political process or not, so long as they cast Democratic ballots. Among the foreign elements in the cities, and particularly among their fraternal orders, Democratic organizers labored as they never had before. Democratic registrars naturalized immigrants at a phenomenal rate, as many as 900 a day at the peak of the state campaign. By the use of various stratagems they also evaded the inadequate state constitutional provision on suffrage.

Thus, when Jewell was defeated by the greatest Democratic majority in years, the Republicans attributed it to the immigrant vote. The Democrats soon learned that these comments were not idle journalistic speculations. O.H.

Platt, chairman of the Republican state central committee, sent a secret circular letter to party members in the legislature, which declared bluntly that if the Republicans were to carry the state for Grant, the legislature must take steps to frame a revised election law. He urged the attendance of all Republican members of the legislature at a special caucus for that purpose on May 25. The caucus met and appointed a committee headed by William T. Minor to draw up a new bill, doubtless a labor of love to the former Know-Nothing governor. At any rate, his committee wasted no time in drawing up two comprehensive bills that struck at the very heart of the Democratic immigrant vote.[35]

Democratic leaders at once recognized the threat to their political future. Their minority position in the legislature meant certain passage of the bills unless they could protract debate long enough to secure final adjournment. They could count on a veto from Governor English, but this could hold up passage for only two weeks at the most. Under the constitution the governor was allowed but three days to consider a bill after it reached his desk. If unsigned in that period, it became law automatically; if vetoed within the time limit, a simple majority of both houses could override.[36] Republicans took care to prepare themselves for all eventualities by hastily adopting a fifteen-minute cloture rule in the house and senate. They were able to choke off debate and pass both bills.[37]

On July 28 Governor English vetoed both bills. He subjected the election bill to a searching analysis, reasoning as the state supreme court had when it nullified the Soldiers' Voting Law in 1862. In that decision the court had determined that electoral qualifications were clearly outside of legislative power, because any legislature might have a direct interest in the qualifications of those voters who elected it. The vetoes were an eloquent defense of civil rights, but they failed to make any impression on the Republican majority. Within minutes after their reading, all opposition was crushed and both bills were made laws of the state. Jubilant Republicans who read the results in their evening papers must have noted a general belief that the state would be safe for Grant in the fall.

Three years of party strife, during which a Republican majority in Congress had enacted laws designed to reconstruct the South and had nearly succeeded in removing Andrew Johnson, were fast drawing to a close. What effect had these momentous events on the political climate of Connecticut? Any answer to such a difficult question must necessarily be qualified, but it would be a reasonable assumption to say that the struggle in Washington was the greatest single political determinant of public opinion and parties for the three postwar years. To a lesser degree, the same sharply divergent views on the nature of the Union, on reconstruction, and on economic policies were present in Connecticut. Connecticut Radicals, in common with their associates in Washington, had been keenly aware of their minority status, and when the people rejected Negro suffrage they had utilized their legislative majority in an effort to reduce the immigrant vote of the Democrats. The political expediency that evolved the Naturalization and Registration Laws of 1868 bore after all a resemblance to those measures that were taken to ensure Republican Party supremacy in the Southern states.

Political reaction in Connecticut had gone generally along conservative lines. Citizens in the "Land of Steady Habits" refused to accept the proposals of the more extreme Radicals. The stand of the Democratic party undoubtedly had much to do with shaping this attitude. It had developed a realistic program that transformed a band of bitter malcontents to a group of responsible citizens whose views on government and society provided a haven for all conservative men of Union principles. And new leaders had emerged—men like English and James Gallagher, the Irish-American cigar-maker—who held conservative views on the role of government, but at the same time were willing to listen to the demands of workingmen for legislation that would limit the hours of labor and improve the lot of working women and children.[38] It had also been a time of devotion to local issues and a wholehearted support for an orderly transition to peace-time pursuits.

Compelling economic reasons, combined with political and constitutional motives, had been largely responsible for this change of direction. Older wealth, whose interests were tied up with the commercial rather than the crop aspects of the Southern market, still managed the Democratic organization in the state. And New Haven Democrats, though increasingly troubled by the aspirations of the restive Irish under their political control, still looked to the Trowbridges and the Ingersolls, families who had made shipping fortunes in the West India trade and then invested their money in carriage factories, the manufacture and transport of hardware, and other items for the southern trade. Accustomed to dealing with the white planter class, these influential Democrats assumed that Congressional reconstruction was primarily responsible for the economic prostration of the South. They lent all the power and all the wealth at their command to a drive for the restoration of their old economic and political ties. The interests of Hartford Democrats differed somewhat from their New Haven colleagues. Most were former Jacksonians, the Burrs, Thomas H. Seymour, Isaac Toucey, and W. W. Eaton. Well-to-do journalists and lawyers, they had once been young ambitious men, mildly liberal for their day, but long since conservative, property-minded citizens, who had never thought slavery wrong, who had all but worshipped the doctrines and the ritual of the old Democracy. Although over-shadowed by the new leadership, they made their presence felt on the platform committees and in the legislature.[39]

The Republican Party, like the Democratic, had also changed under the pressures of the postwar years, but unlike the Democratic organization the transition had not been accomplished so smoothly. From the onset there had been friction between Radical and conservative, between the state faction and the Congressional faction. But in 1867 a more dangerous quarrel was touched off within the party itself. Politically, the tendency of the Republicans to engage in factionalism stemmed from the make-up of the party—former Whigs, Americans, and Free-Soil Democrats, a quarrelsome mixture—the uncertain forays of Washington Radicals, moderates and conservatives into local patronage, and the jealousies of local machines, which had been built up over years of continuous victory. Then too, the tug of war between the President and Congress had certainly caused a state of flux and apprehension among Connecticut Republicans, which abetted inconsistency.

Little difference existed in the underlying political philosophy of the Radical and moderate factions; but heightening industrial acceleration had sharpened the intrasectional competion between the two foci of Connecticut industry: New Haven and Hartford. It was inevitable that the industrial hopes and fears, the jealousy and the pride of these two areas should find expression in politics, that each area should strive to secure legislation for its own benefit. The New Haven area was more urbanized, had more heavy industry, a greater immigrant population, more taxable property than the Hartford area. Furthermore, much of New Haven's capital was invested locally, while Hartford insurance and banking capital, the greatest single aggregate in that city, was dispersed throughout the state and nation. The heavy financial stake of Hartford in the textile industry of eastern Connecticut was an important factor in determining the moderate to Radical politics of New London, Windham, and Tolland counties. Litchfield, the only county more or less independent of Hartford or New Haven influence, was dominated economically and politically by the iron interests of William H. Barnum. New Haven and Hartford were staunch defenders of their own individual wealth, progress, and prestige. It was no mere coincidence that Sperry, leader of the New Haven Republicans, and Democratic Governor English were the busiest real estate speculators and building contractors in New Haven; nor that James G. Batterson, a pillar of the Hartford Radicals, owned acres of the choicest land in Hartford, was the wealthiest quarry owner in the state, and one of its most prominent insurance men.[40]

Radicalism made one final stand in Connecticut in 1869. At the instigation of Hawley, Mark Howard, a prominent member of the Hartford Radical circle, prepared a bitter indictment of Sperry for publication in the *Courant*. As a precautionary measure, however, the *Courant* editor thought it best to have the opinion of Marshall Jewell, by now the leader of the moderate Republicans in Hartford. Jewell was horrified at the bitter tone of the letter and vehemently opposed its publication; in fact, urged its immediate suppression. Confronted with a possible division among Hartford Republicans, Hawley wavered, but the Hartford Radicals insisted that the letter be made public. At their request, Howard sent the letter to the Radical *Meriden Republican*, which published it on January 25.

Entitled "Republicanism in Connecticut, Why Its Poor Progress?", the Howard letter charged that "the party has been controlled by enemies of its ideas . . .by a combination of reactionists devoted chiefly to plunder . . . installed . . . and sustained by the Federal patronage through Senator Dixon." Contemptuously referring to Sperry as "the Johnson Postmaster of New Haven," Howard stormed that officeholders loyal to him "are now attempting to intimidate the Republicans of the State, especially of New Haven, from all efforts to have the Federal offices placed in faithful hands." Though the letter immediately became a political sensation, and though the *Republican* revealed its origin, the *Courant* maintained silence for a week; then disclaiming any knowledge of approval, curtly suggested that the incident be closed. In the same issue, however, Hawley announced his candidacy for Congress, which, in view of his obvious connection with the Radical sentiments Howard expressed was too much for the moderates. Jewell refused to support him.

If Hawley seemed too Radical for the moderates, by refusing to stand publicly on the Howard letter he also appeared too moderate for the Radicals. Caught between two divergent opinions, Hawley realized his position was untenable, and two days after accepting the nomination he withdrew from the campaign.[41] Hawley's withdrawal did not completely silence cries for a return to Radicalism in Connecticut, but most observers thought it questionable that any "reform movement" could develop enough strength to threaten the Jewell organization. Few were surprised when the moderates seized control of the preconvention caucus and easily nominated the entire 1868 slate on February 3, 1869. Although Radical attempts to head off Jewell's nomination met a crushing rebuff, their more vocal delegates persisted in trying to shape the platform. They introduced a Negro suffrage resolution, only to have it promptly rejected by a two to one majority.

The Democratic convention, held a week earlier, had also been reluctant to rock the boat. There had been considerable sentiment for change, but the 1868 slate was rammed through by acclamation. Moreover, the Democrats in demanding gold redemption for government bonds were as dogmatic about sound money as the Republicans. "Our Government when its debts fall due must pay them," said Thomas M. Waller, the temporary chairman, "true to the letter and the spirit of the original contract. Paying gold when gold is specified and in doubtful contracts construing doubt in favor of our creditors." The only significant difference between the two parties was a Democratic plank urging the Grant administration to be more conciliatory toward the South.

A similar treading of water marked the Democrats' New Haven Congressional convention, which nominated James Babcock, formerly a nativist Johnson supporter and now a recent convert to the party. The high-handed tactics of the *Register* group in forcing the Babcock nomination developed a dangerous mood among the Irish. For fourteen years they had chafed under the control of conservatives who took their cue from Minott Osborne, editor of the *Register*. Utilizing its control of the local party apparatus, the Osborne machine had been able to deny proportional representation to the Irish wards in the city conventions and thus not only dictate policy, but reserve all city offices for its retainers.

Prior to 1855 Democratic delegates to all conventions had been elected by mass meetings, customary party procedure throughout the state. In that year of Know-Nothing power, however the *Register* clique had managed to alter representation by alloting three delegates to each ward, regardless of population, subject to approval of a mass meeting of the party. This arrangement had continued in force, until a split over the presidential electors in 1861 forced the clique to compromise. Each voting district would retain two delegates, but one additional delegate would be allowed for every 100 Democratic votes.

During the war, immigration had been slight, and the influence of the old guard over city politics predominant. However, a nice balancing of interests had permitted James Gallagher to secure the chairmanship of the state committee and English, a warm friend of the Irish, to be nominated for governor. The workingmen's movement, and especially the wholesale naturalization of Irish voters in New Haven during the 1868 campaign, had troubled some members of the city's Democratic oligarchy, even as it had alarmed Republican managers. Under the 1861 Compromise, Irish wards were gaining delegates so rapidly that they threatened to submerge the representation of the *Register* group and destroy its power. Furthermore, Gallagher was showing signs of independence and personal ambition.

The *Register* clique decided it was high time to discipline the unruly Irish leader. A city convention was called early in 1869 in which the anti-Gallagher Democrats still maintained a precarious majority. By skillful manipulation, it obediently adopted a return to the 1855 representation, which cut large ward representation from 15 delegates to 6 and reduced the total number of delegates from 72 to 28, insuring that 22 of these represented small wards completely under the clique's control. These were the delegates who had nominated Babcock while the Irish majority sat helpless. Gallagher served notice that he and his following would not support Babcock and even hinted that he might bolt the ticket, but the *Register* Democrats felt certain that he could be kept within bounds. Still, the undisguised anger of the New Haven Irish over the Congressional nomination would carry the ticket down to defeat.[42]

Republican Congressional nominations, though undistinguished, did not reflect the querulousness so evident among their opponents. Events on the national scene were not encouraging, however. A monumental debate was taking place in Congress over the proposed Fifteenth Amendment, which would permit adult male blacks to vote, an unpopular subject in a state where it was freely conceded that the plans of Charles Sumner and Henry Wilson to enfranchise such blacks by federal law had been responsible in part for the Republican defeat of 1867. No one appreciated this fact more than ex-Senator Dixon, whom the Democrats had nominated for Congress from Hartford County. Exploiting the suffrage question, Dixon sent a series of carefully written letters on the subject to the *Courant* and *Post.* The former Senator saw a Radical plan to secure a permanent Republican ascendancy in the United States by securing a solid black Republican vote in the South. The *Courant* asked him on March 24 if he would favor a Negro suffrage amendment to the state constitution. Dixon replied with an emphatic "no!" "If," said he, "the enfranchisement of the black race at the South was honestly based upon the principle of impartial suffrage, it would furnish to many minds a reason for extension of the right of voting . . . but . . . the Radical party have disenfranchised tens of thousands of white citizens in the Southern states and are now attempting to make the Negro vote a controlling element in our national politics."[43]

In addition to the Negro suffrage question, nativism reappeared as an issue when the Republican press opened a drumfire attack upon James Babcock. The Radicals even induced a Catholic priest, the Reverend Stephen Carmody, to pen an indictment of him in the *Courier* and the *Palladium.* The Democrats fought back by attacking corruption in the national government, with particular reference to the millions of acres of national domain that were going to railroad speculators. Carefully sidestepping the lobbying activities of Connecticut railroads, notably the New York and New Haven, whose president was a prominent Democrat, the Democrats contrasted national policies of waste and extravagance with the state administration of Governor English.[44]

The Democrats fought a strenuous campaign, but the Republicans won a considerable victory, every bit as striking as their defeat in 1867 had been. The Republicans would have a two to one majority in the state senate and a majority of 30 members in the house. As usual, the two state tickets ran much closer. Jewell eked out a tenuous 409 vote victory over English. Dixon's defeat, after a campaign in which he had attacked the proposed Fifteenth Amendment, partially invigorated a waning Radicalism in Connecticut and made the Republicans more confident about popular support for Negro suffrage. They hastened their preparations to make it one of the first items of business when the legislature convened.

On May 3, 1869 the state senate passed the Fifteenth Amendment; on May 13 the house concurred. One week later to celebrate ratification a Negro clergyman of Hartford opened the session of both houses with a prayer. Political reconstruction finally seemed complete in Connecticut. The labor movement had been broken, a vigorous temperance movement contained, the

Registry and Naturalization Laws had hemmed in the Irish Democrats, and upwards of 2,000 Negroes would soon be voters. The central political goals for postwar Republicanism had been met and the Democracy placed in a difficult political position.

To the utmost chagrin of Connecticut Radicals, however, Negro votes were of no assistance in the campaign of 1870. Though the requisite number of states had ratified the Fifteenth Amendment well in advance of the Connecticut election, Congress was dilatory in enacting the necessary enforcement legislation, and Grant was annoyingly tardy in having it proclaimed. Since the amendment did not go into effect until March 30, angry Radicals saw their own Registry Law bar Negro enfranchisement for a year and cheat them of what would have been a certain victory at the polls, for English defeated Jewell by 844 votes, a margin so slight that it would have been erased had Negro suffrage been in force. In those towns and senatorial districts where Negro franchise made little difference, the Democrats led substantially, gaining ten seats in the senate and adding to their strength in the house.[45] The importance of Negro suffrage was borne out in the 1871 election, where 1,438 blacks voted for the first time and almost to a man for the Republican ticket. Jewell and English were again the nominees, and they polled approximately the same vote after an election of interest only for the "dirty tricks" practiced on both sides. The Republicans won handsomely the following year, however, when more than 2,000 Irish Democrats again defied the old city machines in Hartford and New Haven counties and bolted the ticket.

In November 1872, Irish voters went solidly for Grant over Horace Greeley, who received only lacklustre Liberal Republican and Democratic support. Grant carried the state by a more than 5,000 majority, most of which had come not from traditional Republican strongholds in the countryside but from the state's nine cities. Indeed, the Republican vote in the countryside declined by almost exactly the same amount as Grant's majority. In the main, the Irish Democrats had carried Connecticut for the Grand Old Party.[46]

This was to be the last Republican triumph, however, during the reconstruction years. With industrial depression hanging heavy over the state after 1873, the Irish returned to their traditional allegiance and a new Prohibitionist Party cut into formerly Radical Republican constituencies. Charles R. Ingersoll, the Democratic candidate for governor from 1873 to 1875 carried in the state ticket with ever increasing majorities. And by 1875 Connecticut was represented in Congress by Democrats from three of its four districts and both United States Senators were Democrats. Yet since 1870 there had been little to distinguish the two parties. Ironically, when the Democrats gained control of the legislature in 1873, they made no effort to remove the Naturalization and Registry Laws. Old guard Democratic managers had found these statutes too useful in curbing their own unruly Irish voter, for they had quickly learned how to cope with the nativist legislation. Managing to gain control of urban registry boards, they actually turned the laws to their advantage. As for the vaunted Negro vote that had given the Republicans a solid victory in 1871, it proved of little lasting consequence because the black population remained relatively stable, while immigrants continued to pour into the cities and larger towns and helped swell Democratic majorities.[47]

NOTES

1. John Niven, *Connecticut for the Union* (New Haven, 1965), pp. 429-38.

2. *Norwich Advertiser*, September 22, 1871; *Hartford Times*, April 8, 1869; *New Haven Union*, August 6, 1871; Thomas S. Weaver, *Historical Sketch of the Police Service of Hartford*, 1901, pp. 37, 38, 139 ff.; *Hartford Courant*, December 18, 1871.

3. J. R. Hawley to Welles, December 16, 1865; Calvin Day to Welles, January 14, 1865; William Faxon to Welles, November 7, 1864, Welles Papers, (Library of Congress).

4. J. R. Lane, *A Political History of Connecticut during the Civil War* (Washington, 1941), p. 210.

5. Hawley to Welles, December 16, 1865, Welles Papers, LC.

6. Hartford *Evening Press*, September 18-22, 1865.

7. *Hartford Courant*, May 5, 1865; those who might have been disposed to ignore *Scott v. Sandford* might well reach into Connecticut judicial history where a decision of State Supreme Court Chief Justice Daggett held that the Negro was not a citizen of the state. *Hartford Courant*, June 15, 1865; *Hartford Courant*, June 28, 1865; *Hartford Times*, July 3, 1865; *New Haven Palladium*, October 3, 1865. The vote by counties indicates that it was rejected three to one in Fairfield, by almost 2,000 votes in New Haven. The only county to accept the amendment was Windham, and even in this stronghold of Abolitionism, 1,406 votes out of 3,559 were cast against it. *Norwich Aurora*, October 2, 1865. Joanna Dunlap Cowden, "Civil War and Reconstruction Politics in Connecticut " (doctoral dissertation, The University of Connecticut, 1974), pp. 233, 234, 248.

8. John Niven, *Gideon Welles* (New York, 1973), pp. 510-11.

9. *New Haven Palladium*, October 3, 1865. Other Republican papers took up the hue and cry. The *Press*, apparently speaking for the ultraradicals, was particularly abusive.

10. H. B. Harrison to Hawley, February 23, 1865; C. D. Warner to Hawley, September 8, 1865; Hawley to Harriet Hawley, November 20, 1865; Warner to Hawley, October 19, 1865, Hawley Papers, LC.

11. *Hartford Courant*, April 18, 19, 1866. "We can and ought to speak well of Andrew Johnson for he deserves it," declared Hawley, "but to speak of him in such a way as to imply hostility to Congress to endorse him in any such way as to acknowledge that there is antagonism between him and Congress would be most unwise. (I believe he would think so.)" J. R. Hawley Papers, letter undated, 1866; the third article of Hawley's platform dealt with the Negro. He declared, "that the rights of people in the rebellious states, without regard to color should be secured . . . that is in all the elements of civil liberty, the people shall be equal . . . that the inequalities in representation likely to result from counting blacks without letting them vote be counteracted and the American people as taught by example that 'treason is crime' not in revenge not in anger but that treason is a crime and should be esteemed as such and punished as such"; Hawley to Warner, Jan. 31, 1866, J. R. Hawley Papers, LC.

12. *Norwich Aurora*, December 12, 1865; Lane, *Connecticut*, pp. 166, 236; *New Haven Palladium*, February 8, 1866.

13. Howard K. Beale, ed., *Gideon Welles Diary* (3 vols., New York, 1960), II:452-63; Niven, *Welles*, pp. 524-25; *New Haven Palladium*, March 23, 24, 1866; *Hartford Times*, March 23, 1866.

14. Ibid.

15. *New Haven Register*, March 30, 1866; *Norwich Aurora*, April 28, 1866; *New York*

Tribune, April 31, 1866. A significant upsurge of Democratic strength was indicated. The party received 5,000 votes more than its strongest year, 1863, while Republican increase over that year was half as much. Ibid. Hawley trailed his ticket by an average of 872 to 2,871 votes. *Hartford Courant*, April 24, 1866; *Norwich Aurora*, April 28, 1866.

16. Niven, *Welles*, p. 527; O. S. Ferry to O. H. Perry, Ferry Papers, Connecticut State Library; *Norwich Bulletin*, April 18-22, May 1, 1866; *Norwich Aurora*, May 12, 1866; *New York Tribune*, November 25, 1875; Welles, *Diary*, vol. 2, p. 541; *Hartford Courant*, June 26, 1866.

17. *Norwich Aurora*, October 6, 1866.

18. *New Haven Palladium*, February 7, 8, 1867; *New York Times*, February 14, 1867.

19. *Bridgeport Weekly Standard*, February 22, 28, 1867; corr. *Boston Post* in *Norwich Aurora*, July 7, 1866; Hawley to E. H. Fenn, May 1, 1874, Hawley Papers, LC; *New York Tribune* March 20, 1867; *The Nation* March 20, 1867; *Bridgeport Weekly Standard*, April 3, 1867; *New York Herald*, March 2, 1867 to April 2, 1867. The Radical press in Connecticut in general supported him as the party candidate and nothing more. Two exceptions should be noted, the *Bridgeport Standard* and the *Courant* backed him heartily to the end; P. T. Barnum to Hawley, February 19, 1867, Hawley Papers, LC; *Bridgeport Weekly Standard*, March 31, 1867. After the election P. T. Barnum was to charge W. H. Barnum of gross bribery and demand a Congressional investigation; however, when the facts came out the committee was unable to determine which candidate had spent the most money. *Norwich Advertiser*, May 15, 1867.

20. O. H. Platt to Hawley, February 14, 1867, Hawley Papers, LC; James F. Babcock to Welles, October 23, 25, 1867, Welles Papers, NYPL; Hawley to Tyler, April 8, 1867; S. N. Pardee to Hawley, April 17, 1867; O. S. Ferry to Hawley, April 5, 1867, Hawley Papers, LC; C. H. Mallory Diary, April 1, 1867; Francis Wayland to Hawley, April 20, 1867; W. H. Bannister to Hawley, March 28, 1867, Hawley Papers, LC; *Hartford Times*, April 2, 1867; New York *World*, April 3, 1867; with the exception of Barnum, who trailed his own ticket by 834 votes, the Republicans won the third district with 1,896 votes and lost in the first and second by an average of only 500. *New Haven Register*, April 5, 1867.

21. *New Haven Union*, July 30, August 6, 1871; *New Haven Register*; June 30, 1866; *Norwich Advertiser*, January 22, 1867; John M. Morris to Hawley, February 27, 1867, Hawley Papers, LC; *Hartford Evening Post* Feburary 20, 1867; Hawley to S. G. Nichols, Patrick Maher, and F. M. Groat, Committee, February 19, 1867; H. H. Starkweather to Hawley, April 8, 1867, Hawley Papers, LC; *New Haven Union*, August 20, 1871. Cowden, "Connecticut Politics," pp. 259-71,

22. Compendium of the *Ninth Census* 1870, p. 402. The Irish, 70,630 strong, were by far the largest of the non-native groups constituting about 60 percent of the whole immigrant population or more than one-eighth of the total population of the state. English, Germans, French-Canadians, and Scots in that order made up the remainder of the foreign-born. 1,804 Negroes had emigrated from the South after the war, with Virginia furnishing the most, 753, and Maryland second with 324. They, together with native-born Negroes and those from Northern or Western states, aggregated just over 9,500. 9,668, compendium of the *Tenth Census*, 1880, Part I, p. 339. *Hartford Times*, April 3, 1867; *Norwich Advertiser*, April 6, 15, 1867; Middletown *Sentinel and Witness*, April 4, 1867; *New Haven Register*, April 5, 8, 1867; *Hartford Evening Post*, April 18, 1867; *New Haven Union*, December 16, 1871.

23. Chapter CXXIV, Public Acts of the State of Connecticut, May Sess., 1867; *Boston Post*, quoted in *Norwich Advertiser*, February 16, 1868; *Meriden Republican*, March 17, 24, 1868; *New Haven Register*, April 6, 1868; *Hartford Courant* April 6, 1868. Francis Atwater, a native of Meriden and active in politics there, has left us an unusually clear account of employee coercion as it was described to him. He is especially critical of Charles Parker, a Prohibition leader and Meriden industrialist. Francis Atwater, *Memoirs of Francis Atwater, Half-Century of Recollections* (Meriden, 1922).

24. Ibid.

25. *Norwich Advertiser*, March 20, 28, April 4, 1868; *New Haven Register*, February 8, 1869.

26. *New Haven Union*, July 13, 31, 1873.

27. *New Haven Register*, November 26, 1867; February 23, 1868; Hawley to Bromley, April 9, 1868, Hawley Papers, LC.

28. J. Hammond Trumbull, ed., *Memorial History of Hartford County, 1633-1884* (2 vols., Boston, 1886), I:570 ff;

29. See Jewell's unsuccessful efforts to charter the Southern Planters Co. in 1867, *New Haven Register*, May 15, June 30, 1867.

30. *Meriden Republican*, January 23, 1868; Niven, *Connecticut*, pp. 284, 285.

31. Ibid., *Litchfield Enquirer*, January 22, 1867.

32. A. E. Burr to Welles, February 7, 26, 1868, Welles Papers, LC; *Bridgeport Weekly Standard*, January 3, 1868; *New Haven Register*, January 30, March 21, April 3, 1868; *New York Tribune*, April 9, 1868.

33. *Hartford Courant*, April 4, 1868; *New Haven Register*, May 9, 11, 15, 17, 1868.

34. The radicals had tried again in the 1867 session of the Legislature to pass a Negro suffrage amendment to the state constitution, but were unable to muster the necessary two-thirds majority. *Norwich Advertiser*, August 2, 1867.

35. *New Haven Register*, March 31, 1868; *Norwich Bulletin*, March 9, 1868; *Norwich Advertizer*, June 2, 5, 1868. Cowden, "Connecticut Politics," pp. 273-77.

36. Constitution of Connecticut, Article 4, Section 12, *Connecticut State Register and Manual* (Hartford, 1947), p. 45.

37. *New Haven Register*, July 15, 18, 20, 29, 1868.

38. *New Haven Register*, June 29, 1866; June 13, 1867; *Governors' Messages*, 1868, 1870, Pub. Doc.'s. of the Leg. of Conn., May Sess. 1868, 1870, Doc.'s. #2, #20, #1; *Norwich Advertizer*, August 6, 1867; Chapter CXV *Public Acts*, State of Conn., May Sess., 1868; *New Haven Union*, July 30, December 16, 1871.

39. For intercity rivalries see debates on the railroad bridging question in 1867, 1868 sessions of the Leg. *Hartford Courant*, May-June, 1867, 1868, passim.

40. John Hooker, *Some Reminiscences of a Long Life* (Hartford, 1899), p. 231. J.R. Hawley to Warner, February 27, 1868, Hawley Papers, LC; *New Haven Register*, January 30, 1869, *Meriden Republican*, January 25, 28, 1869; *Hartford Courant*, January 27, 30, 1869; *New Haven Register*, February 1, 1869. Sperry was a partner in the New Haven real estate firm of Thompson, Smith, and Sperry. *New Haven Weekly Union*, February 11, 1875. English's real estate operations are described briefly in *Commemorative Biographical Record of New Haven County*, pp. 12, 13, *James Edward English, A Memoir* (New Haven, 1890), passim, and in Edward Atwater's *History of the City of New Haven to the Present Time* (New York, 1887), p. 578.

41. *Meriden Republican*, January 30, 1869; *Norwich Advertizer*, February 2, 3, 5, 1869; *New Haven Register*, February 4, 5, 1869.

42. Ibid., *New Haven Journal and Courier*, February 19, 1869; Francis Wayland to Hawley, February 22, 1869, Hawley Papers, LC; *New Haven Union*, February 22, 1874.

43. Hawley to Warner, February 28, 1869; Wayland to Hawley, March 5, 1867, Hawley Papers, LC; *New Haven Register*, January 29, 1869, *Hartford Courant*, February 10, 25, March 24, 1869, *Norwich Advertizer*, March 22, 1869; *New Haven Register*, March 26, 1869.

44. *New Haven Palladium*, March 28, 1869; *New Haven Journal and Courier* March 28, 1869. Carmody wrote other condemnatory letters, which were published on March 28, 30, 31, 1869. *Hartford Courant*, March 31, 1869; *New Haven Register*, March 30, 1869; *Hartford Times*, April 1, 1869; *New Haven Register*, February 4, 1869; *Hartford Times*, March 30, 1869.

45. *Norwich Advertizerer*, April 7, 1869; *New York Tribune*, March 29, 1870; *Hartford Courant*, April 6, 1869; *New Haven Register*, April 20, 1869; *Norwich Advertizer*, May 8, 14, 1869; Connecticut was the twenty-second state to ratify the Fifteenth Amendment; *New Haven Register*, May 22, 1869; *New Haven Palladium*, March 13, 1870. The *New York Tribune* attributed the delay to "obstructionism of the Butler Stripe." *New York Tribune*, April 6, 1870; *New Haven Register*, March 11, 14, 27, 1870; *New Haven Palladium*, February 23, 1870; *Hartford Times*, April 5, 6, 1870.

46. *Hartford Times*, January 13, 1874; *Hartford Courant*, March 31, 1871; *Norwich*

Advertizer, April 1, 1871; *Springfield Republican*, January 1, 1874; *New Haven Register*, April 4, 1871; *New York Herald*, April 9, 1871; *New Haven Register*, March 25, 26, 1871; *New York Tribune* February 6, 1872; *New Haven Register*, April 4, 1872 , April 8, 1872.

1868 cities	Grant	Seymour	Total
	14,821	17,254	32,075

1872 cities	Grant	Greeley	Total
	17,049	17,315	34,364

The towns cast 66,872 votes in 1868 and 61,804 in 1872. Temperance and Labor Reform tickets polled 380 votes; all figures from *Norwich Advertizer*, November 8, 1872. The *New Haven Register* felt that the reason for Grant's large majority "was pure and simple. Democrats just wouldn't vote for Greeley. The leaders did their duty but the rank and file were far from unanimous." *New Haven Register* November 8, 1872; *Hartford Times*, November 6, 1872; *Hartford Courant*, November 13, 1872.

47. *Norwich Advertizer*, April 12, 1873; *New Haven Register*, May 14, 1874; *Norwich Aurora*, May 1, 1875, June 27, 1874, July 1, 1875.

3

PENNSYLVANIA

An Eclipse of Ideology

David Montgomery*

For many years it has been customary to regard the Radical Republicans of the post-Civil War era as rather more conservative than their party name would suggest. A generally accepted notion of Reconstruction would identify the Radicals as spokesmen for northern economic interests, heirs to the program of the former Whigs, and proponents of radical social policies only so far as the southern states were concerned. The late Howard K. Beale contended that "on the great economic questions of the day, the 'Radicals' were in general conservative, and the opponents of their reconstruction policy tended toward radicalism of an agrarian type."[1] Others have agreed that the reconstruction measures of Congress were undertaken, in whole or in part, in order to safeguard the interests of "northeastern business" against the threat of a coalition of southern and western forces which were antagonistic to a high tariff, a return to hard currency, and northern economic penetration of the South.[2]

Quite recently, this conventional interpretation of reconstruction has been challenged. Serious doubt has been cast on the unity of "northeastern business" with regard to the major issues of the period.[3] A comprehensive study of the money question argues that the most adamant of the Radical leaders tended to be supporters of the greenback policy and actually blended "soft-money" and tariff protection into a single expansionist approach to economic questions.[4]

*Originally published as "Radical Republicanism in Pennsylvania, 1866-1873" in *The Pennsylvania Magazine of History and Biography* 85(1961):439-57. Reprinted with the permission of the author and publisher.

1. Notes to this chapter are to be found on pp. 61-65.

Perhaps the time has arrived to abandon not only the concept of a mono-
lithic "northeastern business," but also the thesis that the Radicals promoted
social reform only in the South. Certainly a study of Radical ideology and
activities in the key Republican state of Pennsylvania during the governorship
of John White Geary (1867-1873) suggests that some revision may be in
order.

The decade 1860-70 saw an explosive increase in manufacturing production. For the country as a whole, the total value of manufacturing output
rose from about $1.9 billion to $4.2 billion, an increase of 123 percent. In
Pennsylvania, the second state of the Union in both population and manufacturing, the increase was 145 percent, as compared with an already impressive rise of 87 percent during the previous decade.[5] This leap took place
despite two and a half years of heavy unemployment between 1865 and
1868.

The attendant change in the social structure of the nation was equally
significant. At the time of the 1860 census, the rural population outnumbered
the urban four to one, and 59 percent of the working population was engaged
in agriculture. By 1870, although the population as a whole was still overwhelmingly rural, only 53 percent of the workers remained in agriculture. In
the following decade, the percentage fell to 47 percent—in Pennsylvania, 25
percent. More important, by 1870 36.5 percent of gainfully employed Americans were industrial wage earners and salaried employees, and another 23
percent agricultural wage earners, located largely though not entirely in the
South. In other words, by the end of the sixties almost 60 percent of the
American people were dependent for a livelihood on employment by others.[6]

Leading this development was a group of entrepreneurs, or manufacturing
capitalists. Iron smelters and founders were rebuilding their industry with the
new anthracite smelting process, which outproduced the charcoal furnaces of
the old iron plantations only after 1860.[7] Young veterans with carpetbags in
hand were opening the oil fields.[8] Mine operators, largely former miners and
farmers, sank new shafts in the coal country.[9] Mechanics founded engineering
works.[10] The *nouveaux riches* of the shoddy fortunes were reorganizing the
garment and shoe industries on a factory basis.[11] These men saw themselves
as Walt Whitman dramatically proclaimed them:

> Race of veterans—race of victors!
> Race of the soil, ready for conflict—race of the
>   conquering march!
> (No more credulity's race, abiding temper'd race,)
> Race henceforth owning no law but the law of itself,
> Race of passion and the storm.[12]

The temper as well as the interests of this group was manifested in political
life by such men as Thaddeus Stevens, William D. "Pig Iron" Kelley, Edward

McPherson, Alexander K. McClure, and the other Radical leaders of Pennsylvania. It is a mistake to identify the outlook of the entrepreneurs with that of the great commercial capitalists; that is, with the wholesale distributors who intervened between the producers and the national market,[13] the heads of the railroad and shipping corporations, the metropolitan bankers and realtors, or, in short, with the members of the elite Saturday Evening Club of Philadelphia who scorned the manufacturing *arrivistes* and their diamond-bedecked wives.[14] The captains of commerce, unlike their counterparts in industry, were the bulwark of conservatism in both political parties. The identification of Radicalism with "northeastern business" fails precisely because it ignores the sharp conflict of interest and origin between these two sectors of business.

Similarly misleading is the customary equating of Republican with former Whig.[15] Many of the leading Pennsylvania Republicans, including John White Geary, Simon Cameron, John Hickman, William D. Kelley, and John W. Forney, had been Democrats before the Kansas crisis. The stronghold of Republican strength throughout the sixties lay in the farm counties to the north and west of the great arch of the Appalachians, counties which had stood consistently by Jackson in the 1830s.[16] David Wilmot might lie in the graveyard of a Towanda village church, but the spirit of his Proviso and of the Independent Democrats of 1854 still prevailed among the farmers and country businessmen who considered the Republican Party their own creation.[17]

The hard-fought political contests of the reconstruction era were centered in that broad wedge of heavily populated counties which runs northward out of Philadelphia between the Delaware and Schuylkill rivers to the New York line in the north and the Susquehannah River on the west. Here powerful Democratic machines were entrenched, as in Philadelphia's notorious Fourth Ward along the Delaware, and in Luzerne, Schuylkill, and Lackawanna counties where the secret "Molly Maguires" wielded great political power.[18] Of crucial importance is the fact that anti-Negro sentiment was institutionalized in the Democratic Party of Pennsylvania, which sought to bolster its opposition to the Republicans by incessantly fanning the flames of bigotry.[19] Just as the Republicans had a vested interest in "the bloody shirt," so the Democrats had one in the concept of a "white man's country."

Labor in this period did not constitute an effective political bloc. Democratic strength cannot be equated with labor strength. The votes of the workingmen seem to have been determined far less by labor questions as such than by loyalties to local party groupings, religious and nationality questions, and the issues posed by the major parties.[20] Most of the new labor organizations, at least in the politically decisive eastern part of the state, followed the course advocated by Jonathan Fincher, the machinists' leader from Philadelphia, and avoided all party politics. Although the young National Labor

Union advocated quick restoration of the southern states, it sought to bring about a political realignment in the nation on the basis of the greenback question.[21] Only twice did the N.L.U. make a significant impact on state politics. First, in the wake of a long and bitter series of strikes by iron puddlers, molders, and heaters in Pittsburgh in 1867, the unions launched a Labor Reform Party in Allegheny County. Its candidates for the state legislature claimed to have won 3,500 votes and small majorities in nine precincts, but none were elected.[22] It is quite possible that this labor effort spurred the passage of some of the Radical and prolabor legislation which was enacted during the Assembly session of 1868.[23] Second, in 1872 the N.L.U. joined forces with the Republicans in Schuylkill County to elect as judge Cyrus Pershing, who was to use his office to break the power of both the Democratic Party and the "Molly Maguires" in that area.[24]

The election campaign of 1866 was fought over national issues. The Republicans placed themselves squarely behind the proposed Fourteenth Amendment to the Constitution and declared in their state platform that "the most imperative duty of the present is to gather the legitimate fruits of the war, in order that our Constitution may come out of the rebellion purified, our institutions strengthened, and our national life prolonged."[25] The commercial interests of the state were largely sympathetic to Andrew Johnson's program of immediate restoration of the former Confederate states.[26] The most powerful Republican leader, Simon Cameron, who in the spring of 1866 was still hoping to be the dispenser of Johnson's patronage in the state, prevented the party convention from taking an anti-Johnson stand.[27] Only a Radical threat to bolt the party brought about a compromise plank which commended Johnson's wartime position, but appealed to him "to stand firmly by the side... of the loyal masses," who would support all measures by which "the freedom, stability, and unity of the National Union [could be] restored."[28]

The Democratic candidate for governor was Hiester Clymer, a lawyer from "one of the oldest Pennsylvania families."[29] The Democrats praised Republican Senator Edgar Cowan, who had backed Johnson's vetoes, and proclaimed that "the white race alone is entitled to control of the government of the Republic, and we are unwilling to grant the negroes the right to vote."[30] The high point of their campaign was the National Union Convention called in support of Johnson in Philadelphia at which the Massachusetts delegates, led by such men as Robert Winthrop, General Darius N. Couch, Leverett Saltonstall, and John Quincy Adams, grandson of the former President, entered the hall arm in arm with the delegates from South Carolina while the band played "Dixie."[31]

When Johnson arrived in Philadelphia on his "swing round the circle," he was greeted by a committee of businessmen headed by Anthony J. Drexel, one of the leading bankers of the city.[32] George W. Child's influential *Public*

Ledger, the leading commercial paper of the city, gave a coverage to the "swing" that was favorable to the President, although its ardor cooled perceptibly after Johnson's angry performance in the face of hecklers in Cleveland.[33]

As far as Pennsylvania is concerned, it is difficult to picture Johnson and his supporters as defenders of agrarian America. Johnson never opposed the financial policies of Secretary of the Treasury Hugh McCulloch until after the election of 1868. The high tariffs which those who have depicted Johnson as an agrarian radical think he should have vetoed, were, in fact, signed.[34] Indeed, at a great rally in Reading opening the Democratic campaign, the featured speaker, Montgomery Blair, castigated the New England Republicans, especially Senators Sumner and Wilson, for failing to support Pennsylvania's high tariff needs.[35]

The Republican candidate, John White Geary, was a former Democratic leader of California, the onetime territorial governor of Kansas appointed by President Pierce, and a military hero with an almost legendary record.[36] He was nominated as a compromise candidate with strong popular appeal, acceptable to both wings of the party.[37] Republican campaign advertisements consisted of a serialized life of Geary and explanations of the Fourteenth Amendment, described as a measure which would protect the rights of Pennsylvania citizens in all states, prevent one white southerner from having the voting power of two northerners, keep traitors out of office, and end all possibility of compensation for slaves or repayment of Confederate debts.[38] The Democrats, for their part, sought to split off conservative Republicans by indicating possible acceptance of the last two sections of the amendment while attacking the first two,[39] and by using John's patronage powers to have Radical postmasters fired.[40]

In the October elections, the largest vote ever polled in the state returned a more than 17,000 majority for Geary, and gave the Republicans two additional Congressmen and a clear majority in the state legislature.[41] The results established the Republican Party in full control, an advantage which was retained for the remainder of the decade and which improved the ability of the Radicals to operate within that party. As governor, Geary became increasingly a spokesman for the Radical outlook. To demonstrate how this strength was used we might examine the Radicals' image of themselves and their position on the tariff, currency, public education, Negro rights, labor, and the railroads.

The Radicals viewed themselves as part—even as leaders—of a world-wide upsurge of democracy. Throughout their speeches one finds the theme that was expressed in Geary's message to the Assembly in 1869. The governor pointed to England's new law broadening the suffrage, the expulsion of the Bourbons from Spain, and the liberal concessions in France and Prussia, and asked: "What are these but echoes of the dire catastrophe that has overwhelmed aristocracy in the United States?"[42]

The fact that democracy had successfully weathered "The Rebellion" had, for the Radicals, confirmed its superiority over all other political forms. Pointing to every new increase in American production, they challenged "monarchic England" for world supremacy. Their foremost economist, Henry Carey, declared that the overthrow of slavery had ended America's former condition of economic vassalage in which all her railroads had simply moved agricultural products and raw materials to the workshops of England. Now, behind the sheltering wall of the tariff and bolstered by an abundant legal tender and bank note currency, the manufacturing of the United States was outstripping that of the Old World.[43] The twin levers of this success were seen to be the protective tariff and political democracy.

So intimately were the tariff and the ideal of democracy intertwined in the thinking of Pennsylvania's Radicals that Congressman William D. Kelley argued:

> The theory that labor—the productive exercise of the skill and muscular power of men who are responsible for the faithful and intelligent performance of civic and other duties—is merely a raw material, and that that nation which pays least for it is wisest and best governed, is inadmissible in a democracy; and when we shall determine to starve the bodies and minds of our operatives in order that we may successfully compete in common markets with the productions of the under-paid and poorly-fed peasants of Europe and the paupers of England, we shall assail the foundations of a government which rests upon the intelligence and integrity of its people.[44]

Although to many historians of this century the protective tariff has appeared to be inherently reactionary legislation on behalf of special vested interests, to the Radicals it was not only necessary for national economic progress and independence from England, but also a prerequisite for social harmony and for the preservation of a citizen body capable of taking part in democratic government. Kelley warned that free trade even in England had led to "the disappearance of the small farmer, and of the small workshop," to "the concentration of land and machinery in the hands of a constantly diminishing number of persons," and to "the rapidly increasing destitution . . . and despair of her laboring classes."[45]

Quite in contrast to the thesis that the Radicals favored a contraction of currency, Geary called for an expanded money supply to encourage business.[46] His administration funded the state debt, or paid it off rapidly in "legal tenders." The House of Rothschild held $500,000 of the Pennsylvania debt. Through its American agent, August Belmont, it protested vigorously in 1868 against being repaid in greenbacks. State Treasurer William Kemble replied in a brusque note that Belmont's complaint was ridiculous and that the Commonwealth intended to redeem its debt immediately and in legal tender notes. Kemble concluded his reply with an anti-Semitic thrust: "We are willing to give you the pound of flesh, but not one drop of Christian blood."[47]

Beside political democracy and government aid to industrial expansion in the hierarchy of Radical values stood that of universal education. Both developing industry and successful democracy were seen to require an educated population. It may well be that the firm establishment of the state-supported public school system was the most lasting social accomplishment of reconstruction.[48] The Pennsylvania common school system had been founded in 1834 largely through the efforts of Thaddeus Stevens; in an interview just before his death, Stevens called the Pennsylvania schools his greatest achievement.[49] For this county-supported system of elementary education, to which the state legislature made contributions, Geary's administration increased the state appropriations from a level of $340,000 in 1865 to more than $750,000 in 1871. The new constitution of 1874 contained a proviso that the legislature must appropriate at least one million dollars for the common schools each year.[50] These state expenditures were used to centralize the system, to enforce higher standards, especially in the rural schools, to increase the number of teachers from 14,646 in 1860 to 19,522 in 1870, and to stimulate a total increase in public appropriations for common schools during that decade from $2.4 million to $7.2 million.[51]

On the subject of civil rights for Negroes in Pennsylvania the cleavage between the Radicals and conservative Republicans went deep. The conventional view of historians that the Republicans advocated civil rights and Negro suffrage for the South but shunned them for the North may be true of the conservative Republicans, but it is not true of the Radicals.[52] In Pennsylvania, however, the Radical position on this issue was weakened within party deliberations by fear of the Democrats. Suffrage had been taken away from the Negro in Pennsylvania by the Constitution of 1838. In schools, streetcars, poorhouses, and employment the 57,000 Negroes of the Commonwealth were segregated.[53]

The civil rights battle was first joined over streetcars. In 1866 the Republicans in the lower house of the legislature attached to a bill regulating city transit lines a rider prohibiting discrimination against any passenger because of color or nationality, but the measure failed to pass the senate.[54] During the ensuing election campaign the proposal was furiously attacked by the Democrats. Efforts by Negroes to seat themselves in the cars in violation of old patterns of segregation were met with violence and even with the derailing of some streetcars.[55] When the Court of Common Pleas in Philadelphia awarded damages to a Negro woman who was evicted from a car by the conductor for refusing a seat in the Jim Crow section, the state Supreme Court overruled the lower court and upheld segregated seating.[56] While that case was pending in the courts however, the legislature passed an act prohibiting exclusion or discrimination by any railroad or transit line and making conductors who enforced such practices guilty of a misdemeanor. Despite continued Democratic opposition to integration throughout the campaign of 1868, all efforts to repeal the new law failed.[57]

Most of the Radicals felt that the question of Negro suffrage could be approached most effectively from the federal level. In Congress, Radical votes from Pennsylvania would be augmented by those from the New England states where Negroes already voted, from the reconstructed South, and from the homestead states of the West, which were free of a strong Democratic Party and already calling for manhood suffrage.[58] Had Negro suffrage, divorced from the other Radical measures, been put to a special popular vote in Pennsylvania, it would probably have been defeated. It was, therefore, in Congress that the effort was made. The Negro suffrage bill of 1866 for the District of Columbia, considered by William D. Kelley as the opening wedge for a national reform, was commended in a resolution by the lower house of the Pennsylvania legislature. But the day after Johnson announced his intention to veto the bill if it passed Congress, the state senate, over vigorous Democratic objections, sent the resolution back to committee to avoid a vote.[59] Only a handful of staunch Quakers and Pennsylvania Germans from Lancaster and York counties, led by John Hickman and Adam C. Reinoehl, refused to be silenced by the party leaders and pressed a Negro suffrage amendment to the state constitution throughout the session of 1868. The measure went down to a final defeat in a 14 to 68 vote, opposed by the Democrats and by Republicans who were afraid to campaign on the issue.[60] The strong national Republican victory of that year and the fact that Negro votes gave Grant his popular majority[61] brought the Radicals the strength they needed to roll the Fifteenth Amendment through Congress and the state legislatures in 1869. Geary recommended ratification, and the legislature complied by a strict party vote in the session of 1869.[62] In the election of 1871, the first with substantial Negro voting, violence flared in Philadelphia. Three leading Negroes were killed, but the right of all male citizens to vote was firmly established.[63]

The Radical ideology, then, placed its faith in political democracy based on universal suffrage and led by a party closely allied to the independent entrepreneurs of the nation. But where in this credo did the growing class of propertyless wage earners fit? Ironically, the extension of suffrage to them had not weakened but rather strengthened the political influence of the commercial interests, because the enormous expense of campaigning for office made candidates increasingly dependent on backers with abundant cash. To be effective, informed, and independent citizens of a political democracy the workers needed leisure time, the strength of organization, and a standard of living at least sufficient to allow personal dignity and political self-reliance.[64] On the other hand, the achievement of these objectives, so necessary to the political ideals of the Radicals, would at the outset increase labor costs and thus decrease profits for the manufacturers themselves. The Radical approach to the labor question had to be formulated within the context of this dilemma.

Immediately after Appomattox, a new upsurge of labor activity had swept the nation; its efforts were focused on the organization of trade-unions and the shortening of the working day to eight hours. The Pennsylvania Radicals endorsed the eight-hour day, arguing that leisure time was necessary for self-improvement, and passed a law in 1868 establishing eight hours as the legal working day in the state (*provided* no private contract to the contrary was made).[65] The great vexing question both in the Assembly debates on the bill and in the only major strike conducted to enforce the law (the coal miners' strike of 1868) was not whether hours should be shortened, but rather whether the day's pay should be reduced together with the hours. The law left the question unanswered, and in the strike the eight-hour demand was ultimately abandoned in favor of a wage increase.[66] To meet other demands of the miners, the Republicans repealed the brutal "Tioga County Law" of 1865 which had permitted the eviction of striking miners from company houses,[67] enacted the nation's first comprehensive mine safety law in 1870,[68] and in 1872 specifically exempted unions from the conspiracy laws.[69] All these acts were stripped of their force by the Radical insistence on "freedom of contract." They stand, nevertheless, in striking contrast to Republican measures of later decades. The extent of subsequent retrogression is indicated by the fact that the eight-hour law of 1868 was repealed by an act of 1913; the latter, a reform for its time, established a maximum working day (for women only) of ten hours.[70]

The greatest pressure against Radical measures, however, came from the side of commercial capital. The power of the railroads, the extension of the influence of commercial capital within industry itself through the corporate form of organization, and the political activities of this conservative grouping, all exerted a force against the Radicals which mounted as the 1860s drew to a close. To meet the power of the railroads, which was protected by special charters, the Radicals sought the only remedy consistent with their own ideology: more competition. In 1866 the manufacturers of Pittsburgh supported a proposal to extend the Baltimore and Ohio Railroad to their city in an effort to end the monopoly position of the Pennsylvania Railroad.[71] In the same year, Senator Thomas J. Bigham of Allegheny County introduced a group of resolutions designed to promote both the construction of competitive lines to Pittsburgh and the passage of a "free railroad incorporation law" to allow the establishment of new lines without special charters.[72] The proposed measure became so popular that every legislator felt compelled to endorse it, at least in principle. Geary pressed for the bill in the session of 1868 and, by vetoing an original form which would actually have increased the privileges of existing lines, won the law he desired.[73]

Despite these efforts, the power of such "corporation men" as Franklin B. Gowen and Thomas A. Scott, both of whom were lawyers who had risen through corporation channels to railroad leadership, continued to grow. Democrats nominated a railroad executive, Asa Parker, to oppose Geary in 1869. In the face of opposition from many conservatives in his own party Geary won reelection by fewer than 5,000 votes, less than the majority won in Philadelphia where the Republicans had used their 1868 registration law to the utmost. By placing both registration and the counting of ballots in the hands of Republican-controlled boards, this law had enabled the Republicans to enroll fictitious voters whose ballots were cast by faithful repeaters, while frustrating similar frauds by the Democrats in all but the most secure Democratic wards.[74]

In 1871 came a crucial battle. The strong miners' union of the eastern coal counties had struck for a wage increase. Many operators settled, but those under the control of Gowen's Philadelphia and Reading Railroad refused. The railroad tripled its rates, so that operators who had settled could not ship. The independent mine owners were thus hit from two sides. Geary reacted furiously: he proclaimed martial law and declared it unlawful either to prevent anyone from going to work or for any railroad to impose prohibitive freight rates. "By the existing condition of things," he declared to the Assembly, "miners and laborers and those dependent upon them are greatly injured, large classes of our manufacturers are crippled . . . . Chartered privileges were never granted or designed to bring about such results as these; and if, as represented, the corporations have misused or abused their privileges, . . . public duty, justice, and humanity alike appeal to the legislature for adequate and speedy redress."[75]

Geary's drastic steps rescued the mine owners from the immediate emergency, even though the legislature failed to comply with his requests for safeguards against future repetition of such occurrences. By 1875, however, Gowen had established the Philadelphia and Reading Coal Company as master of the area, and, after a bitter strike, had destroyed the union.[76] The Pennsylvania Railroad joined with Andrew Carnegie in founding the huge J. Edgar Thomson Steel Works, which rolled its first rail in 1875. This event heralded the decline of the independent entrepreneur in his second great stronghold, the steel industry.[77] The agreement by which John D. Rockefeller and three major railroads established full control of the oil fields was reached in 1872.[78] New forms of industrial organization relentlessly supplanted the anarchic competition of the small entrepreneur.

Simultaneously, the political assault on the Radicals was intensified. Railroad executives, financiers, and merchants, forming the Philadelphia Committee of one Hundred, attacked the Republican legislature at its most vulnerable point, its unparalleled venality, and backed the Liberal Republican movement in the name of reform.[79] The Democrats, seizing their new opportunity, declared that they were prepared to join the cause of the Liberals by accepting all three of the recent amendments to the federal Constitution, which they had fought so bitterly, and by endorsing former Republican Governor Andrew G. Curtin to oppose the regular Republican nominee, John F. Hartranft, in the gubernatorial campaign of 1872.[80]

By 1871 even Geary had begun to detach himself from the organization of Senator Simon Cameron, which dominated the state Republican Party. Geary appealed to the legislature in his annual message of 1872 to apply the treasury surplus to the immediate reduction of the state debt, a proposal which, if enacted, would have effectively ended partisan use of state funds. In the same message, he endorsed the proposal for a state constitutional convention, attacking specifically the corrupt use being made of private bills, and backed labor's demands for a state bureau of labor statistics and an end to the importation of Chinese coolie labor. Finally, the message supported Senator Charles Sumner's proposal for universal amnesty in the belief that the reconstruction of the southern states had been completed and the time had arrived for an end to the passions of war-time.[81] The means, often fraudulent and even violent, by which the Radicals had held office and pressed through their reforms, were tending to become ends in themselves, and Geary warned particularly against the dangers inherent in using federal troops to supervise elections, as had been done not only in the South but even in Philadelphia in October 1871.[82]

Ambitious to become President, Geary turned to the newly established Labor Reform Party, in the ranks of which he held considerable popularity. At that party's 1872 convention in Columbus, Ohio, Geary led the field on the first ballot, but on the fourth lost the nomination to Judge David Davis of Illinois.[83] The Labor Reform Party collapsed when Judge Davis withdrew from the race after the Democratic convention had been held and threw his support to Horace Greeley.[84] Geary reluctantly returned to the regular Republican fold and endorsed President Grant for reelection.[85] The new political alignments of the early seventies thoroughly obscured the earlier delineations of radical and conservative, Republican and Democrat.

Radicalism in Pennsylvania, in short, seems to have been not the effort of a united "northeastern business" to defeat the threat of "agrarian radicalism" by forcing on a prostrate South social reforms which were scorned in the North, but rather the quite consistent ideology of the self-confident manufacturing entrepreneur in the hour of his ascendancy. The reorganization of Pennsylvania's basic industries by emerging corporations eroded the social realities upon which the Radical outlook was founded. The political realignment introduced by the Liberal Republican movement made the identification of Radicalism with a part of the Republican Party anachronistic. These new tendencies, already evident by 1872, were swept to the forefront by the great depression which broke in 1873, bringing in its wake the consolidation of the major manufacturers into trusts, and undermining the confidence of the Radicals that they had ushered in an era of economic prosperity and social harmony.[86]

NOTES

1. Howard K. Beale, *The Critical Year; A Study of Andrew Johnson and Reconstruction* (New York, 1958), p. 7. Beale's work was first published in 1930.

2. See Charles A. and Mary R. Beard, *The Rise of American Civilization* (New York, 1938), II:105-10, 266-67, 287-94; Vernon L. Parrington, *Main Currents in American Thought* (New York, 1930), III:20-30; Allan Nevins and Henry S. Commager, *The Pocket History of the United States* (New York, 1956), pp. 236, 257; W. E. Burghardt Du Bois, *Black Reconstruction in America, 1860-1880* (New York, 1935), pp. 210-14.

3. Stanley Coben, "Northeastern Business and Radical Reconstruction: A Re-examination," *Mississippi Valley Historical Review* 46 (1959):67-90; Irwin Unger, "Business Men and Specie Resumption," *Political Science Quarterly* 74 (1959):46-70.

4. Robert P. Sharkey, *Money, Class, and Party: An Economic Study of Civil War and Reconstruction* (Baltimore, Md., 1959).

5. "A Compendium of the Ninth Census," *House Documents*, 42nd Cong., 1st Sess. (June 1, 1870), pp. 796-97. My percentage calculations are from the census figures.

6. The percentage calculations are based on the figures given in Warren M. Persons, *Historical Statistics of the United States, 1789-1945. A Supplement to the Statistical Abstract of the United States* (Washington, D.C., 1949), pp. 25, 63; and "The Statistics of the Population of the United States," *Ninth Census* (Washington, D.C., 1872), I:674-87. According to the figures of the Ninth Census, the percentage of the working population in agriculture had already fallen to 47 percent by 1870. I have used the revised estimate of Persons because it bases both the 1860 and the 1870 figures on the same definitions. The estimates of employees are derived from the following figures of the 1870 census: personal service, 1,133,448; manufactures and mining, 2,691,953; trade and transportation, 726, 757; agriculture, 2,885,996. Many laborers were included in the census category "personal service."

7. William A. Sullivan, *The Industrial Worker in Pennsylvania, 1800-1840* (Harrisburg, Pa., 1955), p. 9.

8. A. K. McClure, *Old Time Notes of Pennsylvania* (Philadelphia, 1905), II: 470-74.

9. Joseph F. Patterson, "Reminiscences of John Maguire after Fifty Years of Mining," Historical Society of Schuylkill County, *Publications* (Pottsville, Pa., 1907-14), IV: 305-36.

10. Robert Allison, "Early History of Coal Mining and Mining Machinery in Schuylkill County," Ibid., pp. 134-55; Charles F. Derr, "The Derr Foundry," ibid., pp. 213-32.

11. Virginia Penny, *Five Hundred Employments Adapted to Women* (Philadelphia, 1868), pp. 261-64, 310-11, 333; Terence V. Powderly, *Thirty Years of Labor* (Columbus, Ohio, 1890), pp. 133 ff.

12. Walt Whitman, *Leaves of Grass* (New York, 1954), p. 260.

13. John R. Commons, ed., *History of Labour in the United States* (New York, 1918), II:3-6; Fred Mitchell Jones, *Middlemen in the Domestic Trade of the United States, 1800-1860* (Urbana, Ill., 1937), pp. 13-32.

14. McClure, *Old Time Notes* II:244-54; Sharkey, *Money, Class, and Party*, pp. 238-67, 293, identifies the conflicting groups as "industrial and financial capital." This classification leads him to conclude that Radicalism died in 1868 with the death of Thaddeus Stevens and with the emergence of clear party alignments on the money question. My view goes beyond that, based solely on the greenback question, and sees Radicalism as an effective social ideology until the coming of the depression in 1873.

15. Beard, *American Civilization*, II:287-288; Beale, *The Critical Year*, pp. 8-9; Parrington, *Main Currents*, III:20, 30.

16. See Sullivan, *The Industrial Worker*, pp. 231-33, for a tabulation of voting in the 1830s. Of the counties Sullivan records as most staunchly Democratic in 1832, nineteen

were Republican in 1866, and seventeen, all eastern counties, remained Democratic. Seven Whig counties of 1832 were Republican in 1866 and two Democratic. This count unfortunately cannot analyze the many counties that were divided or consolidated between the two elections.

17. See McClure, *Old Time Notes,* I:331 ff., on "The People's Party."

18. See W. E. Burghardt Du Bois, *The Philadelphia Negro* (Philadelphia, 1899), pp. 40-42; McClure, *Old Time Notes* II:431-34; Walter J. Coleman, *The Molly Maguire Riots* (Richmond, Va., 1936), pp. 61-69. In 1866 the Fourth Ward vote was 2,268 Democrat to 946 Republican. Philadelphia *Public Ledger,* October 10, 1866.

19. See the accounts of Democratic party meetings in Philadelphia during the campaign of 1868, *Public Ledger,* September 3, 24, 25, 26, and 29, 1868.

20. James D. Burn, *Three Years among the Working Classes in the United States during the War* (London, 1865), pp. 247-48; Sharkey, *Money, Class, and Party,* p. 218.

21. Commons, *History of Labour in the United States,* II:93-94. Delegate Krepps from Pittsburgh made a strong appeal to the National Labor Union convention against involvement in party politics. *Chicago Daily Tribune,* August 21, 1867. On the National Labor Union stand toward the South, see John R. Commons, ed., *A Documentary History of American Industrial Society* (New York, 1958), IX:126 ff., 138-39, hereinafter cited as *Documentary History.* Note also the stand of the N.L.U. in favor of cooperation with Negro workers, which distinguished its position from that of the Democrats. Ibid., IX:157.

22. Chicago *Workingman's Advocate,* October 12 and November 23, 1867; Boston *Daily Evening Voice,* October 15, 1867. The same Krepps who had denounced party politics in August was himself a labor candidate for the legislature. *Workingman's Advocate,* September 21, 1867.

23. Three points from the Labor Reform platform were enacted during the legislative session of 1868: a state eight-hour-day law, repeal of the "Tioga County Law," and a free railroad incorporation law. The platform of the party was printed in the *Workingman's Advocate,* September 28, 1867.

24. McClure, *Old Time Notes,* II:434; Coleman, *Molly Maguire Riots,* p. 67.

25. Edward McPherson, *Handbook of Politics for 1868* (Washington, D.C., 1868), p. 123.

26. See the *Public Ledger* editorial "Business and Politics," January 23, 1866, and the editorials of January 27 and August 9, 1866.

27. McClure, *Old Time Notes,* II:193-95.

28. McPherson, *Handbook of Politics for 1868,* p. 123.

29. *Public Ledger,* March 3, 1866.

30. McPherson, *Handbook of Politics for 1868,* p. 123.

31. *Public Ledger,* August 15, 1866. On the Massachusetts delegation, see ibid., August 9, 1866.

32. Ibid., August 29, 1866. The foremost banker of the city, Jay Cooke, in 1866 endorsed the financial policies of the administration, but not Johnson's campaign for a conservative Congress. In the following years, Cooke lent his support even to the Radical views on currency expansion. Unger, "Business Men," pp. 60-61.

33. *Public Ledger,* September 19, 1866.

34. Beale, *The Critical Year,* pp. 235-36, 272. On Beale's view of Johnson's policies as "agrarian," see ibid., pp. 28-29, 115, 244, 299.

35. *Public Ledger,* July 19, 1866.

36. William E. Armor, *Lives of the Governors of Pennsylvania, 1609-1873* (Philadelphia, 1873), pp. 466-90; Harry M. Tinkcom, *John White Geary, Soldier-Statesman, 1819-1873* (Philadelphia, 1940).

37. *Public Ledger,* March 8, 1866; McClure, *Old Time Notes,* II:192-95.

38. *Public Ledger,* September 24, 1866, and subsequent issues.

39. Ibid., September 27, 1866.

40. Ibid., September 22 and 24, 1866. Within six months, Johnson's administration discharged 446 federal officeholders, of whom 120 were postmasters removed expressly for patronage reasons. Ibid., January 17, 1867.

41. Ibid., October 11, 22, and 31, 1866. The total vote was more than 597,000.

42. "Papers of the Governors," *Pennsylvania Archives, Fourth Series* (Harrisburg, Pa., 1902), VIII: 957, hereinafter cited "Papers of the Governors."

43. Henry Carey, "Report for the Committee on Industrial Interests and Labor," *Debates of the Convention to Amend the Constitution of Pennsylvania* (Harrisburg, Pa., 1873), V:470-81; and *Reconstruction: Industrial, Financial, and Political. Letters to the Hon. Henry Wilson* (Philadelphia, 1867).

44. William D. Kelley, *Reasons for Abandoning the Theory of Free Trade, and Adopting the Principle of Protection to American Industry* (Philadelphia, 1872), p. 3.

45. Ibid., p. 12.

46. "Papers of the Governors," VIII: 1038-41. Cf. Beale, *The Critical Year*, p. 278. Geary put far more emphasis on the role of national bank notes in expanding the currency supply than Sharkey's discussion of Radical monetary theories would lead one to expect.

47. *Public Ledger*, February 11, 1868. The currency question was hotly debated in the state legislature in 1868 when a bill was introduced to pay a bonus to state banks to compensate them for the difference between the gold and legal tender values involved in the repayment of funds lent to the state in specie in 1863. Party lines were shattered in the vote that defeated the bill 48 to 33. *Daily Legislative Record, 1868*, pp. 798-801 (March 19, 1868).

48. Du Bois, *Black Reconstruction*, Chap. 15.

49. *Public Ledger*, August 19, 1868.

50. "Report of the State Treasurer," *Public Ledger*, January 4, 1866; *Constitution of the Commonwealth of Pennsylvania* (1874), Art. X, Sec. I. For the sharp debates on this section, see *Debates of the Convention to Amend the Constitution of Pennsylvania*, II:435-37, 470-73; VI:39-40.

51. "A Compendium of the Ninth Census," *House Documents*, 42nd Cong. 1st Sess., pp. 487-88. 491.

52. Adams Sherman Hill, "The Chicago Convention," *North American Review*, 107 (1868):167-86; McClure, *Old Time Notes*, II:280-81. Cf. Beale, *The Critical Year*, pp. 173-87, and Du Bois, *Black Reconstruction*, p. 726. On this point, the views of Beale and Du Bois are diametrically opposed to each other.

53. Du Bois, *Philadelphia Negro*, pp. 25-57. In 1837, the year before the constitutional disfranchisement of the Negroes, the state Supreme Court, overruling a lower court, had declared Negroes ineligible to vote. *Hobbes v. Fogg*, 6 Watts 553.

54. *Legislative Record, 1866, p. 633 (March 16, 1866), p. 777 (April 4, 1866).*

55. McClure, *Old Time Notes*, I:595-96.

56. *West Chester and Philadelphia Railroad Company v. Miles*, 55 Pennsylvania State Reports 209. The validity of this ruling as a precedent with respect to segregation, as distinct from the general right of railroads to make rules for passengers, was sharply questioned in 1876 in the case of *Mount Moriah Cemetery Association v. Commonwealth of Pennsylvania ex rel. W. H. Boileau and Margaret Jones*, 81 Pennsylvania State Reports 235.

57. Act of March 22, 1867, Pennsylvania Session Laws (1867), pp. 38-39; *Legislative Record, 1868*, pp. 228-31 (January 31, 1868); *Public Ledger*, January 29, February 1 and 26, March 20, and September 3, 1868.

58. Negro suffrage was advocated by the state Republican parties of Nebraska, Wisconsin, Minnesota, and Iowa in 1866, and Ohio and California in 1867. *Public Ledger*, March 20 and April 26, 1866; McPherson, *Handbook of Politics for 1868*, p. 352; *Public Ledger*, April 16, 1866, June 20 and July 20, 1867.

59. *Legislative Record, 1866*, pp. 93-94 (January 24, 1866); p. 154 (February 1, 1866); *Public Ledger*, January 24 and February 2, 1866. For Kelley's statement, see *New York Times*, January 22, 1866.

60. *Legislative Record, 1868*, pp. 585-86 (March 3, 1868). See the even more revealing debates on Lancaster County school board elections, ibid., pp. 458-65 (February 21, 1868).

61. Charles W. Coleman, *The Election of 1868: The Democratic Effort to Regain Control* (New York, 1933), pp. 369-70.

62. "Papers of the Governors," VIII:975; Edward McPherson, *Political Handbook for 1870* (Washington, D.C., 1870), p. 470.

63. McClure, *Old Time Notes*, II:284-87; Du Bois, *Philadelphia Negro*, pp. 39-42.

64. This was the appeal of the leading eight-hour-day propagandist Ira Steward. See Commons, *Documentary History*, IX: 284-301, especially 292-97. The same arguments were used by Radical leaders John Conness, Henry Wilson, and Cornelius Cole in Congress on behalf of the eight-hour law for Federal employees. *Congressional Globe*, 40th Cong., 1st Sess., p. 413 (March 28, 1867); 40th Cong. and Sess., 3425-36 (June 24, 1868).

65. *Pennsylvania Session Laws* (1868), p. 99.

66. In the lower house, an amendment requiring ten hours' pay for eight hours of work was adopted 62-26, but the senate struck out this section. *Legislative Record, 1868,* pp. 1199-1202 (April 9, 1868), 1280 (April 13, 1868). On the "Eight Hours Strike," see Joseph F. Patterson, "Old W.B.A. Days," Historical Society of Schuylkill County *Publications*, II:357-59; John Maguire, "Early Pennsylvania Coal Mine Legislation," ibid., IV:337; Chris Evans, *History of the United Mine Workers of America from the Year 1860 to 1890* (Indianapolis, Ind., 1918-19), I:17-18.

67. March 14, 1865 supplement to 1863 Landlords and Tenants Act, *Pennsylvania Session Laws* (1865), p. 6. The law was twice repealed in the 1868 legislative session. Ibid. (1868), pp. 104, 757.

68. Ibid. (1870), pp. 3-12. Geary strongly advocated this bill, "Papers of the Governors," VIII: 1024-27. See also Maguire, "Coal Mine Legislation," pp. 337-38.

69. *Pennsylvania Session Laws* (1872), pp. 1175-76.

70. Ibid. (1913), p. 1034.

71. *Public Ledger,* January 8, 1866.

72. *Legislative Record*, 1866, pp. 61-67 (January 16, 1866).

73. "Papers of the Governors," VIII:869-70; *Legislative Record, 1868,* p. 252 (February 4, 1868); pp. 404, 412-13 (February 18, 1868); pp. 415-17, 492-500 (February 19, 1868); pp. 756-61 (March 18, 1868); pp. 933-37 (April 1, 1868); p. 940 (March 31, 1868); pp. 976-77 (April 2, 1868); p. 1029 (April 2, 1868); Act of April 4, 1868, *Pennsylvania Session Laws* (1868), pp. 62-65.

74. McClure, *Old Time Notes*, I:79-82; II, 233-43, 263-74; Tinkcom, *John White Geary*, pp. 127-28, Geary received 290,552 votes to Packer's 285, 956.

75. "Papers of the Governors," IX:12-13. Geary's martial law orders, ibid., pp. 32-35. On the strike, see Patterson, "Old W.B.A. Days," pp. 364-65; Evans, *United Mine Workers,* I:33-37; Tinkcom, *John White Geary*, pp. 130-32. Note the contrast between Geary's behavior and Professor Beale's thesis that the Radicals *feared* action by the states against the railroads. Beale, *The Critical Year,* pp. 144-45, 217-18, 265.

76. Patterson, "Old W.B.A. Days," pp. 366, 376-83.

77. Edward C. Kirkland, *A History of American Economic Life* (New York, 1951), pp. 407-08; McClure, *Old Time Notes,* II:554-55.

78. Kirkland, *American Economic Life,* pp. 403-05.

79. McClure, *Old Time Notes,* II:292-337. McClure, who joined the Liberal movement himself in 1871, argued that the "debauching" of the state legislature during the sixties had been the necessary price of economic progress. Opposition to important measures was overcome by force or cash. Ibid., II:410-28. If the thesis of the present article is valid, our view of the Liberal Republican movement needs modification. There was far more involved in that movement than the reassertion of "the American sense of fair play" against military rule and corruption seen by Francis B. Simkins, *A History of the South* (New York, 1956), p. 286; or the purely political maneuvers chronicled by Earle Dudley Ross, *The Liberal Republican Movement* (New York, 1919).

80. Edward McPherson, *Handbook of Politics for 1872* (Washington, D.C., 1872), pp. 145-46; McClure, *Old Time Notes,* II:340-51.

81. "Papers of the Governors," VIII: 1127-31, 1156-62; McClure, *Old Time Notes,* II:274-75. Ross, *Liberal Republican Movement*, p. 35, may have overstated Geary's opposition to Grant's Southern policies.

82. "Papers of the Governors," VIII:1160-62.

83. McPherson, *Handbook of Politics for 1872*, p. 210; Commons, *Documentary History*, IX: 272-73; McClure, *Old Time Notes*, II:276-77.

84. Eugene H. Roseboom, *The Civil War Era, 1850-1873* (Columbus, Ohio, 1944), p. 480. Some members of the Labor Reform party held a second convention and merged with the "straight" Democrats to support Charles O'Connor for president.

85. McClure, *Old Time Notes*, II:277. In his final message to the Assembly in January 1873, Geary mixed priase of Grant with pleas for reform of the federal administration. "Papers of the Governors," IX:137, 181-82.

86. For the impact of the depression on Republican ranks, see C. Vann Woodward, *Reunion and Reaction* (New York, 1956) and *Origins of the New South, 1877-1913* (Baton Rouge, La., 1951), especially Chaps. 1 and 2; Du Bois, *Black Reconstruction,* pp. 594-605, 685-93; William B. Hesseltine, "Economic Factors in the Abandonment of Reconstruction," *Mississippi Valley Historical Review* 22 (1935): 191-210.

4

NEW YORK

The De-Politicization of Reform

James C. Mohr

When the Civil War ended in the spring of 1865, the government of New York State was already in the hands of a Radical Republican coalition. The two principal blocs in this coalition were liberal-minded independents, on the one hand, and aggressive power-oriented partisans, on the other. The former, though most of them had once been Whigs, had grown upset by the continued caution of their old champions Thurlow Weed and William Seward, especially on questions of social change and civil rights. The latter, many of whom had joined the Republicans after bolting the ante-bellum Democracy, were anxious for a chance to supplant their Old Whig rivals as the policy-makers and party leaders of New York Republicanism. Led by the state's recently inaugurated governor, Reuben E. Fenton, this coalition, distinguished by its hard line on war-related issues, had gained control in Albany as a result of the November elections of 1864.

Though they controlled the state government, the Radicals in Albany faced several serious political problems. First, like most other Americans at the time, they considered a general political reshuffling quite likely once the war was over. When Weed and Seward began actively to encourage President Johnson's National Union scheme, Radical fears of political betrayal and party disintegration grew acute. Consequently, the Radicals in New York needed a program with which their temporary alliance of liberal-minded independents and power-oriented partisans might be solidified and perpetuated; a program that would help them maintain their control over the state's Republican Party. Second, the Democrats were not exactly moribund in New York. The 1864 elections had been very close, and many rapidly growing

1. Notes to this chapter are to be found on pp. 79-81.

constituencies, particularly in and around New York City and Brooklyn, remained vigorously Democratic. Consequently, the Radical Republicans in Albany also needed an appropriate way to strike out at the resurgent Democracy. Third, New York's Radicals had won their political power by campaigning exclusively on national issues related to the war and its settlement. Since those issues would not always be dramatic enough to sustain victories at the state and local level, and since those issues were beyond the control of state leaders in any event, the Radicals in Albany believed they would soon need some domestic issues as well. Finally, the Radicals of New York broke quickly with the Johnson administration, which left them almost from the beginning of the reconstruction period without supra-state direction and without federal patronage. As a result, they badly needed both a basic approach to state policy and a new source of partisan jobs.

The Radicals of New York discovered an ideal solution to their dilemmas in a program of reform at the state level. The Radicals' approach to reform embodied both a faith that institutional change could produce social change and a belief that the massive problems of postwar New York could best be handled by the central government at Albany. Because this approach appeared entirely reasonable in the context of reconstruction America, and because most of the Radicals' specific proposals were supported by civic-minded pressure groups, the more independent liberal-minded Republicans had no difficulty backing such a program. Because action at the state level vitiated several key institutions dominated by Democrats at the local level, and because the creation of state authorities provided an opportunity for the governor to make new appointments, the more power-oriented Radicals were also willing to back a reform program, both as a way of handicapping the opposition and as a way of rewarding themselves. Because the program focused attention on events at Albany, Radical reform provided some substantive issues not directly related to national events. Steadily developed and expanded during 1865, 1866, and 1867, the Radical approach to reform in New York functioned well politically during the immediate postwar years and produced one of the most significant bursts of activist legislation in the state's history.

The Radicals launched their reform program with an attack upon the New York City fire department, which was then more effective as an adjunct of the Democratic Party than as an instrument of urban fire safety. The Radical-sponsored Metropolitan Fire Department Act of 1865 replaced the city's archaic and locally controlled volunteer arrangement with a paid professional department under the direction of a gubernatorially appointed state board. The monumental Metropolitan Health Act, one of the landmarks of American public health legislation, followed in 1866 after the Radicals resolved a series of internal disputes that had blocked passage in 1865. Like the Fire Act, the Health Law effectively combined the Radicals' activist, centralizing

philosophy of reform and their hard-headed, political self-interest. In 1866 the
Radicals also passed the Normal School Act, which created eight new campuses
around the state and fully committed New York to public higher education.

The Radical Republicans reached what proved to be the apex of their
political power in New York during the first half of 1867. Weed and his
conservative allies, gambling that the National Union idea could be transformed into an effective political alternative, abandoned the Republican
Party organization altogether to the Radicals in the summer of 1866. When
the Republicans captured both houses of the legislature that autumn and
returned Reuben Fenton to the executive mansion, the Governor's coalition
was in an ideal position to push forward with its reform programs during the
new year. Consequently, the legislature enacted a stiff new Tenement House
Act, which for the first time set minimum housing standards in New York,
and a Free School Law, which eliminated the practice of rate-billing and thus
for the first time allowed every child in the state to obtain an elementary
education without fees. The Radicals, in 1867, also created New York's first
state Board of Charities, established a state school for the blind, and took
initial steps toward prison reform.

Contemporary observers recognized a basic similarity between the political
philosophy being implemented so successfully at Albany and the political
philosophy of the Congressional Radicals in Washington. The Chicago *Tribune*, for example, the most important voice of Radicalism in the Mid-west,
applauded the reform program going forward at the state level in New York
and minced no words in justifying it on the grounds that the situation in New
York City was "so inherently rotten" that the intervention of a higher
authority in its local affairs was not only justifiable but "purifying."

> So the great Copperhead metropolis stands before the world a proof of
> the fact, that in some communities the elements of corruption may be
> concentrated together to a degree that incapacitates the aggregate mass
> for self-government, and compels the state to deprive them as far as
> possible of the essential attributes of sovereignty and govern them as a
> conquered province. The Southern States form another illustration of
> the same fact, and it is somewhat singular that in both instances this
> proved incapacity for self-government arises out of, and is coextensive
> with, sham Democracy.[1]

New York's Democrats had been painfully and publicly aware of their role
as surrogate Southerners since 1865, but the parallel between Radical policy
at the state level and Radical policy at the national level became more
obvious than ever before when Governor Fenton's coalition decided early in
1867 to try in New York what Congress had decided to try in the South:
black suffrage. Under the state constitution of 1846, which was still in effect,
black voters were subject to a $250 property requirement not imposed upon

white voters. The requirement effectively disfranchised blacks. The Radicals, partly because they wanted more votes in the downstate areas where the great majority of New York's blacks lived, partly because they were caught up in the national political momentum of the period, and partly because many of them had made a genuine commitment to civil and political rights for blacks, resolved upon a full-scale constitutional convention to eliminate this discriminatory franchise provision specifically and to restructure the state's organic law generally. The Radicals were not reluctant to undertake this as an essentially partisan policy and, despite dogged opposition from the Democrats, Fenton's followers first authorized a state convention and then won a commanding majority in the special election to select delegates. When the convention's Suffrage Committee, chaired by Horace Greeley himself, won floor approval of its revised franchise requirements in July 1867, the greatest triumph yet for New York Radicalism seemed to be within reach. But it was not.

Between July and November 1867, the entire thrust of postwar politics in New York was abruptly reversed. Republican setbacks in other states, especially in Ohio where Radicals at the state level were also trying to revise a racially discriminatory constitution, combined with a vicious but effective racist campaign in New York on the part of the Democrats to destroy the political confidence of many of the Fentonite Radicals. In September the Republicans adjourned their own constitutional convention rather than risk finishing a nondiscriminatory document in time to have to run with it on the November ballot. The action was an undisguised retreat; the Radical coalition at Albany was coming apart. By October even Governor Fenton himself was openly predicting defeat, and the November elections confirmed his fears. Democrats captured the assembly and every state-wide office being contested.

The prime significance of the November elections of 1867, however, lay not in the short-term defeat of a particular party but in the longer-term discrediting of an entire approach to reform. The Radical coalition had depended all along upon an active program at the state level that combined idealistic commitment and partisan efficacy; indeed the latter had frequently given a cutting edge to the former. But this approach to reform had become bound up with the question of race, and the question of race in New York, as in the rest of the United States, proved politically disastrous. What was intended to be the supreme achievement of the Radical program brought not victory, but defeat.[2] "Jacobinism is effectually dead," gloated one of Seward's old friends from Auburn on the day after the election. "In about six months you will scarcely find a man that will acknowled [sic] himself a Rad [sic]."[3] Seward's correspondent was wrong about the use of the word, but right about the end of the Radical coalition as he had known it. The protoprogressives and the partisans went their separate ways after 1867 in New York's Republican Party, and it would take nearly a quarter of a century to revive the philosophy of reform that united them during the immediate post-war period.[4]

Following the defeat and dissolution of the Radical coalition in the fall of 1867, New York State endured two years of political deadlock and policy stagnation. Fenton remained governor through 1868, and the gerrymandered state senate remained narrowly Republican as well. But the successful racist campaign of 1867 had won for the Democrats a solid majority in the state assembly. William Hitchman, a loyal follower of newly elected state senator William Marcy Tweed, became speaker in the lower house. Control of the assembly gave the Democrats an effective veto over any programs around which the Fentonites might have tried to rally, though it did not put them in a position to carry through any policy decisions of their own.

New York Republicans, their formerly vigorous program at the state level now stilled by electoral defeat, their recently effective coalition now broken and disspirited, and their previous power at Albany now neutralized, became, significantly enough, the first state party in the country officially to endorse General Ulysses S. Grant's presidential candidacy, notwithstanding the fact that Grant was known around the state primarily as Thurlow Weed's choice.[5] This endorsement was made early in February 1868, only six months after the triumphant convening of the Radicals' constitutional convention, and may be taken as the characteristic response of a party defeated at the state level: try to identify with an external winner. The retreat from Radicalism continued when the state convention of July rejected Horace Greeley, chief publicist of the postwar coalition, and nominated for governor, John A. Griswold, a man who had once backed McClellan for President and who would shortly favor reelection of the cautious centrist Edwin D. Morgan to the United States Senate. The 1868 Republican state platform was eloquently silent on the question of suffrage.[6]

In November former governor Horatio Seymour carried the state over Grant by some 10,000 votes for president, and Tweed's choice for governor, John T. Hoffman, then mayor of New York City, beat Griswold by nearly 28,000 votes for Fenton's old job. But those state-wide totals were run up primarily in New York City itself and apparently resulted at least in part from wholesale frauds perpetrated by Tammany.[7] Elsewhere around the state the Republicans did better then they had in 1867 and recaptured a majority in the assembly. Thus, though the canvass of 1868 juggled the parties' positions in Albany and confirmed the demise of New York Radicalism, it did not end the period of stalemate. The Democrat Hoffman was in a position to check passage of any politically or substantively important bills agreed upon by the Republican legislators, yet powerless to strike out on a new tack of his own. Hoffman, in fact, was unable to win confirmation for his gubernatorial appointees during 1869.[8]

The legislative stand-off of 1868-69, coupled with unresolved struggles for leadership and a general absence of policy direction at the state level within the major parties, created an ideal political environment for skillful lobbyists and individual manipulators. And Albany did not lack for either with railroad and canal boosters ensconced at local hotels and Tweed in the state senate. The sessions of 1868 and 1869 produced faulty building contracts, fraudulent railroad franchises, irregular canal deals, and Tweed's infamous New York City tax levies. Together those two sessions ranked among the worst back-to-back sessions of any state legislature in American history. Even Fenton, who had spent three years writing courageous justifications for a steady barrage of antirailroad vetoes, succumbed to the chaotic cross-pressures of a deadlocked political system during 1868 by signing the infamous Erie Railroad bill. Like many less well-known members of both parties, the former chieftain of New York's Radical coalition apparently thought first of himself in this period of uncertainty; the Governor was alleged to have received political donations in excess of $20,000 in return for his approval of that single piece of legislation.[9]

The 1868 and 1869 sessions of the New York legislature brought forth condemnation from contemporaries and historians alike. The vitriolic Greeley, the sanctimonious Godkin, and the properly appalled Adams brothers all cited those sessions when they penned their most famous critiques of American political venality.[10] In retrospect, however, the venality does not appear to have been as much political as it was apolitical; less the product of partisanship and conflict than the result of party dissolution and stalemate at the state capital. Nor can this era of corruption be attributed, as such periods sometimes are, to some vague sense of moral deflation following a war. Wartime politics led directly to the proto-Progressivism of the Albany Radicals during the early postwar years, not to corruption. It was the defeat of that postwar spirit, not its elevation, and the subsequent inability of either party to win support for functional and attractive alternative methods of meeting the state's problems that produced the quagmires of 1868 and 1869 at the state level in New York.

The one issue of significance addressed during those two years of deadlock, appropriately enough, was the issue that had largely brought the deadlock about: the issue of race. During 1868 the Democratic majority in the assembly voted to place the Radicals' 1867 suffrage amendment on the November ballot.[11] They remembered how well they had done "running against the nigger" in 1867, even when he was not on the ballot, and they would no doubt have been delighted to see the issue reappear in a presidential year. But the Republicans, with equally vivid memories of the 1867 debacle, blocked that move in the senate.[12]

Political circumstances in 1869 pushed the issue forward once again. In 1867 black suffrage had been associated in New York with the Radical coalition, and the defeat of the Fentonites on the race question in November of that year had cost the Radical coalition not only its control over the state's

Republican Party but its very existence. In 1869, however, New York Republicans found themselves facing the paradoxical fact that black suffrage for the entire country had become a policy of the Republican Party at the national level, the level to which state party regulars had looked for help after the disasters of 1867. Hence the party was under some pressure to take up the issue once again. Second, since the Republicans held both houses of the legislature, they could place their old constitutional suggestions on the ballot in whatever form they considered politically least dangerous. They took advantage of this situation to isolate not only the suffrage amendment but also a judicial amendment and a taxation amendment as separate referenda, though the Fentonites had fought this tactic bitterly in 1867 when the Democrats had proposed it. In 1869 the ploy was designed to protect a much more cautious Republican Party from its own issue.[13] Third, the 1869 election involved few major offices. Assuming that the question would have to be put to the people sometime, it seemed preferable not to jeopardize the Congressional nominees of a party that was again depending upon federal patronage and national leadership. Early in the year even Horace Greeley had hoped that 1869 would "take the everlasting negro question forever out of national politics," and *Harper's Weekly* later struck a similar note with regard to New York's own suffrage amendment as well.[14] In short, it seemed the right time to try to get the whole business over with. Fourth, Governor Hoffman would almost certainly approve the referendum, for its presence on the ballot promised to help his party at the state level and thus strengthen his own power in Albany. Finally, and of most importance, the Republican state legislators were in the unique position of being able to cover their bets on the suffrage question in 1869 by ratifying the proposed Fifteenth Amendment to the federal constitution. Ratification, in fact, was one of the few substantive actions the Republican legislature could legally take during that deadlocked session which would not require approval from the hostile governor.[15] This had advantages: it would link New York's state issue more closely to the larger national question, and, by making the suffrage issue look like a fait accompli, it might defuse some of the racist hostility evoked so effectively by the Democrats in 1867. For all of these reasons, the Republican legislature of 1869, two full years after its Radical predecessors had authorized a constitutional convention, finally voted to put the chief result of that convention before the people of New York.

Although a Republican legislature had both authorized the suffrage referendum and ratified the Fifteenth Amendment, and although that party's state committee prepared ballots in support of the franchise amendment, Republicans tried to play down the race question. John Griswold, the party's gubernatorial nominee of the previous year, studiously avoided the issue in his charge to the delegates at the state convention, and both in their platform and in their campaign, Republicans disingenuously presented the race question as a kind of ethno-cultural problem.[16] But the Democrats, especially those who spoke for the upstate districts where the composition of the next state legislature would ultimately be decided (the Democrats already controlled the downstate Tammany dominated districts), hammered effectively and incessantly at black suffrage with heavy handed racist rhetoric.[17] No less a spokesman than Samuel J. Tilden reminded delegates to the Democratic state convention, for example: "We reject [black suffrage] as we would reject the doctrine that an African or a negro has a right to marry our daughter without our consent."[18] Greeley ultimately felt compelled to devote his final editorial of the campaign to a desperate appeal to Democrats to rise above their party's stand on Negro suffrage.[19] Consequently, the elections of 1869 became the second off-year canvass in a row in which the political status of New York's black population was the chief rhetorical issue.[20] And like the one before it in 1867, the race-oriented campaign of 1869 both benefited the Democrats and inaugurated a new phase in the political history of New York during the reconstruction era.

The Democrats in 1869, for the first time since the 1840s, won majorities in both houses of the state legislature, thereby ending the two-year deadlock at Albany. The most significant inroads they made were along the southern tier of counties through which the Erie Railroad struck west. Tweed, for legislative services rendered, had been made a member of that corporation's board of directors and profited from its stocks to the amount of some $650,000, some of which was apparently pumped back into the Erie counties in support of Democratic candidates.[21] While the state-wide offices went Democratic by margins of roughly 20,000 votes, the black suffrage referendum was defeated by over 32,000 votes. Because Hoffman's term continued into 1870, the Democrats were finally in a position to enact a program of their own for postwar New York. Republicans realized that a new era was at hand. On the Friday following the elections, the *Tribune* dejectedly predicted that reforms begun by the Radicals would now "be swept away," and the prediction proved completely accurate.[22]

The Democrats' approach to the problems of New York State in 1870 was virtually the direct opposite of that developed by the Radical Republicans between 1865 and 1867. Where the Radicals had favored centralization and the imposition of rationalized administration from above, the Democrats counterattacked with a program based upon decentralization and local autonomy. Where the Radicals had tried to expand the role of the state and the power of officials at Albany to meet the needs of a rapidly urbanizing and industrializing society, the Democrats, as befitted the state's surrogate Southerners, championed "home rule" and defended those governmental units closest to the people as the most appropriate agencies to solve the people's problems. "I unhesitatingly recommend," thundered Hoffman in his first annual message, "the repeal of all laws creating [state commissions such as the Metropolitan Board of Health], and the restoration to the people of every county and city in the state of the constitutional power to regulate and manage their own local affairs. . . . I recommend the repeal, not only because the legislation to which I object is a usurpation of power and an evasion of the Constitution, but also because the commissions themselves have been to a great extent partisan in their character and conduct, and because the majority of the people in the respective districts have had no effective representation in them"[23]

At least two aspects of the Democratic philosophy of 1870 are worth careful note. For one thing, there was no logical or inherent reason why a strategy of popular responsibility at the grass roots level would be any less legitimate, less reformist, or less appropriate as an approach to the problems of the state than the postwar Radical strategy had been. Theoretically, in other words, it was neither better nor worse as a political philosophy, in any absolute sense, than the proto-Progressive philosophy that the Radicals had adopted immediately after the war; it was simply different, an alternative approach to reform. Second, despite Hoffman's complaints about the partisan overtones of Radical reform, his own counterphilosophy was far from non-partisan. Local control enhanced the power and political effectiveness of the state's most solidly Democratic areas, and it represented a sort of political pluralism, or partisan laissez-faire, upon which the Democrats were prepared to gamble their party's fortunes in the same way that the Republicans had bet that the imposition of a rationalized order from above would shape a political universe more to their party's liking.

Both these aspects of the Democrats' strategy, its potential for reform and its partisan nature, were evident in the single most important piece of legislation passed at Albany during 1870: the so-called Tweed Charter for New York City. This document restored home rule to the city and placed each of the Republican-imposed commissions back under the control of local officers. That the law was baldly partisan goes without saying; it gave Tammany virtually complete control over the largest concentration of people and capital in the United States, and it dismantled the most impressive structural remains of the Radical period.[24] Also important, however, is the fact that other than partisan Democrats could view the program as a reform. No less an organization than the Citizen's Association itself, the very same pressure group that had proved so effective in backing the Metropolitan Health Law of 1866 and the Tenement House Act of 1867, publicly endorsed the new city charter when Hoffman signed it into law in 1870.[25]

Except for the Tweed Charter, the period of Democratic control inaugurated at Albany in 1870 was characterized less by what was carried out than by what was not carried out. Sticking closely to their strategy of local responsibility, the Democrats permitted the Republican-inspired Board of Charities to make its annual reprots, then buried the Board's suggestions for action at the state level. The recommendation of a Republican-appointed prison commission was also laid on the table indefinitely. The state's Tenement House Act went blithely and openly unenforced.[26] A telling index of Democratic rule lay in the annual state school budgets, which were relatively nonpartisan in comparison to any of the foregoing issues. Under the Republicans, New York's educational expenses had risen after the war at an average annual rate in excess of 16 percent. During the period of deadlock the annual average increase tapered off to approximately 10 percent. Under the Hoffman administration the state school budget not only stopped increasing but actually fell, notwithstanding fairly steady rates of slowly increasing attendance.[27] Finally, the Democrats took a negative action even on the lingering question of black suffrage by voting early in 1870 to rescind the previous legislature's ratification of the Fifteenth Amendment.[28] This action, however, proved futile when President Grant and Secretary of State Fish declared the amendment ratified two months later by the necessary three-fourths of the states, thus settling by federal proclamation one of the most politically significant issues in the history of New York State during the reconstruction period.

With one exception, then, the federal imposition of black suffrage, the Democrats could be pleased with the successful implementation of their own political policies at Albany. Moreover, just as the Radical programs had seemed politically effective in 1866, the Democrats were delighted with their showing in the autumn election of 1870. Not only did they retain control of both houses of the state legislature and reelect Governor Hoffman, but they did so despite the presence of federal marshalls in New York City who had been stationed there by the Grant administration in an effort to block a repetition of the 1868 frauds.[29] Hoffman's annual message of January 1871 exuded confidence and self-congratulation. "The management of their own affairs has been restored to the people of the great cities," the Governor proudly noted, and he anticipated a legislative session "much shorter than usual" because there was so very little that needed to be done at the state level.[30] New York's Democrats appeared to be as strong in the early months of 1871 as the Radicals had been in the early months of 1867.

What brought the Democrats down, and hence ended the third phase of political readjustment in postwar New York, was the spectacular failure of the Democratic strategy of local responsibility when applied to New York City. Seymour Mandelbaum has skillfully sketched the enormous difficulties of making decentralization work in a place like postwar New York, difficulties that drove the Tweed machine to adopt a "big payoff" system of organization and communication.[31] But by the summer of 1871 the price of those payoffs became so great and the methods of obtaining them so flagrant that the city's bankrupt, though still official, government was essentially superseded by an ad hoc directorate comprised of the city's most powerful private citizens. The story of Tweed's fall is well known and does not require retelling here. More important in the present context is the impact of that enormously publicized incident on party policy in postwar New York, for it precipitated within the Democracy a process very like that which was already under way among Republicans.

The defeats of 1867 had cost the Radical coalition at Albany not only its continued control over state legislation, but its ascendant position within the Republican Party as well. Indeed, the defeat over black suffrage that year cost the Radical coalition its very existence. Institutional reform seemed no longer compatible with political success, as it had during the early postwar years, but rather brought defeat and deadlock. And the campaign of 1869 appeared to confirm the lessons of 1867 to any politicians still in doubt. The crucial link between institutional reform and political efficacy, the link upon which Radicalism hung in New York State, had been snapped. In the stalemate period that followed Republicans groped for a long-term strategy to replace the one associated with Fenton's years, and in the short run looked out for themselves personally. Fenton managed his own election to the United States Senate after stepping down as governor at the end of 1868, but the Republican Party that he left behind him in Albany was a party without real direction.

The man who eventually developed a new strategy for the Republican Party in New York, and consolidated his own power on the basis of that strategy, was Roscoe Conkling. Federal patronage, something the Radicals had never enjoyed during the Johnson years, became one aspect of the new Republicanism under Conkling, and dependence upon the specific benefits that a political machine could deliver began to supplant faith in positive programs.[32] When Conkling gained Grant's confidence regarding New York's appointments, Fenton's remaining power at the state level vanished.[33] Business backing became the second hallmark of the new Republicanism in New York, especially under men like Thomas C. Platt, Conkling's lieutenant in charge of rebuilding the party in the southern tier of counties where Erie Railroad money had proved so helpful to Tweed. Campaigns were becoming more expensive, and men like Platt never forgot that Weed, the great political mastermind of the previous generation, had helped to elect the immortal Lincoln in 1860 by trading legislative contracts for campaign contributions.[34] The manipulation of ethno-cultural issues, especially the relationship between church and state on the one hand and the legal status of alcohol on the other, became the third cardinal characteristic of the new Republicansim at the state level in New York. The party struck out upon this tack openly in 1869, when the Republicans headed their ticket in New York for the first time in their history with a non-native American, the German-born Franz Sigel, and left on the table at their state convention a resolution advocating temperance.[35] The effect of Conkling's reorganization of the party, then, was to disassociate Republicanism from institutional reform. Under Radical leadership, the Republican Party had been badly burned trying to tinker with the fundamental institutions of the state; the ascendancy of Roscoe Conkling's approach by 1871 assured that the party would not soon go near the fire again. Federal patronage, full campaign chests, and the manipulation of pre-existing ethno-cultural divisions were politically safer than trying to remake systems, however ineffectually those systems seemed to be working.

Tweed's fall had a parallel impact upon the Democrats. Through 1870 that party too had been willing to take fundamental partisan responsibility for making substantive institutional adjustments in the governance of New York State. They had countered the Radical move toward an active state with legislation designed to effect local responsibility and decentralization. But that approach to reform failed the Democrats as badly in 1871 as the Republicans' approach had failed them in 1867, and as a result the Democrats, like their Republican opponents, turned away from institutional reforms of any sort as partisan issues. Hoffman sensed the new direction of politics in New York clearly, and less than six months after the demise of his old boss the Governor devoted a special portion of his annual message to mending his ethno-cultural fences among the Catholic Irish by trying to explain his controversial role in the widely publicized Orangemen's parade incident of the previous summer.[36] And just as the Republicans found a leader for the new era in the person of Roscoe Conkling, the Democrats found one in Samuel J. Tilden. Tilden, notwithstanding his reputation as a crusading reformer, relied not upon substantive issues for his great success but upon his Weed-like organizational genius.[37]

The depoliticization of institutional reform in postwar New York was neatly symbolized in 1872 when Hoffman, in the same message that explained his role in the Orangemen's affair, called for "a commission of thirty-two (32) eminent citizens, to be made up by selection of an equal number from each of the two great political parties" to consider amendments to the state constitution.[38] Moreover, the Republicans in the legislature subsequently went along with this suggestion.[39] The New York *Times*, which otherwise viewed the 1872 session as another debacle, reserved its one bit of praise for the bipartisan commission bill.[40] In 1867 the Radicals had taken full partisan responsibility for constitutional reform and had run that year's constitutional convention in a frankly political fashion. In 1872 there was no convention at all. Instead, there was an elite group of citizens trying desperately to agree upon scrupulously nonpartisan alterations of the organic law of the state.

Though most of the commission's essentially technical amendments were subsequently accepted in 1874, the people of New York lost rather than gained as a result of the process that produced them. The state constitution thereafter remained untouched until the 1890s, when institutional reform was again given a partisan edge in the nascent Progressive movement.[41] Debates over temperance and appeals to ethnicity replaced debates over the state's ability to meet the problems of health and appeals to operationally different philosophies of running a modern city. By 1872, in other words, neither the Republican Party nor the Democratic Party was willing to experiment any further with genuine changes in the state's archaic governmental institutions. Politicians were no longer prepared to stake their political careers on their abilities to vigorously and effectively implement sharply defined alternative programs to deal with large-scale industrialization and urbanization. This was reemphasized in 1873 when the legislature passed a compromise charter for New York City to replace the discredited Tweed charter. That 1873 document remained in effect until 1897.[42]

One thing was left to complete the process of depoliticizing reform in postwar New York: a redefinition of what "reform" actually meant. To the Fenton Radicals, and to the pre-Tilden Democrats as well, reform had meant institutional change with a partisan edge and could be embodied in specific pieces of legislation at Albany, such as the Metropolitan Health Act of 1866, the Free School Law of 1867, or the New York City Charter of 1870. After 1871, however, reform came increasingly to mean the elimination of "bad" individuals; new management rather than a new system. Many Republicans had begun to drift toward that position in the wake of the disclosures of corruption during 1868 and 1869; the Democrats fell back upon the same ground in self defense after Tammany's peculations came into full view in 1871. "The responsibility for the wrong-doing" in New York City, pleaded Governor Hoffman, "does not rest so much upon the charter as upon individuals who held office in the city before the charter was passed, and took office also under it."[43] That summer the Governor went the whole distance and endorsed the Liberal movement in New York State, although that party's presidential nominee was the local editor who had vilified him for years.[44]

Reform during the 1872 session of the state legislature produced no specific pieces of legislation at all, but rather the impeachment of the most flagrantly corrupt state judges. The judges no doubt deserved removal, but the operational definition of reform had shifted. The Liberal revolt that same year, even though it was a political farce from the outset at the state level in New York, legitimized and publicized the new view of reform as nonpartisan cleanliness.[45] John A. Dix, who had been nominated from the floor of Conkling's regular Republican convention "on behalf of the business men of New York" by a delegate standing in for Weed, succeeded Hoffman as governor and made no pretense of seriously experimenting with structural changes in the system.[46] Although Tilden won a national reputation later in the decade as a reform governor, he was clearly one of the new anticorruptionist reformers rather than a policy-maker willing to gamble his fate on significant alternative approaches to governing the state. The reconstruction era in New York, a period of crucial transformation at the state level, was over.

NOTES

1. Chicago *Tribune,* March 4, 1866.

2. The "extreme Radical Deadheads," wrote George J. J. Barber to Weed, "load [ed] down the Party with all the Niggers." Barber, a veteran politician and former member of the Assembly, longed in the autumn of 1867 for "the good old Whig times." Letter, October 24, 1867, Thurlow Weed Papers, Rush Rhees Library, University of Rochester. See also David T. Neligan to David Neligan, October 25, 1867, and David Neligan to Weed, October 26, 1867, Weed Papers.

3. J.[esse] Segoine to Seward, November 8, 1867, William H. Seward Papers, Rush Rhees Library, University of Rochester.

4. To this point the present essay has drawn heavily upon the author's book-length study, *The Radical Republicans and Reform in New York during Reconstruction* (Ithaca, 1973). For that reason footnotes here have been restricted to direct references not included in that volume. From this point forward conventional documentation resumes. On the impact of the 1867 elections nationally see Michael Les Benedict, "The Rout of Radicalism: Republicans and the Elections of 1867," *Civil War History* 18 (December 1972): 334-44.

5. New York *Times,* February 6, 1868; New York *Tribune,* February 6, 1868; De Alva Stanwood Alexander, *A Political History of the State of New York* (New York, 1909), III:191-92; cf. A. G. Browne to J[ohn] A. Andrew, October 22, 1867, Weed Papers.

6. Alexander, *Political History,* III:125-26, 193-96, 215-18, 220; *Tribune,* July 9, 1868.

7. The federal government subsequently investigated the 1868 elections in New York. See United States Congress, William Lawrence, *Report on Election Frauds in New York, House Reports,* No. 31, 40th Cong., 3d sess., February 23 and March 1, 1869 (Washington, D.C., 1869).

8. New York State, *Journal of the Assembly ... 1869* (Albany, 1869); New York State, *Journal of the Senate ... 1869* (Albany, 1869).

9. The state senate subsequently investigated the whole Erie business, and its findings, though little more than a whitewash, are contained in *Documents of the Senate of the State of New York at Their Ninety Second Session, 1869* (Albany, 1869), V, No. 69.

10. *Tribune,* Nov. 7, 1868, July 24 and 29, 1869; *The Nation,* Oct. 29, 1868, March 18, 1869; Charles Francis Adams, Jr., "A Chapter of Erie," *North American Review* 109 (July 1869): 30-106, and "An Erie Raid," ibid., 112 (April 1871):241-91.

11. New York State, *Journal of the Assembly ... 1868* (Albany, 1868), I:648, 710, 775; II:877-78, 983-84.

12. New York State, *Journal of the Senate ... 1868* (Albany, 1868), pp. 724, 957, 962-63, 1072-73.

13. New York State, *Journal of the Assembly ... 1869,* I:453, 782, 923, 942; II:1374, 1386-87; New York State, *Journal of the Senate ... 1869,* pp. 31, 61, 100, 106, 128, 134, 136, 148, 153, 191-92, 211, 222, 234-35, 241, 736.

14. *Tribune,* February 27, 1869; *Harper's Weekly,* September 25, 1869.

15. *Journal of the Assembly 1869,* I:453-54, 543-44; II:1159; *Journal of the Senate 1869,* pp. 299, 314, 514, 542, 582, 589-91.

16. See *Times,* September 23, 29, and 30, 1869; *Tribune,* September 29 and 30, 1869. Phyllis Field of Cornell University very kindly made available to the author three excellent, meticulously researched, draft chapters of her dissertation on the evolution of the black suffrage issue in New York State between 1846 and 1869, which was then still in progress. Ms. Field's fine study explores in depth both the ethno-cultural and the political factors involved in black voting in New York, and demonstrates the ways in which Republicans tried to obfuscate the issue of race per se in 1869 by introducing

extraneous allusions to religion, property, and the rights of immigrants. The long-term shift from black suffrage as a fringe issue to black suffrage as a party position is also explored. The dissertation in its final form, "The Struggle for Black Suffrage in New York State, 1846-1869," is now available from University Microfilms.

17. See, e.g., New York *World*, September 22, 1869.
18. New York *Herald*, September 23, 1869.
19. *Tribune*, November 1, 1869.
20. See Greeley's bitter comments in ibid., November 3, 1869, and Alexander, *Political History*, III:227. Cf. Field, who argues that black suffrage was an important but not the predominant issue in 1869.
21. Alexander, *Political History*, III:227; Alexander B. Callow, Jr., *The Tweed Ring* (New York, 1966), pp. 218-19; Alexander C. Flick, ed., *History of the State of New York* (New York, 1935), VII:140; Seymour J. Mandelbaum, *Boss Tweed's New York* (New York, 1965), p. 73.
22. *Tribune*, November 5, 1869.
23. New York State, *Documents of the Assembly ... 1869* (Albany, 1869), No. 2, John T. Hoffman, "Annual Message of the Governor," p. 29.
24. New York State, *Journal of the Assembly ... 1870* (Albany, 1870), I:193, 226, 520, 657, 749, 777-79, 862; New York State, *Journal of the Senate ... 1870* (Albany, 1870), pp. 525, 558-70; *Times*, March 25, 1870.
25. Mandelbaum, *Boss Tweed's New York*, p. 72; Alexander, *Political History*, III:243.
26. Mohr, *Radical Republicans in New York*, pp. 150-52, 271-75.
27. These calculations are based upon the data in New York State, *Documents of the Assembly ... 1873* (Albany, 1873), IX, No. 166, Abram B. Weaver, *Nineteenth Annual Report of the Superintendent of Public Instruction*, pp. 22-23.
28. To appreciate this vote in a larger context see William Gillette, *The Right to Vote: Politics and the Passage of the Fifteenth Amendment* (Baltimore, 1965, 1969), p. 115.
29. Hoffman, quoting DeWitt Clinton, formally protested the presence of federal troops in New York. See New York State, *Documents of the Assembly ... 1871* (Albany, 1871), No. 2; John T. Hoffman, "Annual Message of the Governor," pp. 33-39; Alexander, *Political History*, III: 243-44.
30. Hoffman, "Annual Message," 1871, p. 2.
31. Mandelbaum, *Boss Tweed's New York*, especially pp. 46-86.
32. Alfred R. Conkling, *The Life and letters of Roscoe Conkling, Orator, Statesman, Advocate* (New York, 1889), pp. 316-19, 329, 338-47; Alexander, *Political History*, III:173-74.
33. "For more than a year," complained Greeley in 1872, "to be an avowed friend of Governor Fenton was to be marked for proscription at the White House," quoted in Sullivan, *New York*, V:1762.
34. Louis J. Lang, ed., *The Autobiography of Thomas Collier Platt* (New York, 1910), pp. 55-60; Harold F. Gosnell, *Boss Platt and His New York Machine: A Study of the Political Leadership of Thomas C. Platt, Theodore Roosevelt, and Others* (Chicago, 1924), pp. 14-15.
35. The rise of ethno-cultural issues to prominence among Republicans may be traced in many ways. The Field dissertation is excellent on this subject. Alexander, *Political History*, III:235-40, 250-64, discusses Conkling's role specifically. Still another perspective is Morton Keller's *The Art and Politics of Thomas Nast* (New York, 1968), which traces the emergence and rise to prominence of nativistic, especially anti-Catholic, themes in the work of the party's most famous and effective cartoonist between 1868 and the middle 1870s.
36. In July 1871, Governor Hoffman overruled New York City's Mayor A. Oakey Hall when the latter, pressured by Irish Catholics, had rescinded a parade permit previously issued to Irish Protestants who wanted to celebrate the anniversary of the Battle of the Boyne. Hoffman alienated a traditionally Democratic bloc with his order allowing the Orangemen's parade to go forward under police and military protection, but gained the plaudits of Protestants and defenders of civil rights, including many Republicans, around

the state. The decision backfired, however, when the parade sparked a violent incident that left forty-nine people dead and some eighty-seven wounded. Six months later Hoffman was still trying to explain away his role in the affair in such a way as to preserve his old political bases. For one description of the incident itself see Denis T. Lynch, *"Boss" Tweed: The Story of a Grim Generation* (New York, 1927), pp. 366-69. New York State, *Documents of the Assembly . . . 1872* (Albany, 1872), I, No. 2, John T. Hoffman, "Annual Message of the Governor," pp. 31-33.

37. See, e.g., Horatio Seymour to Tilden, September 20 and 23, 1874, in John Bigelow, ed., *Letters and Literary Memorials of Samuel J. Tilden* (New York, 1908), I:338 and 341; Alexander C. Flick and Gustav S. Lobrano, *Samuel Jones Tilden: A Study in Political Sagacity* (Port Washington, N.Y., 1939, 1963); Alexander, *Political History,* III:265-75; Keith I. Polakoff, *The Politics of Inertia: The Election of 1876 and the End of Reconstruction* (Baton Rouge, 1973), especially pp. 70-93; Flick, *New York,* VII:151-59.

38. Hoffman, "Annual Message." 1872, p. 53.

39. New York State, *Journal of the Assembly . . . 1872* (Albany, 1872), I:993, II:1692, 1770, 1859-60, 2095-96, 2126; *Journal of the Senate . . . 1872* (Albany, 1872), 167, 988, 1005, 1052, 1076, 1155, 1198, 1203, 1243, *Times,* May 16, 1872.

40. *Times,* May 18, 1872.

41. Flick, *New York,* VII:206-14.

42. Mandelbaum, *Boss Tweed's New York,* pp. 105-13. Mandelbaum notes tartly, p. 107, "The creation of bipartisan boards, as a protection against gross party manipulation, did not ensure effective government."

43. Hoffman, "Annual Message," 1872, p. 39.

44. Part of the New York City Democracy, unable to swallow Greeley, ran Charles O'Conor on a separate ticket. Tilden, too, endorsed Liberalism, though he campaigned exclusively for candidates at the state and local level. See Sullivan, *New York,* V:1762, and Flick and Lobrano, *Tilden,* p. 241.

45. Many key politicians in New York, of course, Roscoe Conkling being chief among them, never accepted even this new and limited operative definition of reform. Conkling became famous for his withering attacks upon reform and reformers during the 1870s and is still much quoted on those subjects by historians. See, e.g., Ari Hoogenboom, *Outlawing the Spoils: A History of the Civil Service Reform Movement, 1865-1883* (Urbana, Ill., 1968). Many others could accept the new definition of reform, but hesitated to act upon it. See, e.g., Andrew Dickson White, *Autobiography of Andrew Dickson White* (New York, 1905), I:160,164-72.

46. *Times,* August 22, 1872.

5

OHIO

A "Perfect Contempt of All Unity"

Felice A. Bonadio

When the Civil War ended, the Republican Party seemed to be in firm command in Ohio. But the superiority of the Republican Party appeared more impressive than it actually was. Indeed, in the period following the war, the party was often on the brink of political disaster, a situation that contrasted sharply with its victories during the war.[1] The party's difficulties, in turn, had their basis within the Republican ranks. Since the birth of their party, Republicans had been avid, internecine fighters. The party arose in the 1850s as a loosely formed political coalition of several diverse and conflicting groups. As likely as not, Republican leaders were former political enemies who discovered in opposition to slavery an issue barely able to overcome personal hatreds and the scars of prior partisan battles. Various factions arranged themselves according to their own standards of party membership and tried to exclude all who were not "orthodox" Republicans by their particular definition. When the Republicans won control of the state, as they did on the eve of the Civil War, it was often with men who represented only a section of the party, usually with limited cooperation from the others.[2] The crisis of the war helped Republicanism to survive as a political organization, since all depended upon party unity. But in 1865, after peace had been restored to the nation, old resentments reappeared. A new struggle among Republicans began, more bitter, more unhappy than ever before.

Of all the divisions within the Republican Party, the most serious lay between the ex-Democrats and ex-Whigs. The contempt that these two groups of Republicans felt toward each other turned the party into a battleground in Ohio and extended to almost every Congressional district and county in the

1. Notes to this chapter are to be found on pp. 100-103.

state. It is not difficult to understand why. A decade earlier, ex-Democrats had formed the original nucleus of the Republican movement in Ohio, but in the political upheaval of the 1850s they had to accommodate themselves to a heavy influx of Whigs, who soon constituted the largest element in the new party.

The presence of the Whigs raised the critical question of which group would control the party. Ex-Democrats spoke angrily of "eleventh-hour" workers, and this anger, they said, was justified by the failure of the Whigs to give assistance of any kind to the crusade against slavery until their own party had disintegrated. Ideologues that they were, the ex-Democrats looked upon the Whigs as mere opportunists who had joined the Republican movement for reasons of expediency. Some former Democrats also suggested, with much justice, that the Whigs were engaged in a devious attempt to restore their old party to renewed life and power.[3] It was inevitable that relations between the ex-Democrats and the ex-Whigs would become even more bitter in the period after the war, for the problem of reconstruction was uniquely suited for division and dissent.

A second internal division that plagued Republicans involved the regulars, on the one hand, and the War Democrats, who joined the party soon after the outbreak of the Civil War, on the other. Most Republican leaders had welcomed the War Democrats for two reasons: to strengthen their own party and to maintain the semblance of a bipartisan war effort. Animosities arose, however, when some of the older Republicans claimed that the share of political offices received by the War Democrats outweighed their actual worth to the party. It seemed not only unjust but absurd that special favors be granted to those who had so recently become converts to the Republican Party. "I am tired of having the state governed by that element [War Democrats] of the Union forces," wrote one Republican worker. "It furnishes about a tenth of the votes and has gotten about nine-tenths of the offices." This argument was true neither during the war nor after it, but the fact that the War Democrats gained any offices at all was enough to plant jealousy in the hearts of local politicians in many parts of the state.[4]

It is a great error to suppose, therefore, that the Republican Party emerged from the war with either unity or strength of purpose. On the contrary, the party was torn by severe internal conflicts. A number of dissident Republicans, in fact, soon abandoned all hope of living within their party. As a result of their various disappointments, they decided to form their own political parties in the state. These third party, or "independent," movements had not been unknown to Republicans in earlier eras. Several minor defections had taken place during the war. But as intra-party warfare increased in the years following the war, Independent mutinies spread throughout the state, causing turmoil and confusion unlike anything Republicans had experienced before. In the eyes of several political observers, the Republican Party seemed to be "in a fit condition of self-murder."[5]

What brought the Republicans' internal difficulties to a painful head was the controversy over reconstruction. In the simplest terms reconstruction involved two questions: the restoration of the Southern states and the issue of Negro rights. But these two problems were closely connected to a third issue: the supremacy of the Republican Party. Republicans believed that if their party was to preserve its supremacy in national politics, it would need the votes of freedmen in the South. They pointed out that support for their party in the North was not sufficient to keep them in power at Washington, because, ironically, the abolition of slavery had increased the political power of the South. Once restored to the Union, Sourthern and Northern Democrats might strike a political bargain that would drive the Republicans from national office. Most Republicans understood, therefore, that voting rights for Negroes were of the greatest importance to their party.[6]

One consequence of Republican factionalism, however, was that the party found itself in a weak position to deal with important issues, much less those of a controversial nature. Republican leaders in Ohio were sensitive on this point even before the debate over reconstruction began. Jacob Cox, who became governor of the state in 1865, had little hope that Republicans would pull together in the interest of their party. "Everyone talks about the need for party unity," he wrote, "yet we do not hesitate to cut each other's throats in perfect contempt of all unity when the advantage of a part of the party may be found in it." Murat Halstead, Republican editor of the *Cincinnati Daily Commerical,* regretted the large number of "soreheads" who made party unity impossible. "If we suffer ourselves to be divided," he warned, "we shall find our opponents united and ready to take advantage of our weakness." Indeed, the Democrats were quick to see the advantage of waiting, during the coming crisis, for the violently controversial and politically dangerous issues of reconstruction to tear the Republican Party to pieces. As the *Cleveland Plain Dealer* told its readers: "The Republicans have a passion for hating each other. It is only a matter of time before the Republican party will be reduced to its original elements."[7]

As a consequence of their own divisions, paradoxically, most Republicans could agree that exclusion of the South, at least until after the presidential election of 1868, was a good policy. In that way Republicans could preserve their control over the federal government long enough to unify their party at home before facing a resurgent South. This "solution" to the reconstruction probelm was especially popular among Ohio's moderate Republican leaders. John Sherman's speech at Circleville was characteristic of the approach. "I would leave them [the South] under military rule until they provide the only secure security for the future." Other leaders of the party took exactly the same position. James Garfield told his constituents that he would keep the South "on the mourner's bench for some time," and make certain that "the military ruled over them." Edward Noyes, who later became governor of

Ohio, expressed confidence in "the establishment of a . . . military force in each Southern state."[8] The moderate policy, however, while it precipitated an early break with President Johnson, was based upon a dubious hope that a definitive program of reconstruction would, if left to time and compromise, emerge of itself.

Opposition to the moderate program emerged at once from the ex-Democrats. These Republicans argued that a reconstruction program without substance, without proposals for radical changes in the South, was the design of timid conservatives who would not hesitate to dilute the idealism of the party. To the ex-Democrats it was clear what was happening: the ex-Whigs were beginning to dominate the party. The men who had fought the long battle against slavery, organized the Republican movement, and inspired the new party with moral zeal and energy, were now looked upon as old-fashioned, no longer entitled to give orders. The ex-Democrats heard with indignation that they should surrender their authority to Republicans who considered themselves, by skill and temperament, more attuned to the party's postwar needs.[9] The reaction of the ex-Democrats was not merely surprising, it was startling. They counterattacked by proposing that the Republican Party support a program to make the Negro a full voting citizen not only in the South but also in Ohio, and they insisted that only those Republicans who agreed with their position should be nominated by the party for public office. "Negro suffrage," one Republican leader complained, had suddenly become "the high test of party loyalty."[10]

It is not surprising that many Republicans in Ohio were dismayed. The scheme for Negro suffrage in the South was not the primary object of their concern. Some sort of franchise program was inevitable, if, as was generally expected, the Republicans would need the votes of the freedmen to retain control over the national government. But most Republicans were not prepared to grant the franchise to the Negro in Ohio. Only too clearly party leaders realized that what their race-conscious constituents might accept for the South would probably be rejected for Ohio. The desire of the militants to extend political equality to the Negro may have reflected a sincere desire on their part to advance the cause of human freedom, but many moderates feared that the policy reflected a desperate attempt by the militants to retain their positions of leadership in the party. As Jacob Cox wrote in a private note: "The Negro suffrage question is in itself grave enough, but it is likely to be complicated by the ambition of politicians to make it a leverage on one side or the other."[11]

These difficulties came openly to a head during the state elections of 1865. At the Republican convention in July militants tried to force their party to adopt a resolution endorsing Negro suffrage in Ohio. The proposal was defeated amid squabbles that broke out between the militants and army delegates at the convention. The convention finally passed one of those "glittering generalities," which John Sherman "liked to see from time to time" in the interest of party unity. But the issue did not fade away.[12]

When their first anger was over, the militants decided that it would be advantageous to force all Republican candidates to take a stand on the issue of Negro suffrage. A group of "Oberlin radicals" addressed an open letter to Cox, the Republican candidate for governor, and insisted on a reply. Cox, boiling with rage, was suddenly placed in a situation which, he believed, demanded honesty and courage. Rejecting Negro suffrage completely, he explained his own plan for "racial harmony" in America: the colonization of all Negroes in America in the three Southern states of Georgia, Alabama, and Florida, a proposal that "fell like a bombshell" upon his party.[13] Cox's proposal seemed as extreme in its own way as the militants had been in theirs. Arguments and counterarguments flew back and forth between Republicans. If the militants had shaken party unity during the campaign, so had Cox's proposal. The Republican attempt to present a united front on the issue of Negro suffrage had failed.

The Democrats, of course, were delighted by the difficulties of their opponents. They believed that it was the opening of an opportunity for them to recover from their flirtation with the peace movement during the Civil War. In 1862 the "peace without victory" crusade had contained a most alluring prospect for the Democrats, and under the leadership of men like Clement Vallandigham, Congressman from Dayton, and Washington McLean, editor of the *Cincinnati Daily Enquirer,* many of them embraced it. The result of this policy was the direct opposite of Democratic expectations, for among the electorate there was widespread disapproval of it. The political damage to the Democrats was severe. In the postwar years, no issue was so politically embarrassing to the Democrats as the failure of their party to give complete support to the Northern war effort.[14]

The Democrats hastened to praise President Andrew Johnson's reconstruction program as a model of statesmanship, and they pledged their party to support his proposals. Next, the Democrats made much of a "radical conspiracy" within the Republican Party, determined at whatever cost to overthrow the President and to defeat his program. "The Democracy have had private meetings here," wrote a Cincinnati Republican to Cox: "I am this morning, in confidence, put in possession of some of the results. Their effort is to capture President Johnson. . . . They expect aid from our divisions. They hope the radicals will make war on Johnson on the question of negro suffrage. They will come to his support, hold out to him expectations but finally treat him as they did Tyler. This is the purpose of the enemy. To be forewarned is to be forearmed."[15]

The test of the Democratic position came in the Congressional elections of 1866. Prior to the elections, Johnson had called for the formation of a new political organization, the National Union Party. The long agonizing relationship between Johnson and the Republican Party was over, for they now faced each other as members of opposing political parties. In Ohio, as in other states of the North, the Congressional elections of 1866 were fought with intense bitterness. For their part, Republicans avoided the controversial issues of reconstruction, and confined their campaign to a denunication of the South and President Johnson. The election itself, cast as it was in terms of Johnson versus the Republican Party, was enough to allow Republican leaders to revive the issues of the Civil War and thus impose on their party a sense of unity more extensive than had existed since the end of the war.

In the Congressional elections of 1866 the Republicans were triumphant. Yet Johnson's defeat was accomplished mostly by his own mistakes and miscalculations; popular support for the National Union Party in Ohio failed to materialize. Consequently, the 1866 elections could hardly be called a popular endorsement of the Republicans. Indeed, in their review of elections, the apprehension of Republican leaders about the future of their party increased. Such victories as the Republicans had achieved were clearly misleading and had a doubtful relationship to the actual condition of the party. Far from being delighted with the result, Republican leaders were plainly worried.

Their fears were fully justified. In most of Ohio's Congressional districts Republican majorities were much lower than they had been in 1864. In ten of the state's nineteen districts the reduction in Republican support was dangerously low, and the figures appeared to indicate a trend that did, in fact, continue into 1868.[16] The deep-seated antagonisms within the Republican Party, moreover, were hardly hidden from public view. Only the blindest of voters could fail to see that beneath the facade of party unity the Republicans treated each other with increasing harshness. In some parts of the state they openly detested one another. As the Democrats put it: "They [the Republicans] have lost their cohesive force. In fact, instead of being a united party, the Republicans have divided into two or more discordant factions, hating each other worse than either of them hates the Democracy."[17] The Democrats, however, were not without their own difficulties. They had not fully recovered from their minority position. It was most unlikely that they would be sufficiently recovered by 1868 to capture the presidency. And in any case what victories the Democrats had achieved depended upon the factionalism of the Republicans.

At the beginning of 1867, however, the Republican Party in Ohio found itself facing a new dilemma: a re-emergence of the Negro suffrage issue. Some Republicans were furiously angered by this development. They believed the issue of Negro suffrage had been disposed of during the 1866 Congressional campaign. At that time, the Democrats had seized on the question with great delight, convinced that no better issue could be found with which to discredit the Republicans. Again and again during the campaign the Democrats accused the Republicans of being advocates of Negro suffrage, arguing that the Fourteenth Amendment had the result of granting both social and political equality to the Negro. The Republican reaction was to deny the charge completely. "The Fourteenth Amendment has absolutley nothing whatsoever to do with the franchise," wrote the *Cincinnati Daily Gazette,* echoing the sentiments of most Republicans. Nevertheless, the Democratic argument proved so telling and effective that Republicans throughout Ohio were forced to rival their opponents in professions of loyalty to the dogma of white supremacy.[18]

But Republican extremists were not to be shaken in their determination to impose Negro suffrage on their party, including suffrage for the Negro in Ohio. Accordingly, in the months following the election, they demanded that Republicans in the state legislature support a resolution to change the state constitution in order to allow "all adult males" in the state the right to vote. Such a resolution, because of state law, would be submitted to the people for their approval in the fall elections of 1867. To some Republicans this was a disturbing thought; it was no comfort to realize that their party might be forced to battle the Democrats in those elections on the issue of Negro voting in Ohio.[19] To others, however, it was less upsetting.

By the early months of 1867 certain circumstances had made the issue of Negro voting in the state more palatable to many Republicans than it had been in 1865. Some were reminded that, if the party rejected the issue, the Radicals would simply continue to press their demands until they became impossible to control. Then too, there were those Republicans who argued that justice to the Negro was dead if they forced the South to adopt a policy that they refused to accept at home. Others supported the proposal in order to "get the nigger out of politics."[20] Still others accepted the proposal for Negro suffrage in Ohio for more strictly political reasons; they believed that the votes of Negroes could be used to defeat the Democrats in many parts of the state.

There were approximately 10,000 Negroes in Ohio. Their votes could be decisive to Republicans, particularly in the so-called doubtful counties of central Ohio, where the margin between the two major parties was extremely close. In Muskingum County, for example, the Republican majority in 1865 had been 65 votes; the 400 Negroes of voting age who lived in the county would certainly increase that majority. In Ross County, the Democrats had won the election of 1865 with a majority of 103 votes; the 460 Negroes of voting age who lived in that county would certainly have taken victory away from the Democrats. In 1865 the *Columbus State Journal* published a complete list of those counties in Ohio in which the vote of the Negro would mean the difference between victory or defeat. "This may be regarded as a selfish appeal to our friends in behalf of the amendment," the *Journal* commented, "but it is such an appeal thay may well reach many men on whom any argument as to the abstract justice of manhood suffrage would be lost."[21]

That was in 1865, when Republicans could hardly conceive that their party would soon lose so much popular support. But in 1867, in the months preceding the state elections, the *Portage County Democrat* was happy to show the great effect that a mere 6,000 votes might have on the fortunes of the party in the forthcoming fall elections.

> In the election of members of the House at the next election, a change of 3,000 votes from the Union ticket, as the vote stood in 1865, will change the political complexion of the House, while in the Senate the same change will be effected by a change of 3,622 votes. Deducting from the last number of the votes of those counties included in the House estimate, and it would require but 6,035 votes to change the political complexion of both branches of the Legislature, giving the Democrats control of both Houses, a majority on joint ballot and therefore a successor to Wade in the Senate.

To prevent this result, the *Democrat* concluded, the only alternative was for Republicans to support suffrage for the Negro in Ohio.[22]

The Negro suffrage proposal also contained an element of danger. How could Republicans produce a formula for Negro suffrage without losing the support of their white constituents? Certain Republicans, of course, genuinely believed that anti-black sentiment in the state was not as severe as some maintained. Other Republicans argued that since the actual number of Negroes in Ohio was so small the mass of the white population would not object to granting the franchise to them. But for a great number of Republicans, particularly in the southern part of the state, it was not easy to see how the party could sponsor Negro suffrage without destroying itself politically.[23]

Moreover, at the national level events did nothing to assure Republicans that the enormous burden of Negro suffrage could be placed with any degree of confidence on the tottering structure of their party. In the early months of 1867 Congress passed the First Military Reconstruction Act, which left as many problems as it attempted to solve. Compared with the Fourteenth Amendment there were numerous advantages to Republicans in Northern states, like Ohio, in sponsoring a reconstruction program that subjected the South to definite actions before it could be readmitted into the Union. At the same time, however, the bill could not and did not satisfy each of the several factions within the Republican Party in Ohio, and the reaction of many Republicans to the bill was one of deep disappointment. The *Cincinnati Daily Gazette* expressed the sentiment of these Republicans in clear and unequivocal language. "The measure has brought neither the supremacy of law, nor public or personal security, nor peace, nor does it promise to bring them."[24]

In March 1867 an amendment was introduced in the Ohio house of representatives that would eliminate from the state constitution the provision that
only "white male adults" could vote. The amendment was defeated by a vote
of 56 to 38, with most of the Republican opposition coming from the
southern part of the state. Meanwhile, in that same month, a similar proposal
was introduced in the Ohio senate, where it passed by a strict party vote. One
month later, the amendment was again introduced in the house, and this time
the measure passed by a strict party vote.[25]

For days it remained a mystery how Republican legislators from southern
Ohio had been persuaded finally to support the resolution. But when the full
text of the resolution was published, the mystery was at once cleared up. The
resolution fell into two main parts. First, as expected, it proposed a change in
the state constitution by which the Negro in Ohio had now the right to vote.
Second, it provided that those men who had given aid to the Confederacy
during the war, or who had deserted from the Union army, were to be
disfranchised. The Republicans, in short, had fused together two separate
issues: Negro suffrage and the disfranchisement of disloyal whites.[26]

This second issue turned out to be the price of Republican support in
southern Ohio for the Negro suffrage resolution. The number of white voters
who could be disfranchised was approximately 37,000 and most of these
lived in the southern counties. Not only had the Republicans added Negro
voters to their party, they had also taken the "political risk" out of Negro
suffrage by reducing the number of hostile white voters in the state. If there
was to be a "white back-lash" in Ohio against Negro suffrage, the Republicans
tried to make certain that their party would not suffer the full consequences
of it.[27] The resolution, therefore, was the work of cold political calculation.
The plan seemed perfect. But its success turned upon an important question:
would the Republican Party remain united?

The answer was not long in coming. Municipal elections in Ohio were held
in the spring of 1867, one month after passage of the resolution. The result of
these elections was disastrous for the Republicans. Three of the four largest
cities in the state went to the Democrats; two others, Dayton and Toledo,
were barely retained by the Republicans—Toledo, for example, by a mere
forty votes. The Democrats won control of many smaller cities—Portsmouth,
Fremont, Newark, Circleville, Zanesville—in many cases for the first time in
over a decade. If these elections were any signal, the Republican Party seemed
doomed in the coming fall elections.[28]

For many Republicans, the catastrophe of the spring elections had but a
single cause: Negro suffrage. They were frightened and confused. It was now
inconceivable to them that they should face the Democrats in the fall on the
issue of Negro suffrage. Of all their mistakes, this one, apparently, was the
worst. However, there was still time to repair the damage. Open opposition to
Negro suffrage was clearly out of the question, for the party was too closely

identified with it. But they could, if they chose, both ignore the issue and refuse to admit that the action of Republicans in the state legislature was binding on all Republicans in the state. The Republicans of Brown County, anticipating their colleagues in other parts of the state, adopted this tactic almost immediately. "We do not believe," they announced, "that the Constitutional Amendment should be made a party question, but left for Union men to vote upon as they may chose without prejudicing their standing in the party."[29]

In this emergency, political expediency became the supreme consideration. This meant that Republican candidates for office would use their energies not in support of Negro suffrage, but for their own political survival. Negro suffrage, the issue which Republicans had demanded as a matter of "principle" earlier in the year, was all but discarded as the fall campaign approached. It was a sorry spectacle.

Already reeling over the black suffrage issue, the party had next to nominate a candidate for governor. In the division between Republicans over this matter the ex-Democrats and the ex-Whigs were once again on opposing sides. Edwin Cowles, editor of the *Cleveland Plain Dealer*, led the ex-Democrats. He and his followers had several goals in mind. First, they desired to win the nomination for Benjamin Cowen, a former adjutant-general of the state. Next, they hoped to control the nomination of candidates for the state legislature. This objective was extremely important, for Benjamin F. Wade, Ohio's senior Senator, was up for reelection, and the ex-Democrats wanted desperately to replace him. All these plans and maneuvers could, in turn, be traced to an even larger purpose: the nomination of Salmon P. Chase for President at the Republican national convention in 1868. If the ex-Democrats could control the next legislature, then Wade would be eliminated from politics, and Chase would have a clear field.[30]

The ex-Whigs, led by William Henry Smith, were seething, and in a letter written in the spring of 1867 Smith described the scheme of the ex-Democrats. "Some foolish men in the interest of Chase are endeavoring to complicate the matter [the Republican gubernatorial nomination] with presidential politics. Cowen is as bitter as death . . . and threatens everlasting vengeance."[31] Smith's distaste was understandable. The ex-Democrats, in the interest of Chase, had been responsible in the first instance for raising the issue of Negro voting in Ohio, and since this issue had resulted in great difficulties for the Republicans, the blame must rest with them. Undismayed by the recent results of the municipal elections, however, the ex-Democrats refused to admit that anything was wrong, and were now determined to see Chase nominated for the presidency, quite possibly at the expense of the Republican Party, at least in Ohio. They had acted on their own account without consulting other Republicans, had arranged to defeat Wade in his bid for reelection, and had planned to control Ohio's delegation at the Republican national convention in 1868.

This was more than Smith and many other prominent Republicans were willing to tolerate. Consequently, in order to thwart Cowen in his amibtions, Smith and his supporters brought forward Rutherford B. Hayes, Congressman from Cincinnati, for the gubernatorial nomination at the Republican convention in July. Hayes won and his nomination was a vote of censure on the ex-Democrats.[32]

The ex-Democrats had been defeated, but their determination not to forgive their opponents was still high. Their reaction was instant. If their candidate could not have the nomination, then they were determined to see that the candidate of their opponents would not win either. Unfortunately for Hayes and the Republican Party, Cowen, as chairman of the executive committee, was in a position to inflict serious injury on the party. Every consideration but that of defeating Hayes went by the board. Hayes suddenly found himself the target of a savage attack by the Cowen-Cowles faction of the Republican Party during the campaign. "He [Cowles] circulated lies about Gen. Hayes and resorted to every trick and mean act at the time of the convention," wrote Smith in a personal letter. "When disappointed there, he proclaimed through his nearest friend that now he should lay back and go to cutting throats."[33] Cowen's vindictiveness was particularly damaging because he was responsible for the organization of the Republican campaign, and he did not hesitate to use his authority to defeat the candidate of his own party.

A painful defeat for the Republicans in the fall elections followed. The political position of the Republicans, identified as it was with the issue of Negro suffrage, had been difficult to begin with. But Cowen's deliberate sabotage of the Republican campaign made matters much worse. Defeat for the Republicans was almost inevitable. Hayes won the governor's election, but by a bare majority of 2,000 votes. The Democrats captured control of both houses of the state legislature. Wade would lose his seat in the Senate. As for the constitutional amendment, it was rejected by a majority of over 50,000 votes. For Republicans, there seemed no end to weariness, disillusion, disappointment.[34]

It was, said some Republicans, a singular comment upon the internal politics of their party that the very men who had brought the issue of Negro suffrage into prominence in 1865 were largely responsible for its defeat in 1867. The ex-Democrats had, indeed, raised the issue of Negro suffrage for political leverage, just as Cox had warned, and not for the triumph of justice to the Negro. "The people," warned the *Cincinnati Daily Gazette,* "are tired of this continued chaffing, bickering, scheming, and trickery ... of partisan interference for purely selfish ends."[35]

It was this "continued bickering" that largely explained the failure of the Republican Party to pass any meaningful legislation in the state during the crisis over reconstruction. On a host of problems, whose solutions grew daily more urgent, Republicans accomplished nothing or almost nothing of consequence. In some parts of Ohio the cost of public transportation and an increase in gas rates aroused a public demand for the regulation of municipal utilities. On this matter, however, Republicans took no action. At the same time, urban workers throughout the state complained about their long hours of labor and demanded the passage of legislation that would guarantee to them an eight-hour working day. But here, also, the Republican Party failed to satisfy, a fact that led to the creation of Workingmen's parties in the state.[36]

Even in areas where legislative action seemed possible, opponents of various proposals took advantage of the ruinous contests between Republicans either to defeat the proposals or to render them, if passed, ineffective. This was the case in March 1867, with the railroad commissioner's bill. One year earlier, in response to popular demand, a special committee of the Ohio senate undertook an investigation of several powerful railroad companies in the state. The committee discovered a number of abuses, which included rate manipulation, inadequate passenger service, and widespread breeches of the law with respect to the ownership of railroad stock. The result of these disclosures was the passage of a bill creating a state commissioner of railroads, whose duty it was to investigate complaints against the railroads in Ohio, and to issue reports. However, the force of the bill was counteracted by the railroad interests, who made use of their power to deprive the commissioner of all authority to take legal action against railroad corporations. Although most Republican leaders in Ohio supported the bill, the splitting up of their party into rival factions contributed in large part to the success of the railroads in shaping a measure acceptable to themselves. Critics of the Republican controlled state legislature were deeply angered by this outcome. They were convinced, more than ever before, that the chief object of Republican politicians in the legislature was political power itself rather than the public good. "Take the public institutions and the officeholders out of Columbus," one Republican newspaper declared, "and the state legislature would fall into irredeemable decay."[37] Nor was public frustration limited only to a few close observers of state politics. A large number of people—not merely those who were eager for reform—were disgusted by the unending divisions between Republicans—divisions that made the record of the Ohio legislature in the enactment of local laws so disappointing.

Much of this infighting in Ohio reflected the rival ambitions of the state's two most prominent presidential hopefuls, Chase and Wade. Although the Chase forces had been defeated at the Republican convention in 1867, they were still able to make themselves unpleasant. Cowen's activities during the campaign were aimed not only at making difficulties for Hayes, but in seeing to it that Wade would lose his seat in the Senate to the Democrats. The victory of the Democrats in the elections produced exactly this result and had the additional effect of reducing Wade's chances for the Republican presidential nomination in 1868. Thus, by the end of 1867, the "throat cutting" and "internal slaughter" in the ranks of the Republican Party had reached a climax. It was at once evident that only a Republican candidate of immense popularity could save the party from utter defeat in the presidential election of 1868.

That candidate was Ulysses S. Grant. As early as 1866 Grant had been recommended for the Republican nomination by some Ohio Republicans, who understood the advantages he possessed. He was a national hero. He had never been identified with either of the two major parties. He had taken no part in the political issues of the day. But even so, not all Republicans were happy with the possibility of Grant's leadership of the party. For them, the consideration of overwhelming importance was that the Republican candidate in 1868 must be a man of clear political principles. They had discovered in their experience with Johnson how dangerous it was to have a standard-bearer whose primary qualification had been his ability to attract support outside the party. "We hope the party will shun the nomination of non-committals," wrote the *Columbus State Journal* in 1866, "take nothing for *Grant*ed, but know all about the principles of the man chosen."[38]

By this time, however, support for Grant was being organized by several leading Republicans in the state, and in the localities by numerous lesser politicians, who looked upon him as the salvation of the party. One year later, in the months following the state elections of 1867, this preference was transformed into a frantic, desperate demand for Grant's nomination. William Bickman, editor of the *Dayton Journal*, saw in the results of the elections a clear warning for "all civilian candidates" to stand aside "in the interest of Grant." "What a rush for Grant," wrote one Chase supporter, "and a cowardly rush it is." James Garfield, Congressman from the Western Reserve, wrote to William Dean Howells, editor of the *Ashtabula Sentinel*, that the Grant movement in the state was "irresistible." Howells bitterly agreed. "The Republican party has put a padlock upon their mouths," he answered, "through the corners of which they squeek Great is Grant."[39]

Republicans like Howells could hardly be unmoved by this situation. Only a decade earlier they had been among the original founders of the Republican Party, and they had agreed that this new party would endure because it had been founded on principle, not expediency; righteousness, not self-interest. But now principle and men of principle had become luxuries the Republican Party could no longer afford. The elevation of Grant represented not only the end of political idealism but also the loss of their positions within the Republican Party.

Ohio's Republican delegation supported Grant's candidacy at the party's national convention in June 1868. And while the General's nomination produced a great deal of enthusiasm among most Republicans in Ohio, it produced deep disappointment among several of the party's veterans—the men who had formed the nucleus of the Republican movement in the 1850s. Their correspondence is filled with warnings of disgust and despair. In vain, they pointed out that Grant represented a surrender to political expediency, that his election would result in the death of political idealism. His chief supporters in Ohio, they argued, were "pothouse politicians"—a generation of Republicans who cared only for victory, even if it came at the expense of the party's principles.[40]

By 1868 dissatisfaction among Ohio Democrats was very nearly as widespread as it was among the Republicans. The war had been over for three years. During this period, the Democrats had made remarkable gains, and their victory in the state elections of 1867 was especially sweet. But the Democrats remained uneasy. For one thing, it was clear that in almost every case Democratic success had come as a result of Republican factionalism. In addition, the Democrats were also split into rival factions over the so-called "Ohio idea," a proposal to redeem government bonds with greenbacks rather than gold. This proposal was introduced by the Democrats in the state elections of 1867, and, while the measure was approved by the party, it was by no means acceptable to all Democrats. With a strong sense of urgency, the Ohio idea was denounced by the "hard money" element in the Democratic Party—old-line Jacksonians, for example, who condemned the measure as "a bare faced falsehood and bad law and worse morality and arithmetic." These Democrats at once made it clear that they would sooner leave the party than support the Ohio idea.[41]

Difficulties over the Ohio idea were, however, of minor importance compared with the supreme cause of Democratic disaffection: the control of the party by the old peace Democrats, men like George Pendleton, Clement Vallandigham, and Allen Thurman. For Democrats who had supported the war, the leadership of this powerful triumvirate made the complete rehabilitation of the party in the period following the war an almost impossibly difficult task. They now judged the time had come to give the party new leadership. But while the position of the peace Democrats was secure, the authority of their opponents in party affairs and party politics was by no means established. This fact had been made clear to them by Thurman's nomination as governor in 1867 and by his election to the Senate one year later, to replace Wade. It was, wrote Thomas Ewing, Jr., a "great tragedy" that the Democratic Party remained in the hands of the "peace Democrats" rather than the "sensible Democrats" who had supported the war.[42]

By the spring of 1868, Democrats like Ewing accepted the fact that a major failure for the party was about to occur, when it supported Pendleton for the presidential nomination in 1868, and they accordingly prepared plans. They decided to defeat the peace Democrats by supporting Chase at the Democratic national convention.[43] This plan was received by Chase with great enthusiasm, for it was clear to him that he could not receive the Republican nomination over Grant. But there was a major problem for Chase. He was closely identified with support of Negro suffrage, a proposal that most Democrats in Ohio had vigorously opposed.

Chase at first attempted to persuade Ohio Democrats to change their position, but under the leadership of peace Democrats his suggestion was ignored. Chase overcame initial exasperation, because his ambition was great, and suddenly decided to pursue a policy that might ensure the full support of the Democratic Party in Ohio. In an extraordinary change of mind, he abandoned his views on Negro suffrage, arguing that the question was a matter for the individual states to decide and not for "outsiders" to determine for them.[44] The Republicans were savage in their denunciation of the Chief Justice. "The degradation of Salmon P. Chase is complete," one Republican newspaper proclaimed. "He has gone down into the mire to seek the embrace of a harlot; he has disavowed and repudiated sentiments he has held for a lifetime." "He is a political vampire," wrote another. "He is sort of a moral bull-bitch."[45]

No change of policy, however, could, in fact, persuade the Democratic Party in Ohio to give its support to Chase. At the Democratic national convention, the Ohio delegation was divided between the friends of Chase and Pendleton, but the latter were more powerful. They bitterly opposed Chase's nomination. Vehement controversy followed. "We want no disappointed negro worshipper like Chase," wrote one of his critics.[46]

Seymour's nomination was a great disappointment to many Ohio Democrats. The Pendleton wing of the party found it impossible to accept his denunciation of the Ohio idea, particularly with the undisputed fact of the popularity of currency inflation in Ohio. At the same time, the Chase Democrats found it equally impossible to understand why their party had selected a presidential candidate who had been a peace Democrat during the war. "A complete disaster," wrote Ewing, when he learned of Seymour's nomination.[47]

For both wings of the Democratic Party, therefore, Seymour's nomination seemed to be a mistake. They did not suggest what direction they and their followers would take in the future, but they certainly considered the condition of their party difficult and undesirable. One Ohio Democrat stated the matter in a clear and unequivocal statement. "We must lay the foundations for a new Democratic party. This canvass [1868] *will finish the old one.*"[48] This disappointment, by elements in both the Republican and the Democratic parties, may have reflected, for some, only a temporary disapproval. For others, however, it reflected an attitude of deep hostility which was neither sudden nor temporary; a hostility that had been part of their outlook at least since the end of the war.

This was clearly the case with one group of Republicans. Among their leaders were James A. Garfield, Jacob D. Cox, Rutherford B. Hayes, William Henry Smith, and Isaac Sherwood. All were young when the war ended, their average age was thirty-three. All had attended college, recipients of an education far above average for the era. Garfield and Cox became lawyers; others, like Halstead, Whitelaw Reid, and William Henry Smith, went into journalism. They moved easily from college into a profession, often to relatively comfortable positions. This background of education, comfort, and rapid promotion was very different from that of many of the original founders of the Republican Party. Benjamin Wade, for example, had been poor, was self-educated, and studied law while working at various occupations.[49]

The Civil War catapulted these younger, professional types into political office. Service in the military as commissioned officers was responsible to a considerable degree for their sudden rise in politics. Most of them had become Republicans on the eve of the Civil War, when they were newcomers to the party and to state politics. As such, they had no ties with prewar politics, either as Whigs or Democrats, and, consequently, no public identification with the issues of the past. They were, therefore, especially disgusted with the animosities and antagonisms that proved to be a source of such difficulty, discontent, and even ruin for the older members of the party in the postwar era.

These younger Republicans were also distinguished from the older members of the party in their approach to politics. To them party politics was a "specialty," every aspect of which needed careful attention, organization, and, above all, strict discipline. They compared their view of politics to the administrative methods of large business corporations. They proposed various reforms that would make the Republican Party more "businesslike" and "efficient": the creation of a state executive committee with the power to exercise its authority in city wards; the nomination of candidates for state and national office at the district rather than the county level; the abolition of the open primary; and a "test oath" that would require Republicans to declare their allegiance to the party. One of the first objects of these reforms was to avoid the divisive bickering and bolting that so disrupted party politics in the prewar period.[50]

The annoyance of these Republicans with their party in 1865 went deeper than its lack of organization. They were critical also of the party's veteran leadership. These veterans, the younger Republicans argued, were no longer suited to lead the party for their roots were in the past, when the issue of Negro slavery had all but dominated public affairs. The war had abolished slavery and, more importantly, had ushered in a new America that demanded an appreciation of economic purposes and economic needs. The old crusaders against slavery, the younger Republicans declared, knew nothing about these problems.[51]

At the end of the Civil War the younger Republicans were anxious to strengthen the supremacy of their party, both in the nation and in the state. They supported a policy of impartial suffrage, hoping to create a Republican Party in the South; and they insisted that a decent time should elapse before the South was admitted back into the Union. The controversy over reconstruction, as far as these Republicans were concerned, was deplorable. It spread despondency and alarm deep into the ranks of the party. They blamed Johnson primarily, but they were critical also of the "fanatics" and "opportunists" who encouraged and exploited the controversy for what seemed to be reasons of pure self-interest.

Although these younger Republicans could not ignore the reconstruction impasse, they did their best to avoid taking a leading part in it, preferring instead to let the matter run its course. Behind the scenes they worked furiously at creating a strong political base for themselves in the state. Patronage was important and distributed widely to Democrats, Independents, and National Unionists, as well as Republicans. Men like Garfield, Hayes, and Sherman had managed by 1868 the creation of political machines that were the envy of other Republicans in Ohio. Sherman, for instance, was said to have established "the most powerful political ring in state politics."[52] As the Grant era dawned these men flourished.

Not all Republicans, however, were willing to acquiesce in this feeling of bland satisfaction with their party. Many felt apprehensive about the future of Republicanism itself during this period. Several of these Republicans were newspaper editors of wide respect and considerable influence. They had experience and a serious involvement in politics, and their object quickly became the creation of a third political party in Ohio. A few, like Murat Halstead, had made this suggestion at the end of the war. Others, like Whitelaw Reid and Fredrick Hassaurek, supported this proposal only after the election of Grant.[53]

The dissatisfaction of these Republicans fell into three categories. The first was their concern that the party had deserted the high idealism that, they believed, had been responsible for its birth. The qualities of blind party loyalty, political compromise, and partisan favoritism might help win elections, they argued, but would not ensure honest government or efficient public service. They had no intention, as Reid put it, of including themselves among "the numbers of party slaves, who fear to believe as the party may direct, and blindly follow their leaders, no matter where their course may take."[54]

The second and most important source of disaffection stemmed from the issue of political corruption. James Comly, Republican editor of the *Columbus State Journal*, called the years of his party's leadership in the affairs of the state "the era of embezzlement." There were blatant cases involving theft of money from the state treasury, improper use of tax money, and personal enrichment. Suspicion of Republican leaders in these circumstances was inevitable, and a storm of criticism was directed at certain of them who had added relatives to their payrolls, bribed rival candidates, and received financial favors from the special interest groups that swarmed around the state legislature.[55]

Most regular Republicans either ignored these charges or refused to admit that anything was wrong. But before they had time to mount a counteroffensive, they were startled once more. In June 1868, Donn Piatt, leader of the Republican Party in the Ohio house of representatives, published an editorial that burst upon the state like a thunderstorm. In it, he called his party "the most corrupt that ever existed." He charged that the level of decency of Republicans at the state capital was unbelievably low. "From the lowest officials, up to Senators and Cabinet officers," he wrote, "the taint of corruption runs until the people dazed and confused confound the right and listen with indifference to threats of exposure."[56] As a remedy, Piatt proposed a program of civil service reform in Ohio in order to ensure that the public business of the state would be conducted on a basis not of favoritism, but of merit. This proposal was warmly accepted by the other Independent Republicans.

A third source of disaffection concerned tariff reform. Frederick Hassaurek, a highly respected Republican, and editor of the *Cincinnati Volksblatt*, strongly protested against the tariff rates, which had been increasing since the end of the war. "The age of Chinese Walls has passed away," he declared in his newspaper. "The prosperity of the nation cannot happen by preventing competition."[57] By the middle of 1868 the Republican reformers had come to focus their activities in Cincinnati, primarily because their movement was strongest in that city.

At this stage, the reformers suddenly received support from an unexpected source—Washington McLean, editor of the *Cincinnati Daily Enquirer*, and perhaps the most powerful Democrat in the state. At the end of the war, McLean had been a "straight party" Democrat, and during the controversy over reconstruction he remained faithful to the Democracy. Meanwhile he worked furiously at the reorganization of his party. His purpose was to place his party in the hands of Democrats who were free from the emotions and the convictions of the past. By the end of 1868, however, it became only too clear to McLean that the leadership of the "old line peace Democrats" was still distressingly prevalent. In the early months of 1869, he took a major step forward. He urged Democrats in Cincinnati to align themselves with the Republican reformers in the formation of a new political party.

Strong objections to McLean's proposal arose from Cincinnati Democrats reluctant to leave their old party. "The Democratic party split into older and younger members," the *Cincinnati Daily Gazette* reported, "between those who would not compromise with the base of the party or its name, and those who wanted a new party composition and a new name to go along with it." In the split McLean's strategy was defeated. Angered and frustrated, he and his supporters bolted the regular Democratic Party and joined forces with the Republican reformers.[58]

By the summer of 1869, these groups formed a new political party in Ohio, the Citizens Reform Party. Advanced in all good faith, the platform of this new party consisted of three major objects: political reform, civil service reform, and free trade. The influence of the Citizens Reform Party in the state elections of 1869 was impressive. They elected their entire ticket in Cincinnati and sent seven Reformers to the state legislature. While the Republicans managed to reelect Hayes as governor, these seven Reformers held the balance of power in the state legislature.[59]

It was perhaps the supreme irony of postwar politics in Ohio that the legislature of 1870, in which elements of the old Republican Party were at last openly divided into separate organizations, was the one that ratified the Fifteenth Amendment. Regular Republicans believed that the amendment increased their chances of maintaining control over state politics, and this was widely acknowledged to be the chief reason for their support. The Reformers, for their part, voted with the Republicans in order to eliminate the issue of Negro suffrage from politics, believing that the end of the old would make way for continued growth of the new. That hope proved hollow, but the vote signaled the end of an issue and the end of an era.

NOTES

1. For voting returns in Ohio, in both state and national elections, see, Joseph Smith, *The Republican Party in Ohio* (Chicago, 1898), pp. 39-278; See also, Eugene Roseboom, "Southern Ohio and the Union in 1863," *The Mississippi Valley Historical Review* 39 (June 1952): 29-43.

2. The divisions between the various factions in the Republican party in the prewar period are discussed in David Potter, *Lincoln and His Party during the Secession Crisis* (New Haven, 1942), pp. 40-52; See also, Edward Noyes to William Smith, May 10, 1865, William Smith MSS., Indiana Historical Society; Rush Sloane to John Sherman, May 19, 1865, John Sherman MSS., Library of Congress.

3. For the hostility of the ex-Democrats toward the ex-Whigs see, Alphonso Taft to Benjamin F. Wade, September 8, 1864, Benjamin Wade MSS., Library of Congress; *Portage County Democrat*, June 23, 1865; *The Mahoning Register*, July 12, 1865; *The Cleveland Leader*, June 25, 1865; See also, William Dean Howells, *Years of My Youth* (New York, 1916), pp. 147-48.

4. R. Stephenson to William Smith, March 15, 1865, William Smith MSS., Ohio Historical Society. A detailed account of the peace movement in Ohio is found in Elbert

Benton, "The Movement for Peace without Victory during the Civil War," *Western Reserve Historical Society Collections,* No. 99 (Cleveland, 1918), passim; See also, George H. Porter, *Ohio Politics during the Civil War Period* (New York, 1968), pp. 128-87; For the opposition of some Ohio Democrats to the peace movement see, Samuel Cox to Manton Marble, March 3, 1865, Manton Marble MSS., Library of Congress.

5. Aaron Perry to Jacob Cox, June 4, 1865, Jacob Cox MSS., Oberlin College Library; see also, *Cleveland Plain Dealer,* June 23, 1865; *Cleveland Herald,* September 21, 1865; Edward Noyes to Smith, May 10, 1865, Smith MSS.

6. See, in this connection, C. Vann Woodward, "Seeds of Failure in Radical Race Policy," *Proceedings of the American Philosophical Society,* 110 (February 1966): 1-9.

7. Jacob Cox to Charles Cox, August 7, 1865, Cox MSS.; *Cincinnati Daily Commercial,* December 26, 1865; *Cleveland Plain Dealer,* August 21, 1865.

8. See speech by John Sherman at Circleville, June 10, 1865, in *Cincinnati Daily Gazette,* June 10, 1865; speech by James Garfield at Ravenna, July 4, 1865, in *Portage County Democrat,* July 12, 1865; speech by Edward Noyes at Columbus, September 1, 1865, in *Columbus State Journal,* September 2, 1865; see also, *Dayton Journal,* November 7, 1865; *Toledo Blade,* November 30, 1865.

9. See, for example, Simon Nash to Sherman, January 12, 1866; A. Denny to Sherman, January 17, 1866, Sherman MSS.; E. B. Taylor to James Garfield, December 21, 1864, James Garfield MSS., Library of Congress.

10. Cox to Garfield, July 30, 1865, Cox MSS.; *Cincinnati Daily Commercial,* August 11, 1865; *Mahoning Register,* July 5, 1865.

11. Cox to Aaron Perry, June 4, 1865, Cox MSS.

12. R. P. L. Baber to Andrew Johnson, July 4, 1865, Andrew Johnson MSS., Library of Congress; Cox to Garfield, July 30, 1865, Cox MSS.; Edward Noyes to Smith, May 30, 1865, Smith MSS.; *Cincinnati Daily Commercial,* August 11, 1865; *Mahoning Register,* July 5, 1865; see also, speech by John Sherman at Circleville, June 10, 1865, in *Cincinnati Daily Gazette,* June 12, 1865.

13. Aaron Perry to Cox, July 28, 1865; Cox to Garfield, June 1, 1865; Cox to William Dennison, July 9, 1865, Cox MSS.; William Sherman to John Sherman, August 2, 1865, Sherman MSS.; *Coshocton Age,* August 11, 1865.

14. For a discussion of the differences between Ohio Democrats on the issue of the war see, Charles R. Wilson, "The Cincinnati Daily Enquirer and Civil War Politics: A Study in Copperhead Opinion" (Ph.D. dissertation, Department of History, University of Chicago, 1937).

15. William Dickson to Cox, May 31, 1865, Cox MSS.; see also the editorials in the following Democratic newspapers: *The Marietta Times,* November 30, 1865; *The Crisis,* October 4, 1865; *Cleveland Plain Dealer,* December 1, 1865; *Cincinnati Daily Enquirer,* December 7, 1865.

16. The results of Congressional and state elections in Ohio are tabulated by districts in Felice A. Bonadio, *North of Reconstruction, Ohio Politics, 1865-1870,* (New York, 1970), pp. 64-65.

17. *Cincinnati Daily Gazette,* January 9, 1866.

18. *Cincinnati Daily Gazette,* September 14, 1866. For an excellent discussion of the issue of Negro suffrage and the Republican party see, C. Vann Woodward, "Seeds of Failure," passim.

19. *Columbus State Journal,* January 16, 1867; see also, *Cleveland Plain Dealer,* January 17, 1867; Richard Smith to William Smith, March 20, 1867, Smith MSS.; Henry Martin to Sherman, March 29, 1867, Sherman MSS.

20. Murat Halstead to Sherman, February 22, 1867, Sherman, MSS.

21. *Columbus State Journal,* September 11, 1865.

22. *Portage County Democrat,* August 7, 1867.

23. For Republican opposition to Negro suffrage see, *The Cincinnati Daily Commercial,* June 16, 1865; Larz Anderson to Cox, June 22, 1865, Cox MSS; Edward Noyes to Smith, May 30, 1865, Smith MSS.; R. P. L. Baber to Johnson, July 4, 1865, Johnson MSS.

24. *Cincinnati Daily Gazette*, June 27, 1867; see also, Cox to Aaron Perry, January 25, 1867, Cox MSS.

25. Richard Smith to William Smith, March 20, 1867, Smith MSS.; Henry Martin to Sherman, March 29, 1867, Sherman MSS.; *Portage County Democrat*, March 28, 1867; *Dayton Journal*, April 5, 1867.

26. *Portsmouth Times*, April 20, 1867; *Elyria Democrat*, June 19, 1867; *Miami Union*, April 20, 1867.

27. For a contrary argument see, John and LaWanda Cox, "Negro Suffrage and Republican Politics: The Problem of Motivation in Reconstruction Historiography," *Journal of Southern History* 33 (1967): 315-30. For Democratic reaction to the resolution see, *Cleveland Plain Dealer*, April 8, 1867; *Cincinnati Daily Enquirer*, April 4, 1867.

28. For the voting returns in these cities see, *Toledo Blade*, April 5, 1867; *Columbus State Journal*, April 2, 1867; *Cleveland Plain Dealer*, April 3, 1867.

29. *Cleveland Herald*, April 22, 1867; *Cleveland Leader*, July 13, 1867.

30. Benjamin Potts to Benjamin Cowen, March 26, 1867; Chase to Cowen, March 28, 1867, Benjamin Cowen MSS., Ohio Historical Society; C. S. Hamilton to James Comley, May 11, 1867, James Comley MSS., Ohio Historical Society; Henry Martin to Warner Bateman, May 9, 1867, Warner Bateman MSS., Western Reserve Historical Society.

31. Smith to Warner Bateman, July 23, 1867, Bateman MSS.; A. E. Candle to Wade, June 14, 1867, Wade MSS.

32. Smith to Whitelaw Reid, June 22, 1867; Smith to Joseph Barrett, June 29, 1867; Smith to Robert Mussey, June 29, 1867, Smith MSS.; Samuel Wilkenson to Bateman, June 26, 1867, Bateman MSS.; *Columbus State Journal*, June 24, 1867; *Cincinnati Daily Gazette*, June 20, 1867.

33. Smith to Joseph Barrett, November 2, 1867; Smith to General Schneider, November 2, 1867; Smith MSS.; see also, *Cincinnati Daily Gazette*, October 10, 1867; *Toledo Blade*, October 11, 1867; *Dayton Journal*, October 9, 1867.

34. *Cincinnati Daily Gazette*, November 14, 1867; see also, Smith to Joseph Mussey, October 27, 1867, Smith MSS.

35. *Cincinnati Daily Gazette*, October 20, 1867.

36. For the establishment of Workingmen's parties see, *Cincinnati Daily Gazette*, September 11, 1867; see also, *Dayton Journal*, August 14, 1865; *Cleveland Plain Dealer*, June 20, 1865; *Cleveland Leader*, July 17, 1865.

37. Donn Piatt to Bateman, January 9, 1867; James Worthington to Bateman, March 13, 1867; Samuel Wilkenson to Bateman, July 15, 1867; Henry Martin to Bateman, May 9, 1867, Bateman MSS.; William Smith to Edward Noyes, March 7, 1867, Smith MSS.; *Portage County Democrat*, January 20, 1867.

38. A. Denny to Sherman, February 27, 1867, Sherman MSS.; Lyman Hall to Garfield, December 28, 1867, Garfield MSS.; *Dayton Journal*, November 11, 1868; *The Elyria Democrat*, September 25, 1867.

39. Donn Piatt to Smith, October 28, 1867, Smith MSS.; William Howells to Garfield, February 23, 1868, Garfield MSS.

40. Garfield to Harry Rhoades, March 12, 1868, Garfield MSS.; W. P. Denny to Sherman, October 24, 1867, Sherman MSS.; Smith to Whitelaw Reid, November 5, 1867, Smith MSS; Samuel Shellabarger to James Comley, June 15, 1868, Comley MSS.

41. Thomas Ewing To Thomas Ewing, Jr., June 23, 1868, Ewing Family MSS., Ohio Historical Society; see also, Charles M. Destler, *American Radicalism, 1865-1901* (New London, 1948), pp. 32-43.

42. Thomas Ewing, Jr. to Thomas Ewing, June 23, 1868, Ewing Family MSS.

43. Milton Sutliff to Salmon Chase, May 28, 1868; Chase to John Van Buren, July 11, 1868, Salmon Chase MSS., Library of Congress; see also, Chase to Alexander Long, April 18, 1868, Alexander Long MSS., Cincinnati Historical Society.

44. *Cincinnati Daily Enquirer*, January 23, 1868; *The Coshocton Age*, August 7, 1868.

45. *Sandusky Register*, July 11, 1868; *Columbus State Journal*, June 10, 1868; *The Toledo Blade*, June 5, 1868.

46. William Allen to Charles Brown, June 20, 1868, William Allen MSS., Ohio Historical Society.

47. For an account of Chase and the Democratic convention see, Thomas G. Beldon, *So Fell the Angels* (Boston, 1956).

48. James Wilson to Long, August 19, 1868, Long MSS.

49. The best biography of Wade is by Hans L. Trefousse, *Benjamin Franklin Wade: Radical Republican from Ohio* (New York, 1963).

50. John Sherman to William Sherman, October 24, 1862, William Sherman MSS, Library of Congress; Smith to Whitelaw Reid, June 5, 1865, Smith MSS.; Richard Smith to Bateman, December 29, 1864, Bateman MSS.; *Cincinnati Daily Commercial*, June 23, 1865.

51. See, for example, William Dean Howells, *Years of My Youth* (New York, 1916), p. 109; see also, E. B. Taylor to Garfield, December 21, 1864, Garfield MSS.

52. Samuel Cary to Sherman, April 27, 1866; Murat Halstead to Sherman, February 26, 1867, Sherman MSS.; J. M. Connell to Thomas Ewing, Jr., June 24, 1866, Ewing Family MSS.; Smith to Samuel Shellabarger, February 5, 1867, Smith MSS.; Halstead to Rutherford B. Hayes, June 20, 1869, Rutherford B. Hayes MSS., Rutherford B. Hayes Memorial Library.

53. *Cincinnati Daily Commercial*, December, 23, 28, 30, 1865; *Cincinnati Daily Gazette*, September 4, 1869; *Cincinnati Daily Enquirer*, September 5, 1869.

54. Royal Cortissoz, *The Life of Whitelaw Reid* (2 vols., New York, 1921), pp. 37-38; see also, Howells, *Years of My Youth*, pp. 147-48.

55. *Columbus State Journal*, August 13, 1867; *Cincinnati Daily Commercial*, March 2, 1869; *Toledo Blade*, September 9, 1865.

56. Don Piatt to Bateman, January 9, 1867, Bateman MSS.; *Portage County Democrat*, October 23, 1867; *Columbus State Journal*, June 8, 1868.

57. James West to Frederick Hassaurek, February 14, 1868; Hayes to Hassaurek, February 14, 1868, Fredrick Hassaurek MSS., Ohio Historical Society; *Cincinnati Volksblatt*, April 21, 1869, quoted in *Columbus State Journal*, April 23, 1869.

58. *Cincinnati Daily Enquirer*, September 5, 1869; September 12, 1869; *Cincinnati Daily Gazette*, October 2, 1869.

59. For the results of the state elections of 1869 see, *Cincinnati Daily Gazette*, October 9, 1869.

6

ILLINOIS

Disillusionment with State Activism

Philip D. Swenson

For the people of Illinois, the end of the Civil War was more than a transition from war to peace. With victory came feelings, shared with other Americans throughout the North, of desire, determination, and optimism—desire to return to normalcy, determination that the progress begun by the war's triumph over secession and slavery would continue, and optimism that the lessons of the war could be applied to peace-time pursuits. Peace also involved a process that took place throughout the United States after the war, but that historians have traditionally identified only with the South after Appomattox.[1] American historians have long applied the term "reconstruction" almost exclusively to the South. The word has meant different things to different historians, but most agree that Southern reconstruction on one level involved important, even if sometimes ephemeral, state reforms in the areas of race relations, democratic government, health, education, and welfare.[2] Yet the postwar history of Illinois indicates that this reform aspect of reconstruction was not a strictly Southern phenomenon. In this sense, Illinois, as much as South Carolina and Mississippi, was reconstructed after 1865. Illinois' reconstruction in fact foreshadowed and paralleled in many respects the aspirations and accomplishments of the reconstruction governments in the South. The history of Illinois between 1865 and 1871, moreover, strongly suggests a reciprocal relationship between developments in the North and the South during the era of reconstruction, a relationship that defined the direction and duration of reform in both sections of the country.

The keynote of Illinois' reconstruction was sounded by the state's wartime leader, Governor Richard Yates. On his way to a Senate seat in Washington in 1865, Yates observed in his final gubernatorial message: "The war now being waged has tended, more than any other event in the history of the country, to militate against the Jeffersonian idea, that 'the best government is

1. Notes to this chapter are to be found on pp. 116-118.

that which governs least.' The war has not only, of necessity, given more power to, but has led to a more intimate prevision of the government over every material interest of society."[3] Yates spoke not simply of the national government, but of all levels of government in the federal system. In this he reflected another reality of the civil conflict. Organizationally, even if not theoretically, it was indeed a war between the states. Insofar as concerned the raising of armies and the supplying of the tools of war, the states had governed most, as historian James G. Randall noted years ago when he characterized every Northern governor as his own little minister of national defense.[4] As the execution of the war had demonstrated this truth, so did the North's original objective of preserving the Union. As historian Harold Hyman has recently reminded us, "by reaffirming the permanent nature of the United States, the Civil War enhanced further the pre-eminence of the Union's states."[5] Both practically and ideologically, then, the war taught that government power applied at the state level could solve interstate problems of massive social and economic dimensions.

This experience of successfully applied state power was something new to most Americans in the nineteenth century. Traditional American Constitutional theory recognized the states' plenary adequacy under the police power to serve public wants. Yet prewar practice diverged sharply from theory, as most of the states had remained wedded to do-little notions. There were, of course, exceptions, such as asylum construction, water supply provision, common school support, levee maintenance, canal and railroad subsidies, and slave controls. These undertakings, however, had always been fragmented, isolated, and aimed at very limited objectives. It took the war to demonstrate dramatically how state powers could be applied on a broad front to effect sweeping improvement. Such a forceful exhibition could not be forgotten just because the guns had fallen silent. Numerous postwar reformers throughout the North insisted that if their own states would only use their power they could easily solve many peace-time problems previously neglected. For these reformers Appomattox signaled not an end, but the beginning of a new period of intrastate improvement and progress to match the interstate achievements of the war.[6] These reform advocates might well have composed a Republican campaign song of 1868 entitled, "It Is an Age of Progress."[7]

The most ardent advocates of reform in Illinois seemed to come from the old Whig, upstate, mercantile elements of the Republican Party. Their views were most consistently reflected in the pages of Horace White's newspaper, the *Chicago Tribune*, which during this time became the leading Republican organ in the Mid-west.[8] Behind this leadership, Illinois readily embraced the postwar improvement urge under state auspices. The optimistic spirit derived from the war experience had become widespread by 1871. Governor John M. Palmer observed in his biennial message of that year that the people of Illinois "familiarized with the quick and decisive rule of armies," had "become some-what impatient of the slower and less energetic methods that characterize the reign of law."[9] For many people in Illinois, patience indeed was no virtue during the heady years before 1871. How could it be when there was so much to be done and for such uplifting purposes? Palmer's predecessor, Richard J. Oglesby, had sounded the tone well in his biennial message of 1867. "In all the states," he rhapsodized, "peace once more holds universal sway. Our state maintained a high position during the fearful strife. . . . And now in the grand march of civilization, responsive to the invocations of peace, let her be equally true to the higher obligations of national prosperity, and her own considerate welfare."[10] He urged his fellow-citizens "to bravely meet every requirement necessary to the full development of our natural advantages; to cherish the arts and sciences; to foster education, the soul of the State; and, with charitable hands, to meet and lift up the unfortunate." Oglesby had caught the spirit of what the *Chicago Tribune* favorably described as "an increasing tendency towards the adoption of that principle known as the 'interference theory' of government."[11]

This tendency manifested itself in many ways in Illinois. On one level, it could be seen in increased demands for state regulation of allegedly immoral behavior. Agitation for prohibition and Sunday laws and for action against prostitution increased immediately after the war. The temperance question became one of the more important local issues in the Illinois elections of 1867, as it did in other Northern states. Most people in Illinois, however, undoubtedly agreed with the *Chicago Tribune*'s judgment that no reform group could "depend upon success when it . . . [devoted] its energies to the regulation of the social affairs of men by sumptuary laws."[12] They were much more concerned about assuring the public's health, education, and welfare than with its morals. This concern prompted the state legislature to enact between 1865 and 1871 a number of reform measures touching upon these more vital interests. In 1865 the General Assembly passed a new voting registry law and a statute strengthening the state's public health structure. The year 1867, perhaps the most fruitful, witnessed the passage of a Texas cattle law designed to prevent the spread of a dread cattle disease, the estab-lishment of the University of Illinois, the passage of a law taking the manage-ment of the state penitentiary out of the hands of corrupt lessees and giving it to a commission appointed by the governor, the enactment of an eight-hour law, the creation of a metropolitan health district in Chicago, and the estab-lishment of a state board of equalization. Illinois legislators in 1869 estab-lished an Illinois normal college, created a state board of charities, and passed bills facilitating the establishment of municipal parks in Chicago. All of these measures, and the list is by no means exhaustive, represented substantial if unspectacular exercises of state power to bring about social progress.

Yet important as these enactments were in marking out the state's new directions, they did not excite much interest among the state's people as a whole. Often their impact was diffuse and temporary, as most affected only limited segments of the population at any given time. Even such an apparently broad measure as the establishment of the university was of more immediate concern only to those educators who wanted to preserve the state's private, denominational colleges, or to citizens who lived in towns that were being considered for the site of the new school. The voting law of 1865, in similar fashion, was more important to the people of Chicago, where electoral abuses were rampant and difficult to monitor, than it was to inhabitants of rural districts, where life-long familiarity with each other effectively curtailed fraudulent voting.[13] For the entire people of postwar Illinois, the most vital reform matters concerned not Texas cattle, public health in Chicago, or the like, but centered on issues that would affect all of the state's people for all time. The true tests of their dedication to progress and their optimism regarding government action were to be found in the areas of race relations, corporate regulation, and constitutional revision.

Before 1865 Illinois had contributed little to improving race relations in America. On the contrary, the state was one of the most Negrophobic in the nation. Its power had been exercised repeatedly, not to expand the area of human freedom, but to pass the infamous "black laws," which placed severe restrictions upon the liberties of Negroes within the state.[14] After becoming the first state to ratify the Thirteenth Amendment, however, Illinois moved quickly to obliterate her own peculiar institutions. Following the recommendations of both outgoing Governor Yates and incoming Governor Oglesby to repeal all laws bearing unequally upon Negroes, the Republicans in the 1865 legislature set out to remove the obnoxious black laws from the books.[15] Democratic opposition and Republican political timidness had frustrated earlier attempts at repeal, but Republicans took courage from their resounding victory in 1864. The senate judiciary committee report on repeal of the black laws concluded in recommending repeal on January 18: "The election which took place on the 8th day of November last was of itself a virtual repeal of these odious laws. From that verdict of the masses there is no appeal, no method of escape. And, in this instance, your committee yield a cheerful acquiescence in the motto, 'Vox populi, vox Dei.'"[16] Democratic legislators apparently did not hear as well and threatened to filibuster against repeal. Their threats, however, did not materialize, and the laws were easily stricken on February 7, 1865.[17]

Encountering much more difficulty were efforts to extend the franchise to the state's Negroes through state action. A movement in the Republican Party to establish impartial suffrage began in late 1866, following the lead of the *Chicago Tribune*, one of the first papers in the country to embrace the principle.[18] Many Republicans, however, especially those in Egypt, the southern portion of the state, were not anxious to risk their party's future on such an explosive issue. Their reluctance, combined with the determined resistance of the Democrats, who were still trying to save white America from the "thralldom of Niggerism," foreclosed attempts by the General Assembly in 1867 and 1869 to strike from the state constitution all political discriminations against color and race. With the failure of the legislature, the question was not finally resolved until 1870, when the voters in a special constitutional election overwhelmingly approved a new constitution that contained an article striking the word white from the state's suffrage provisions.[19]

In a sense, the history of suffrage reform in Illinois represented a failure of the state government to act. This failure undoubtedly reflected a lack of common purpose among the people of Illinois respecting Negro rights, at least until 1870. They exhibited more unity of both thought and action behind another state-wide concern that had its roots in the state's old frontier fear and hatred of economic monopoly. During late 1865 and throughout 1866, much of Illinois experienced an antimonopoly revolt directed against railroads and grain warehouses. The revolters posed the simple choice, "whether Illinois is a vast farm to be worked for the profit of . . . corporations, or whether the people thereof have any voice left in controlling their own rights, interests and liberties."[20] Complaining of discriminatory rates and practices against both individuals and localities, the "antimonopolists" demanded state regulation of these overweening corporate interests. By the time the Illinois General Assembly convened in January 1867, the antimonopoly forces had already gathered in Springfield, the state capital, to press their demands. As a result of this intense agitation, the legislature passed a warehouse law aimed at curtailing unfair practices. Efforts to pass a railroad law failed, although three regulatory bills were introduced and thoroughly debated.[21]

The legislature took up the railroad question again in 1869, after the new governor, John M. Palmer, unexpectedly devoted a large portion of his inaugural address to the need for railroad law reform. The legislators responded by passing a maximum passenger-rate bill, but Palmer vetoed it. A second bill, taking his objections into account, was enacted. The new law, which simply stipulated that all rates must be uniform, went into effect on March 10, 1869, but it, along with the warehouse law of 1867, soon proved ineffective against the circumventions of the railroad and warehouse interests.[22]

Undermining the effectiveness of the laws were the state constitution's provisions protecting contracts from legislative encroachments. When Illinois, therefore, convened a convention in 1869-70 to revise the state's organic law, the friends of corporate regulation succeeded in embodying in the new constitution express provisoes for regulation of both railroads and warehouses. Taking these provisions as a mandate for further legislative action, the

General Assembly of 1871 passed two tough new railroad and warehouse laws, to be enforced by the first railroad and warehouse commission in American history. Both laws represented one of the boldest assertions in Illinois history of the state's police power to enforce principles of justice.[23]

The struggle over corporate regulation, like the effort on behalf of Negro rights, had resulted in substantial alterations in the state's body of laws. The two movements differed only in that one added, while the other deleted, statutes from the books. In a very important respect, however, the legal impact of the two movements registered in the same way. Both prompted revisions in the state constitution. The need for those changes indeed provided part of the impulse for the calling of Illinois' second constitutional convention since 1847. The Illinois constitutional convention of 1869-70 was another reflection of the same spirit of state activism that imbued the movements for corporate regulation and Negro rights. Many features of the constitution of 1848 needed reform by 1869, but much of the initial postwar impetus for calling a constitutional convention flowed from a desire among state power activists to strip the constitution of its restraints on legislative power. "The times have changed," editorialized the *Chicago Tribune*, "but the law of twenty years ago remains; the interests of the State have become enlarged, and . . . .legislation of the most important character [is needed], but the old limitation survives."[24]

The activists criticized the old constitution at several points. The authority of the legislature to enact private laws was undesirable because sessions of the General Assembly had become clogged with special interest bills, often passed in omnibus form, that prevented the law-makers from legislating for the welfare of the whole state. There were too few senators and representatives, enabling small cliques of men in both houses to block progressive legislation. The biennial sessions of the General Assembly were too infrequent and too short to keep up with the growing needs of the state. Finally, legislative salaries were too low to induce legislators to serve the expanding interests of the state on more of a full-time basis. The convention rectified all of these shortcomings. When the voters approved the new constitution on July 2, 1870, they outlawed special and omnibus legislation, increased the size of the General Assembly, lengthened its sessions, and augmented the salaries of its members.[25] Thus the state's organic law was streamlined to bring it more into step with the state-centered reform tendencies of the period.

The years between 1865 and 1871 clearly represented a fruitful reform period in Illinois, and its documentation comprises a very important dimension of the state's postwar history. This information assumes even greater importance in view of the lamentable practice of many American historians of relating the history of the United States during the era of reconstruction only in terms of what happened in Washington, D.C., and the South. The history of the North during reconstruction has been neglected, yet there is much in the postwar story of Illinois to suggest that developments both North and South of the Mason-Dixon line can never be fully understood without reference to each other. The benefits that Illinois derived from the state's reform movement of 1865-71 found parallels in the achievements of the reconstruction governments in the South. These similarities simply demonstrate that both the Illinois and Southern reform movements were politically based in the Republican Party. The Republican presence in both instances, however, did not mean that the party played the same role in both places. It was the differences in the party's function within the context of the respective reform movements that provided a crucial factor in the political history of the two regions.

In the South, the Republican Party was the proclaimed vehicle of reform. In Illinois, perhaps the most intriguing aspect of the state's reform accomplishments was the Republican Party's failure to identify with them. This is not to say that Illinois Republicans did not support reform. More Republican legislators voted for reform than did their Democratic counterparts. It is no coincidence that the largest number of reform measures were passed during the 1867 legislative session, when the Republican majority in the General Assembly was its greatest.[26] Illinois reform was obviously conducted under Republican auspices, but at no time between 1865 and 1871 did the party, as an organization, embrace reform at the state level as a rallying principle. Although the party needed a new organizational base, as the issues of slavery, secession, and war faded, no prominent Republicans in the state ever publicly pressed for a party reorganization around the reform issue, and their private correspondence is equally barren of such urging.[27] There were many reasons for this failure, and they can best be understood in reference to the broad reform movements already sketched in the areas of Negro rights, corporate regulation, and constitutional revision.

The most obvious arena for Republican state reform leadership involved the Negro question. At the beginning of 1865, with the ratification of the Thirteenth Amendment and the repeal of the black laws, it looked as if the Republicans meant to act radically and progressively. Yet the true test of radical racial reform during reconstruction was the franchise, and in this test Illinois Republicans were found wanting. Although the Democrats constantly tried to saddle the Republicans with the odium of Negro suffrage, the party itself was much too divided over the principle to embrace it wholeheartedly. The decision not to press the suffrage question was undoubtedly a wise political move. A recent study shows that the strength of the Democrats and the depth of racism in Illinois worked in tandem to reduce support for Congressional reconstruction among Illinois Congressmen.[28] Those same factors meant that suffrage reform undoubtedly would have been suicidal for the state's Republican politicians. They would have met the same fate as their brethren in New York, whose attempts to achieve franchise reform only undermined their party's position in the state.[29] Suffrage reform in Illinois eventually came about only through the efforts of delegates at the nonpartisan constitutional convention, who in most, cases, whether they were Republicans or Democrats, had nothing to lose politically. This nonpartisanship merely emphasized the reluctance of many Republican politicians to act unilaterally in this touchy area. Even after the convention, Republican office-seekers did not have to take an active stand on suffrage, but only had to acquiesce in the ratification of the Fifteenth Amendment, which was imminent even had the Illinois legislature not approved it. It was racial progress by default.

The movement for regulation of the railroads and warehouses presented the Illinois Republican Party a particularly inviting opportunity to assume state reform leadership. Corporate reform would have provided continuity with the party's prewar ideology, which depicted Southern slavery as an aristocratic, oligarchic obstacle to the nation's general prosperity and progress.[30] Likewise, the corporate monopolists were seen as impediments to the state's welfare. The *Chicago Tribune* repeatedly drew the public's attention to the sinister similarties between the monopolies of business and the monopoly of human flesh. "After the settlement of the slavery question," the paper prophesied in 1866, "the next great problem for the American people to grapple will be that of monopolies. Slavery itself, the greatest of all monopolies, required a war of four years ... for its final adjustment. It has been brought down at last, and sooner or later, all the lesser monopolies which are drawing the life blood of the people, will come tumbling in ruins after it." The railroad oligarchy especially was "an incubus on our industry and legislation only less oppressive than that from whose 'great rebellion' we have so lately emerged." There was a real danger, the paper went on, of the state becoming subservient to the corporations because they were "as far above the power of the law as the late slaveholders of the South were when they carried their own State governments in their breeches pockets."[31] Despite this ideological affinity, the Republicans were unable to organize a crusade against corporations as they had against slavery. The reason for this was that the cleavage within the state over regulation took not partisan, but sectional lines. Legislators from southern Illinois, Republican and Democrat, tended to oppose corporate regulation measures because they wanted to attract railroad development to their part of the state and feared that their support of regulatory laws would antagonize railroad capital. On the other hand, legislators from the northern part of the state, where railroad development had been most extensive, were the most antimonopolistic regardless of political affiliation. The three men who spearheaded the drive to regulate the railroads—Stephen J. Hurlbut, Allan C. Fuller, and Jesse S. Hildrup—all represented upstate constituencies. Regional breakdowns of the votes on the railroad and warehouse laws show that opposition to regulation came from representatives of down-state, have-not constituencies. Also, in the popular vote to ratify the state's new constitution in 1870, the articles dealing with railroad and warehouse regulation, which were submitted to the people separately, received less support in the west and south, where the demand for corporate development was greatest.[32] A united Republican campaign against corporate abuses was utterly impossible within the state's geographic and economic setting.

Unlike the movements for Negro rights and corporate regulation, the Illinois Republican Party did play an active role in the effort on behalf of constitutional revision. The interest of the Republican Party in constitutional reform went back to 1860, when a convention movement had been initiated under Republican leadership. The convention that met in 1862, however, had been taken over by the Democrats and produced a highly partisan document, which the Republicans successfully urged the electorate to reject. The Republican press, nevertheless, kept the idea of another convention incessantly before the public. When it was called in 1869, it was due largely to Republican efforts.[33] The Republicans, however, remembering what had happened in 1862 and fearing that the Democrats might turn the tables on them and impugn the integrity of the convention, launched a campaign for a nonpartisan assemblage.[34] The appeal to nonpartisanship reflected wisdom among Republicans who anticipated that the voters would reject, as they had in 1862, a constitution that they thought was overly partisan. Yet in an important respect it was a mistake. Because the convention was notable for its even distribution between Republicans and Democrats, its work could as easily be claimed by one party as the other.[35] Republican strategy was self-defeating because it did little to associate the party in the minds of the people with the reform impulse of the convention.

The failure of the Illinois Republican Party, as a party, to march under the banner of state reform was attributable in large part to intrastate considerations of political strategy and geographic and economic sectionalism. There was, however, another factor at work from outside the state that was of equal, perhaps even greater, importance. As long as the issue of reconstruction in the South remained unsettled, the Republicans in Illinois had no compelling reason to reorganize the party around state reform; it made more political sense to wave the bloody shirt. On that single issue, advised the *Chicago Tribune*, "the Republican party is about the best drilled, best officered, most resolute, determined, overwhelming, and irresistible political party the country has ever known. . . . On no other issue can we so easily preserve the *status quo* of Republican ascendency."[36] The Illinois Democracy, moreover, did little to compel a change in Republican councils. Most Democrats preferred to wallow in antediluvian, ante-bellum states rights principles that had little application to the postwar situation within Illinois. The Democrats saw no ideological principle at stake within Illinois because they had long insisted on the primacy of state action within its respective sphere in the federal system, but their insistence that the federal government's intervention in Southern affairs jeopardized states rights meant that partisanship was channeled into national concerns, not state concerns.

This lack of opposition pressure combined with internal party conditions to militate further against the Republicans abandoning the bloody shirt and unfurling the state reform banner. The Republican Party in Illinois had always been an uneasy coalition of disparate elements, held together only by their hostility to slavery.[37] When the war settled that burning question, ideological unity became difficult to maintain. Organizationally, moreover, the party was very loosely constructed, and so the position of the ostensible head of the party became crucial if unity were to be preserved. War-time conditions gave Yates considerable leverage within the party, but after the war, both Oglesby and Palmer found themselves increasingly at odds with Republican majorities in the General Assembly. The Republican controlled legislature repeatedly overrode gubernatorial vetoes, which became more frequent during the tenures of Oglesby and Palmer.[38] The internal disintegration of the party became even more pronounced the further it was removed in time from the issues of war and reconstruction. During the campaigns of 1869 and 1870, divisions within the party became increasingly visible and difficult to patch over, and they appeared at all levels of political activity—municipal, county, state, and national. In 1869 a special election in the Third Congressional District to fill the resigned seat of Elihu B. Washburne saw John V. Eustace run on the Democratic ticket while claiming to be a Republican. The same year, Republicans and Democrats in Chicago, Will County, and Kane County united on "Citizens' " tickets to defeat regular Republican nominees in city and county elections. The following year's campaigns witnessed even more serious rifts between the supporters of the regular party candidates and challengers in the First, Second, Fifth, Eighth, and Twelfth Congressional Districts, and a "Business Men's" ticket appeared in Chicago to oppose the Republicans in the city election.[39] Given these chaotic conditions, it was no surprise that party regulars waved the bloody shirt frequently and fervently after 1868.

Another important element in the party's deteriorating position was its increasing identification in the public mind with spoilsmen and corruption. The Illinois legislature during this period was better known for its alleged extravagances and excesses than for its accomplishments. Numerous citizens of the state would have seconded one judgment: "Long experience has created a doubt in many minds whether the general public have more to dread from a session of the Legislature or from the absence of all legislation."[40] Charges of legislative corruption filled the newspapers of both parties as successive sessions of the General Assembly passed special interest legislation of all sorts. Concern over bribery was so intense that an antibribery clause was included in the new constitution of 1870.[41] The Republicans, of course, were no more venal than the Democrats, but for the average voter it was easier to associate corruption with the party in power. Democratic legislators, meanwhile, were in the envious position of being able to line their pockets with the blandishments of lobbyists, while at election time they could hang any tainted legislation on the majority party. With the issues of war and reconstruction subsiding, and with the failure of the Republicans to identify themselves with a viable state program, there was very little else to remember about the Republican Party by 1871 except corruption.

The most significant consequence of this corruption was not the decline of the Republican Party in Illinois, although its strength in the General Assembly began to erode after 1869.[42] It was rather a growing disillusionment in the state concerning the ability of the state government to legislate wisely. By 1869 the optimism, born of the war, that government action at the state level could insure continued prosperity and progress had become a civilian casualty of the special interest battles in the legislature. Many Republicans reflected their disillusionment as the time for the state's constitutional convention and election approached. Whereas initial calls for the convention had often emphasized the need to streamline the constitution to facilitate legislative action, by 1869 many spokesmen for constitutional revision were decrying the lack of constitutional restraints on the legislature. "The real point to be decided at the [constitutional] election," declared Governor Palmer, "is whether the people will live in the future, as they have done for several years past, under a government that has such powers as the Legislature . . . *may choose to claim for it!*"[43] This shifting sentiment was perhaps most dramatically recorded in the *Chicago Tribune*, which in 1866 had scoffed at the "ever present dread that if the Legislature was invested with the slightest discretion, it would reduce the State to penury and want." Yet in 1869 it warned that "the discretion of a Legislature is not the most certain protection to public interests."[44] After the constitution was adopted and the voters had approved it, the *Tribune* intoned, "The governing idea of the new constitution . . . is to protect the people against an abuse of the legislative power."[45] Such a climate of opinion did not invigorate state reform, and a great reaction against such activities soon set in.

The failure of the Illinois Republican Party to articulate and execute a program of state reform had repercussions that transcended the state's boundaries and contributed to the larger failure of national reconstruction after the Civil War. At the end of the war, the people of Illinois were ready to utilize their state's power for public improvement. The logical agent of that power was the Republican Party. Illinois Republicans, however, as a party, eschewed state reform and cast their political fortunes on the Southern question. They took this action because they were at least as concerned about party unity as they were about Southern affairs. Southern reconstruction furnished a basis of party unity, while political, economic, social, and geographic conditions in

Illinois prevented the party from consolidating around state reform as a party principle. By the time public solicitude for the South began to fade away, by 1869, the great reaction against state power, growing out of legislative abuses, began to set in. Popular sentiment for state reform action soon dissipated. Illinois Republicans not only lost a great opportunity to bolster and prolong their political power in the state but also, as a consequence, helped to undermine the Republican Party's national position on Southern reconstruction, which depended upon maintaining a strong political base in the North. These circumstances contributed to the early demise of reconstruction in both Illinois and the South. Caught between state and national pressures, the Illinois Republican Party could deal effectively with neither.

The same interplay of state and national forces vitiated extended support in Illinois for the reconstruction program in the South.[46] From 1865 to 1868 the desire to push on with progress at home circumscribed any long-range commitments to interference in the South. Southern reconstruction was a distraction, an obstacle to be removed. In this sense, the election of 1866 was not so much an endorsement of Congressional reconstruction as it was a repudiation of Andrew Johnson's obstructionism. Many concerned persons in Illinois could not tolerate Johnson because he was keeping them from more important matters in their own state. "Instead of moving onward in the path of progress and prosperity," lamented the *Chicago Tribune*, "that ill conditioned Tennesseean compels . . . [Northern] freedmen to continue to labor as scavengers in the Augean stables of slavery."[47] This attitude was partially reflected in the voting patterns of Illinois Congressmen during the 40th Congress, elected in 1866. Only three of the fourteen-member delegation consistently supported the Congressional reconstruction program, whereas in the preceding Congress, nine members were stalwart Congressional supporters.[48] This was hardly the kind of backing for Congressional reconstruction to be expected had Illinois voters been deeply concerned about Southern affairs. Likewise, Ulysses S. Grant's "Let Us Have Peace" slogan of 1868 appealed to the same determination to get on with essential state business. After 1868 the public temper in Illinois, conditioned by a carnival of corruption in the state's affairs, made it easier for people to believe the sordid tales drifting north of unmatched corruption and venality in the Southern reconstruction governments. Since most white Northerners viewed Negroes as inferior beings, their participation in the supposedly lax Southern governments reinforced this credulity. This readiness to believe the worst about Southern government, flowing partially from disillusionment with their own state's capacity to bring about improvement in society, helped to discourage many in Illinois from supporting sustained federal intervention in the South. Reconstruction thus served as both the beginning and end of a promising, but never fully realized, era of reform and progress for blacks and whites alike in both the North and South.

NOTES

1. An increasing number of studies have appeared in recent years that point either implicitly or explicitly to the necessity of viewing the reconstruction era as a national, rather than a strictly Southern development. See Felice A. Bonadio, *North of Reconstruction: Ohio Politics, 1865-1870* (New York, 1970); William R. Brock, *An American Crisis: Congress and Reconstruction, 1865-1867* (New York, 1963); Ira V. Brown, "Pennsylvania and the Rights of the Negro, 1865-1887," *Pennsylvania History* 28 (1961):45-57, and "William D. Kelley and Radical Reconstruction," *Pennsylvania Magazine of History and Biography* 85 (1961):316-29; Stanley Coben, "Northeastern Business and Radical Reconstruction: A Re-examination," *Mississippi Valley Historical Review* 46 (1959):67-90; LaWanda and John H. Cox, "Negro Suffrage and Republican Politics: The Problem of Motivation in Reconstruction Historiography," *Journal of Southern History* 33 (1967):303-30, and *Politics, Principle, and Prejudice, 1865-1866: Dilemma of Reconstruction America* (New York, 1963); David Donald, *The Politics of Reconstruction, 1863-1867* (Baton Rouge, 1965); William Gillette, *The Right to Vote: Politics and the Passage of the Fifteenth Amendment* (Baltimore, 1965); Joseph B. James, *The Framing of the Fourteenth Amendment* (Urbana, 1956); James C. Mohr, *The Radical Republicans and Reform in New York during Reconstruction* (Ithaca, 1973); David Montgomery, *Beyond Equality: Labor and the Radical Republicans, 1862-1872* (New York, 1967), and "Radical Republicanism in Pennsylvania, 1866-1873," *Pennsylvania Magazine of History and Biography* 85 (1961):436-57; Robert P. Sharkey, *Money, Class, and Party: An Economic Study in Civil War and Reconstruction* (Baltimore, 1959); Irwin F. Unger, *The Greenback Era: A Social and Political History of American Finance, 1865-1879* (Princeton, 1964).

2. W. E. B. Du Bois, "Reconstruction and Its Benefits," *American Historical Review* 15 (1910):781-99; Jack B. Scroggs, "Carpetbagger Constitutional Reform in the South Atlantic States, 1867-1868," *Journal of Southern History* 27 (1961):475-93.

3. January 2, 1865, *Chicago Tribune*, January 5, 1865.

4. J. G. Randall, *Lincoln the President* (2 vols., New York, 1945), I:361.

5. Harold M. Hyman, *A More Perfect Union: The Impact of the Civil War and Reconstruction on the Constitution* (New York, 1973), p. 290.

6. This entire discussion relies heavily on ibid., Chaps. xvii-xx.

7. Advertisement in *Chicago Tribune*, May 20, 1868.

8. Philip Kinsley, *The Chicago Tribune: Its First Hundred Years* (3 vols., New York, 1943-46), I:16-20; Joseph Logsdon, *Horace White, Nineteenth Century Liberal* (Westport, 1971), pp. 39, 117-18.

9. January 4, 1871, *Chicago Tribune,* January 5, 1871.

10. January 7, 1867, ibid., January 8, 1871.

11. Ibid., November 13, 1867.

12. Ibid., September 12, 1867.

13. During the legislative session of 1871, rural legislators led an attempt to have the law of 1865 repealed or modified because it had caused their constituents more trouble than it was worth.

14. Eugene H. Berwanger, *The Frontier against Slavery: Western Anti-Negro Prejudice and the Slavery Extension Controversy* (Urbana, 1967), pp. 23, 25, 32, 49, 51n; Leon F. Litwack, *North of Slavery: The Negro in the Free States, 1790-1860* (Chicago, 1961), pp. 67, 69, 70, 70n, 71, 93, 263; Tom LeRoy McLaughlin, "Popular Reactions to the Idea of Negro Equality in Twelve Nonslaveholding States, 1846-1869: A Quantitative Analysis," (Ph.D. dissertation, American Studies Program, Washington State University, 1969), p. 70; Jacque V. Voegeli, *Free but Not Equal: The Midwest and the Negro during the Civil War* (Chicago, 1967), passim.

15. Yates' Biennial Message, January 2, 1865 and Oglesby's Inaugural Address, January 16, 1865, *Chicago Tribune*, January 5 and 16, 1865.

16. Ibid., January 20, 1865.

17. Ibid.; Arthur Charles Cole, *The Era of the Civil War, 1848-1870,* vol. III of *The Centennial History of Illinois,* Clarence Walworth Alvord, ed. (5 vols., Springfield, 1918-20), pp. 387-88.

18. *Chicago Tribune,* December 22, 1866.

19. The quote is from Paul Kleppner, *The Cross of Culture: A Social Analysis of Midwestern Politics, 1850-1900* (New York, 1970), p. 108; Cole, *Era of Civil War,* pp. 406, 417-18; Ernest Ludlos Bogart and Charles Manfred Thompson, *The Industrial State, 1870-1893,* vol. IV of *Centennial History of Illinois,* pp. 14, 27. It should be noted that the suffrage article was not voted upon separately; to reject the suffrage provision, the voters would have had to spurn the entire proposed constitution.

20. *Chicago Tribune,* December 29, 1866.

21. Cole, *Era of Civil War,* pp. 357-58, 385-86; George H. Miller, *Railroads and the Grange Laws* (Madison, 1971), pp. 66-70.

22. Palmer's Inaugural Address, January 11, 1869, *Chicago Tribune,* January 12, 1869; Cole, *Era of Civil War,* p. 359; Miller *Railroads and Grange Laws,* pp. 71-73.

23. Bogart and Thompson, *Industrial State,* pp. 89-91; Miller, *Railroads and the Grange Laws,* pp. 75-89.

24. *Chicago Tribune,* December 29, 1866.

25. The proceedings of the convention are fully reported in *Debates and Proceedings of the Constitutional Convention of the State of Illinois* (Springfield, 1870). A convenient summary of its work and the events leading to its formation is available in Bogart and Thompson, *Industrial State,* Chap. I. Also, for an incisive summation of the paramount issues before the convention see *Chicago Tribune,* April 22, 1869.

26. The combined strength of the Republicans in the Senate and the House was 78 out of 110 seats, or 71 percent. *The Tribune Almanac and Political Register for 1867* (New York, 1868), p. 65.

27. This statement is based upon extensive examinations of newspapers, party platforms, and numerous manuscript collections in the Illinois State Historical Library, including the papers of John Clurts Bagby, the Bailhache-Brayman families, John Charles Black, David Davis, Jesse K. Du Bois, Ozias M. Hatch, Robert G. Ingersoll, Charles H. Lanphier, Richard J. Oglesby, John M. Palmer, Lyman Trumbull, and Richard Yates.

28. Philip D. Swenson, "The Midwest and the Abandonment of Radical Reconstruction, 1864-1877," (Ph.D. dissertation, University of Washington, 1971), pp. 101-05. See also the editorial comment of the Chicago *Staats Zeitung,* quoted in *Chicago Tribune,* October 28, 1867, and the *Tribune's* own editorial on November 6, 1867.

29. Mohr, *Radical Republicans and Reform,* Chaps. vii-viii.

30. Eric Foner, *Free Soil, Free Labor, Free Men: The Ideology of the Republican Party before the Civil War* (London, 1970), pp. 1-72; Major L. Wilson, "The Repressible Conflict: Seward's Concept of Progress and the Free-Soil Movement," *Journal of Southern History* 37 (1971):533-56.

31. *Chicago Tribune,* December 7, 1866, December 1 and 21, 1870.

32. Cole, *Era of Civil War,* pp. 358-59; Miller, *Railroads and Grange Laws,* pp. 70, 74-75, 81, 228n.

33. Cole, *Era of Civil War,* pp. 267-72; Bogart and Thompson, *Industrial State,* pp. 1-3.

34. See, for example, the editorials in the *Chicago Tribune,* July 9 and November 9, 1869.

35. Bogart and Thompson, *Industrial State,* p. 4; John Moses, *Illinois, Historical and Statistical: Comprising the Essential Facts of Its Planting and Growth as a Province, County, Territory and State* (2 vols., Chicago, 1892), II:787-90.

36. *Chicago Tribune,* January 11, 1870.

37. Cole, *Era of Civil War,* Chap. vi.

38. In 1869 Palmer established a new veto record of 72 bills, 17 of which were over-ridden. Ibid., p. 416.

39. Ibid., pp. 418-19; Bogart and Thompson, *Industrial State,* pp. 57-58; *Chicago Tribune,* June 7, August 15, September 6, November 3, 1869, October 20, November 8 and 9, 1870.

40. *Chicago Tribune*, February 28, 1867.

41. The clause is quoted in ibid., June 14, 1870.

42. The percentages of Republican strength in the General Assembly between 1865 and 1877 were: 59 percent (1865), 71 percent (1867), 69 percent (1869), 56 percent (1873), 46 percent (1875), and 49 percent (1877). Raw numbers are contained in *Tribune Almanac* for the appropriate years.

43. Quoted in *Chicago Tribune*, June 26, 1870.

44. Ibid., November 16, 1866, and July 26, 1870.

45. Ibid., July 4, 1870. See also, December 17, 1870.

46. That support did decline can be seen in the voting records of Illinois Congressmen during the reconstruction Congresses (39th-44th). The percentages of Illinois representatives who consistently supported Congressional reconstruction during these Congressional sessions were: 64 percent (39th), 21 percent (40th), 21 percent (41st), 14 percent (42nd), 53 percent (43rd), 32 percent (44th). These figures were arrived at through the techniques of Guttman scaling and Rice cluster bloc analysis. Swenson, "Abandonment of Radical Reconstruction," pp. 15-39, 76-77.

47. *Chicago Tribune*, April 7, 1866.

48. Swenson, "Abandonment of Radical Reconstruction," p. 76.

7

MICHIGAN

Quickening Government in a Developing State

George M. Blackburn

Except for Democratic inroads in the legislature immediately following the depression of 1873, the Republican Party controlled Michigan politics throughout the reconstruction era. This control was maintained despite strong Republican Party support of black suffrage in the face of widespread public opposition. This paper surveys the administrations of the Republican governors of the period from 1865 to 1876, Henry Crapo, Henry Baldwin, and John Bagley, and focuses on the increasing involvement of state government in social and economic activities during the reconstruction era. While the Republican Party made but minimal efforts to enact reforms during the early years of the reconstruction era, by 1876 the party had enacted extensive programs of reform at the state level.

During the Civil War, Michigan was fiercely devoted to the Republican cause; in the postwar period a clear majority of Michigan voters ardently supported the Radical program as soon as the lines of battle between President Andrew Johnson and the Radical Republicans became clear.[1] Support for the Radical program was a logical consequence of widely held views regarding the causes of the Civil War and the circumstances that led to the formation of the Republican Party. Although the party had originated in 1854 during the struggle over the Kansas-Nebraska Act for the stated purpose of fighting the extension of slavery, Republicans believed that they were actually fighting "slave power" and "aristocracy." Because of constitutional limitations, however, they could attack slavery legally only in the territories. In 1860, Republicans believed, their party had been successful in mobilizing freedom-loving and democratic northerners against reactionary forces and elected Abraham Lincoln President of the United States. Unwilling to accept that decision of the electorate, the "slave power" brought about Southern

1. Notes to this chapter are to be found on pp. 139-143.

secession and thus precipitated the Civil War. While the South lost the war, the "slave power" did not give up but continued the struggle in a different form.[2] Identifying what he considered a continuing and persistent menace, Michigan's governor, Henry Crapo, in 1866 warned: "It is not *slavery*, but the *spirit* which seeks to make slavery the corner stone of empire, that we have now to guard against—that element of hatred to freedom and equality that instituted the conflict. . . . That spirit is neither dead nor sleeping. . . . Having failed so utterly in the resort to force, it will but recuperate its energies for a more insidious attack in a different method of warfare."[3]

However incomplete or inaccurate they might be, such views were widely held and constituted the bases of the Radical Republican program for a decade after the Civil War. Not only did these beliefs furnish the context within which political actions occurred, but they gave a peculiar cast to reconstruction controversies, a doctrinaire flavor unusual in American politics. Identification of the Republican Party with the promotion of freedom and democracy against "slave power" and "aristocracy" gave Republicans a messianic sense of destiny. Republican identification of the Democratic Party with slavery and treason made Republican control of the government, said its partisans, a patriotic necessity. Furthermore, the Republicans also viewed the struggle as one involving ageless, eternal principles. Because "slave power" and "aristocracy" were resilient, crafty, and powerful, far-reaching and drastic measures were necessary to extirpate their roots.[4] Such attitudes help explain why party regularity was so highly prized.[5] Nonetheless, that regularity did not preclude intraparty disputes.

Factional differences within the Republican Party in Michigan during the reconstruction era frequently involved the popular, narrowly partisan, and intolerant Zachariah Chandler, a resident of Detroit. Elected United States Senator in 1857, reelected in 1863 and 1869, but defeated in 1875, Chandler was widely charged with possessing a "Detroit ring" of officeholders that promoted his interests rather than the good of the party. Nomination and election of Senators and governors frequently involved controversies over the "locality" of candidates. The most serious rifts pitted the so-called outstaters, particularly the followers of Austin Blair, a resident of Jackson, against a "Detroit ring" that was accused of taking more than its share of the offices.

In addition to the "locality" issue, state politics had been profoundly influenced by unfortunate attempts to promote Michigan development. The state's lack of development by 1865 may appear incongruous in view of the early settlements by the French dating from the seventeenth century in the Upper Peninsula and the founding of Detroit in 1701. Yet the settlement not only of Michigan but of the entire Great Lakes littoral lagged until after the construction of the Erie Canal in 1825. "Buffalo lagged behind Pittsburgh," wrote a student of Michigan history, "Cleveland was a raw village when

Cincinnati was a thriving city. In 1820, five-sixths of Indiana's people lived in its south and one-sixth in the center; its north was about as vacant as the adjoining part of Michigan. Chicago's population reached a hundred after Peoria's and, for that matter, after Pontiac's and Ann Arbor's."[6] Although Ohio had become a state in 1803, Indiana in 1816, Illinois in 1818, Michigan did not achieve statehood until 1837. Indeed, within the Old Northwest, Michigan's growth had fallen far behind her neighbors. Wisconsin, which became a state in 1847, had more inhabitants than Michigan in 1860.

Michigan settlement was concentrated in the southern portion of the state, where there was fertile soil as well as access to transportation facilities and mercantile centers. In 1850 over 98 percent of the state's population lived in the southernmost counties, constituting about one-quarter of the state's area.[7] By 1860 the line of settlement had reached the middle of the Lower Peninsula; in addition, timber towns had been founded in the northern part of the Lower Peninsula at the mouths of important rivers. The Upper Peninsula had scattered settlements at Sault Ste. Marie and in the iron and copper country. "A very small portion of the State has yet been reclaimed and settled," said Governor Crapo summarizing the condition of the state in 1865, "and I apprehend it is safe to calculate that nearly five-sixths of her entire territory remains today a wilderness. *We want settlers.*"[8]

At the time of statehood in 1837 the slow rate of development and the perceived need to encourage additional growth had exerted a profound influence on the prevailing philosophy of government. Most of the populace had recently entered an essentially raw frontier and consequently desired certain governmental services, primarily those involving internal improvements and banks. Accordingly, the new government authorized an elaborate system of state-owned railroads and canals. The new state also enacted legislation encouraging the establishment of private banks. But overly ambitious projects, the crash of 1837, the suspension of specie payment, and lax administration combined to bring on financial disaster.[9] Not surprisingly, therefore, the revised state constitution of 1850 placed severe restrictions on the powers of the state government by denying it the right to engage in internal improvements in any manner and restricted severely its authority to charter banks.

In addition to the disquieting record of the state's initial attempt at large-scale intervention in economic affairs, the personal observations and experiences of the political leaders during the 1860s encouraged reliance on individual initiative rather than extensive governmental programs. Most of the leaders had migrated to Michigan in the 1830s when the territory was essentially a wilderness and had lived to see the forests replaced by farms and primitive river crossings become the sites of villages and towns. These transformations had occurred as a result of private enterprise, not governmental, initiation. Most of the state's political leaders were without tangible resources when they arrived in Michigan, yet they had prospered by their own efforts.

Thus they accepted the belief that state government should be limited in its function. Even John Bagley, who proved to be the chief proponent of strong state government among Michigan's three governors in the reconstruction era, shared this restricted view of the proper relationship between government, the economy, and individual effort. "History," he informed the legislature, "has failed to demonstrate that either legislative enactments or executive policies can provide the means of general prosperity or ensure the revival of industries over an extended country, but it has taught the practical lesson that a people, relying upon their own industry and economy for advancement, will most surely succeed, while those who await the aid of government, will find even the most direct and liberal legislative enactments inadequate . . . . The right road to the highest prosperity is productive industry, with reliance on the government only for general encouragement and ample protection."[10]

Thus as the reconstruction era began the state government of Michigan exercised limited authority. In the area of finance the fundamental tenet was to emphasize prudence: reduction and extinction of existing debt was state policy; governors were pleased to recommend reductions in taxes; capital expenditures were not only carefully scrutinized but "pay as you go" was explicitly praised and practiced. State development was also promoted as inexpensively as possible. In 1850 the federal government had granted Michigan some six million acres of swamp lands upon the condition that proceeds from their sale would be used for reclaiming the lands by means of levees and drains. The legislature in 1859 had interpreted the federal terms as allowing grants of land to subsidize road construction, reasoning that roads were a form of levee and, in any event, provided means for reclaiming and opening the lands to settlement. The federal government also financed construction of canals. A canal bypassing the rapids at Sault Ste. Marie had been funded in 1853 by a federal land grant. In 1865 Congress authorized a canal through the Keweenaw Peninsula in the Upper Peninsula; this was also funded by a federal land grant. Besides these internal improvements, the state promoted development by selling land that had been deeded to the state by the federal government.

Another area of state operations in 1865 involved social institutions. Public education had been required in Michigan under the constitution of 1837. The constitution of 1850 directed the state to make primary education free, but the legislature had yet to implement that mandate by 1865. On the other hand, the state did provide limited support for the University of Michigan, the Agricultural College (now Michigan State University), and the Normal School (now Eastern Michigan University). The state also maintained a prison at Jackson, an insane asylum at Kalamazoo, and an institution for the deaf, dumb, and blind at Flint.

State activities in other areas were limited also. Private economic activities were untouched by the state, except for a subsidy for salt manufacture and regulations relating to the establishment of banks. Michigan had made a symbolic gesture in the 1850s against liquor by a constitutional provision forbidding the legislature to authorize the granting of licenses to sell liquor. The result was that the state lacked any real authority to control the liquor traffic.

The first reconstruction governor, Henry H. Crapo, ardently supported a limited role for state government. The epitome of the self-made man, he was born in Dartmouth, Massachusetts, in 1804, of poor, farmer parents. Although Crapo had scant opportunities for formal education, he acquired sufficient knowledge to become a teacher and land surveyor. In addition, he had achieved success in horticulture. Buying a poor piece of land, he planted it to a great variety of fruits, flowers, and shrubbery, and widely exhibited and published on his horticultural endeavors. He also invested in the whaling industry and in fire insurance. In addition to these activities in his home state of Massachusetts, Crapo also made major investments in Michigan pine lands. So extensive were these investments that he moved to Flint in 1856 to manage them and quickly became one of the leading lumbermen in the state. He also was principally responsible for the construction of a connecting line from Flint to the Detroit and Milwaukee railroad.[11]

Early in his Michigan career Crapo became involved in public affairs. He was elected mayor of Flint in 1860, a state senator in 1862, and governor in 1864; he was reelected governor in 1866. Although Crapo attributed support for his gubernatorial candidacy (for which he professed no personal desire) to his forthrightness, energy, and "disinterested concern" for the welfare of the state, there were other factors. The Michigan Senators, Zachariah Chandler and Jacob M. Howard, were both from Detroit, as was Crapo's principal opponent for the gubernatorial nomination, Henry Baldwin. Clearly, it would be too much for both United States Senators and the governor to be Detroit residents. After several close ballots, Crapo received the nomination 106 to 103. The close vote militates against the argument that all major offices in Michigan politics were tightly controlled by a "Detroit ring," and the Crapo manuscripts give no indication that Crapo was a protege of Chandler.[12]

Although Crapo actively campaigned to secure election as governor in 1864, he and other candidates for state office scarcely discussed local issues— a typical pattern in reconstruction in Michigan. The emphasis on national issues, no doubt, reflected a shrewd judgment by Republican leaders that the voters of the state were staunchly Republican and repelled by Democratic rhetoric, particularly the "treasonous" Democratic platform. Inattention to state issues probably also reflected the lack of burning problems at the state level.

Governor Crapo's legislative program reflected his practical, business-oriented mind and his philosophy of limited government. His program principally encompassed two areas: development of the state and efficiency in government. For development of the state he gave high priority to encouraging immigration. He suggested creation of an immigration commission, appointment of an immigration agent, and distribution of literature calling attention to the attractions of Michigan. He also claimed that the varied natural resources of the state provided a basis for manufacturing and argued that the state should manufacture its own products, rather than depend on eastern manufacturers. He recommended measures to attract capital, suggesting as a model the state bounty of two cents a bushel for salt, which had encouraged industry in the Saginaw Valley. He also recommended reactivation of the state geological survey.[13] None of these measures to attract industry and labor, however, gained approval of the legislature during Crapo's administration.

The governor was also much concerned over another feature of state development—the use of swamplands as subsidies for road construction. Crapo's thrifty business sense was outraged because many roads had been constructed only to secure valuable timber; other roads were poorly constructed, and some were never completed. Upon Crapo's recommendation, the legislature required specific approval of the governor before deeding land and created the office of swamp-land commissioner to examine all swamp-land roads.

The most controversial issue of the Crapo administration involved financial inducements offered by local governments to assist railroad construction. Crapo vetoed such measures on constitutional grounds, since the state was forbidden by the constitution to lend its credit or to assist in any work of internal improvement. Local governments were creatures of the state, he argued, hence local governments could not help finance railroad construction. He further charged that local aid to railroads would lead to excessive taxes and depressed bond prices. Finally, he argued, while all would pay taxes to support railroads, not all would gain benefits.

The railroad aid question split the Republican Party, and economic interest, rather than party, was the critical factor in determining attitudes toward the railroad aid question. Many Republican legislators opposed the governor's position, including the Lansing *Republican*, the self-proclaimed official organ of the party. The *Republican* claimed that voters in large towns realized the importance of railroads and the necessity to subsidize their construction, while "the little seven-by-nine towns" lacked such wisdom. On the other hand, Crapo argued persuasively that public opinion was on his side.[14] In the following administration, railroad aid measures would receive the executive's approval, only to meet an adverse decision by the state supreme court in

1871, which sustained Crapo's original constitutional objections. The issue, accordingly, dropped from the political scene.

In addition to his involvement in internal improvement questions, Crapo was much interested in economy and efficiency in government, especially in regard to the state's social institutions. He visited the prison, the insane asylum, and the school for the deaf and blind. His particular concern was that their spending did not exceed state appropriations. He frequently suggested additional capital appropriations to complete unfinished buildings, arguing that it was uneconomical to let unfinished buildings remain idle and exposed to the vicissitudes of the weather.[15]

Crapo recommended an enlarged role for the Agricultural College. He supported the necessity for agricultural research, dissemination of information, and collegiate training for farmers. No doubt Crapo's support arose from his own horticultural background and his realization of the necessity for improved agriculture in frontier Michigan. Despite some rural opposition to college learning and despite the desire of some citizens to transfer the agricultural program to the University of Michigan, the legislature appropriated, with the governor's support, sufficient funds to maintain the Agricultural College as a viable institution.[16]

Crapo was markedly interested in managing state finances prudently. He strongly approved a "pay as you go" state financial policy and looked forward to extinguishing the state debt through the operation of the sinking fund.[17] He was also diligent in completing financial arrangements and securing reimbursement from the federal government for state expenditures during the Civil War. To facilitate such reimbursement, he visited Washington on several occasions.

Along with his state duties, Governor Crapo found time to support the national Radical Republican program. He proclaimed April 19, 1866, as a day of fasting, humiliation, and prayer, in order to seek "Divine aid" for the yet unfulfilled task of "rebuilding" the nation. He issued the proclamation, he said, "to counteract the influence of the Johnson-Copperhead party here, and to keep the Republicans true to the great work of maintaining their principles." In his view, he wrote to his son, "that Proclamation was like firing a whole battery of grape into the bushes where a thousand rebels lay concealed."[18] In accord with the Radical Republican program, Crapo urged, and the legislature promptly voted, state ratification of the Thirteenth and Fourteenth Amendments to the Constitution.

Another feature of the Radical Republican program, Negro suffrage, became a state issue in 1867, when a convention drew up a new state constitution providing for black suffrage. The question had arisen in Michigan during the ante-bellum period, when some Whigs had supported black suffrage as part of a package that excluded aliens from the ballot box. Michigan

Democrats, on the other hand, had consistently opposed black suffrage, while favoring suffrage for resident aliens. Because the black suffrage question was tied to alien voting, and because of substantial racism in ante-bellum Michigan, black suffrage was rejected.[19]

Racism in Michigan did not decrease as a result of the Civil War. Indeed, during the reconstruction era few major political figures within the state argued for black suffrage on moral or humanistic grounds. Instead, the issue entered state politics through the backdoor of national necessity; black suffrage was essential for creation of a strong Republican Party in the South.[20] The official party organ, the *Lansing Republican*, laid down the law: "Every Republican County Convention and the State convention has declared in favor of negro suffrage. It is a test of party fealty. If you refuse to vote for it, you declare yourself no longer a Republican and will be so regarded by the party. Do not vote against suffrage and expect party preferment hereafter."[21] Since Congress mandated black suffrage in the South, Michigan Republicans argued that it would be illogical to deny black suffrage in the North. Democrats replied that blacks were inferior to whites and that suffrage would lead to innundation and miscegenation. Republicans used population statistics to show that the existence of black suffrage in other states had not encouraged Negro migration to those states.

The proposed constitution embodying black suffrage was put to the people in the spring election of 1867 and decisively defeated. Although a prohibition clause, a railroad aid provision, and an increase in the wages of state officials possibly influenced the result, in the opinion of most observers the constitution was defeated primarily because of the suffrage question.[22] The rejection of the constitution, it should be noted, did not hurt the Republican Party. Republican candidates for state office in the spring elections of 1867 won easily.

In addition to proposing black suffrage, some members in the legislature agitated for a variety of reforms. A bill establishing a female college passed the senate but was defeated in the house. On the other hand, the house passed an eight-hour day bill and also a measure adopting the metric system, but both failed in the senate. The bill to prevent traffic in impure milk and to prevent the adulteration of milk, however, passed both houses and received the governor's approval. None of these measures was suggested by Governor Crapo. Perhaps these legislative activities led the Marshall *Democratic Expounder* to criticize the legislature for passing so many laws. "That country is the best and the most prosperous," it claimed, "where the laws have become settled."[23] The *Expounder* in all probability became increasingly unhappy with the administration of Crapo's successor, who would assume an even more active role for state government.

Without substantial opposition, Henry P. Baldwin was elected governor in 1868 and reelected in 1870 to carry on Republican policy in Lansing. Like

Crapo, he had a New England background, having been born in Rhode Island in 1814. After receiving a common school education, he was orphaned at the age of twelve and became a clerk in a mercantile establishment. When he was twenty, he engaged in business of his own, moving to Detroit four years later, where he established a mercantile house and later became a prominent banker. An active member of the Episcopal Church and the Detroit Young Men's Society, Baldwin also contributed generously to St. Luke's Hospital in Detroit. No political neophyte, he had served as a member of the state senate in 1860, and had sought the gubernatorial nomination as early as 1864. Though a Detroit resident, Baldwin had much support throughout the state. He was, however, according to a critic, "a little too much of the Miss Nancy order and would be a very aristocratic sort of a Governor." Another observer noted that Baldwin was "spare and of rather frail physique . . . of nervous temperment, restlessly active." When in earnest conversation, his words, the observer added, "follow one another so rapidly that he seemed to have more to say than time to express it."[24]

During Baldwin's administration certain proposals previously recommended by Henry Crapo reached fruition. The legislature authorized continuation of the geological survey of the state and by the end of Baldwin's administration a survey of the Upper Peninsula had been completed. The legislature also authorized the appointment of an immigration commissioner, to be stationed in Germany. This official disseminated printed information about the state and sought to persuade Germans to emigrate to Michigan. Unfortunately, the outbreak of the Franco-Prussian War severely hampered the commissioner's efforts, and Baldwin seriously doubted whether the results justified the effort.[25]

Internal improvement activities increased under the new governor. During the Baldwin administration, the federal government engaged in major construction that trebled the capacity of the locks at Sault Ste. Marie. The federal government also financed, through land grants, construction of a harbor and a ship canal from Lake Superior to Portage Lake in the copper country. Although the original grant specified a completion date in 1869, later extended to 1870, the construction company encountered problems, and creditors of the company took over; the canal was finally completed in 1873.

Despite limited governmental aid, railroads were constructed at a rapid rate during Baldwin's administration. On January 1, 1869, Michigan had 1,199 miles of track; two years later an additional 1,808 miles had been constructed, though only 457 miles were beneficiaries of land grants. Railroads also continued to be subjects of political controversy. The state supreme court decision of 1871 that municipal support of railroad construction was unconstitutional invalidated municipal bonds issued for construction already completed. Baldwin urged in vain that the legislature initiate a constitutional amendment validating such bonds.

Disposition of the swamp lands, particularly as grants to subsidize construction of wagon roads, continued to occupy legislative attention. In 1869 and 1870, 599 miles of swamp-land roads and ditches were completed; during 1871 and the first ten months of 1872, an additional 332½ miles were constructed. By the end of Baldwin's administration, the only unobligated swamp lands left in the Lower Peninsula were of such poor quality that they could not serve as grants for construction of additional wagon roads. In 1869 the legislature provided that swamp lands in the Upper Peninsula could be used to subsidize the construction of railroads.[26]

For the remainder of the reconstruction era, however, the emphasis was not so much on subsidizing construction of railroads as regulating their operations. In November 1870, the voters approved a constitutional amendment giving the legislature power to establish maximum rates, to prohibit discriminatory rates, and to forbid consolidation of parallel or competing lines. The Lansing *Republican* pronounced the amendment as a "most important" issue in the 1870 election and characterized it as both "just and salutary."[27] In addition, the legislature passed measures providing for increased taxation of railroads.[28]

Baldwin's principal concern as governor seems to have been the social institutions of the state, and in this realm the Republicans expanded state activity. In 1869 the legislature abolished rate bills for the common schools. Thus "the free schools [were] made what their name indicates," and the 1850 constitutional mandate for free schools was finally implemented.[29] In 1871 the legislature passed a compulsory education law, one of the few measures of the Republican era that involved party division. Many Democrats opposed the compulsory feature of the act, though they were highly supportive of education, while Republicans overwhelmingly favored the measure.[30]

Equally significant changes took place in higher education. In 1867 the legislature for the first time had appropriated tax funds to support the University of Michigan. This measure was favored by supporters of the Agricultural College; in return the friends of the university agreed to support increased appropriations for the college. Yet, charged supporters of the college, the university not only opposed appropriations for the college but also sought to take over the college in order to secure its land grant. In 1869, over strenuous university opposition, the legislature made generous appropriations to the college, including funds for a dormitory. Convinced that the college was a viable institution with strong legislative support, the university thereafter accepted the existence of its sister institution.[31]

Indeed, the university itself was under pressure. The legislature suggested that women be admitted to the all-male institution. In addition, several measures were introduced into the legislature to create a female college.

Perhaps as a result of these actions, in 1871 the University of Michigan admitted its first female students. "The presence of women," Governor Baldwin assured the legislature, "thus far has worked most satisfactorily; they rank high in scholarship, and their influence has in no way been unfavorable."[32]

Education was not the only area of social policy to receive attention by the Michigan Republicans during Baldwin's administration. Additions to the school for the deaf, dumb, and blind at Flint were completed and each of the pupils was introduced to a form of "mechanical instruction." This instruction was designed to enable every pupil, "while in the institution, to become self-supporting after leaving it." The capacity of the insane asylum at Kalamazoo was increased so that the facility could house 500 patients. Since the census of 1870 reported 1,183 cases of insanity in the state, many of the afflicted were in county poorhouses and jails, which were "always unsuited to their condition and often atrocious." Baldwin believed it was "the clear duty of the State to provide for the care and treatment" of all the insane; he accordingly recommended, with legislative approval, that a site be selected and plans be submitted to the legislature for an additional insane asylum. In 1871 the legislature also provided for a state public school, which was subsequently erected at Coldwater, for dependent and neglected children. The purpose of the school was "to provide temporary homes until homes [could] be procured for them in suitable families." The institution was based on the household or family system, with a main building and seven cottages, the main building to be used for administrative purposes, the wings for school rooms, and the cottages for dormitories. Baldwin's principal concern with the reform school was that too many boys were there who should not have been. He thought that many could be sent to the more humane state public school.

Baldwin believed that the prison at Jackson was, on the whole, well managed. "The discipline," he claimed, "though decidedly modified, has been uniformly good; severe and degrading punishments have been almost wholly abolished; the prison has been conducted with a due regard to economy, and the constant aim of the Agents and Inspectors has been to remember that the inmates, though convicts, are human beings, and not entirely lost to the better impulses of the human heart." Yet he was equally aware of a number of very serious physical plant deficiencies: the lack of a hospital, the lack of bathing accommodations, the bad condition of the roof of each wing, and the unsafe heating system. The governor was even more concerned about the lack of segregation of prisoners convicted for different types of crimes, both at Jackson prison and in the county jails. "I have long been convinced," Baldwin charged, "that they [the jails] are the hot beds of vice." He was equally disturbed over the county poorhouses, a large proportion of whose inmates were, in his words, "intemperate, debauched, base and vile." Though some inmates did not belong in those categories, all were mixed together. But the worst single feature of the poorhouses was the practice of confining the insane in those institutions.

In conformity with Baldwin's recommendation, the legislature authorized a commission to examine the penal, reformatory, and charitable institutions. After extensive investigation, the commission recommended a reform school for girls; intermediate prisons or work houses; assistance to ex-convicts in securing jobs; a central board for all preventive, reformatory, and penal institutions; an additional insane asylum; a state hospital at Ann Arbor; and a uniform system of record keeping for sheriffs and keepers of poorhouses. Except for construction of the state hospital, Baldwin supported all the recommendations, and Michigan's Republicans worked hard to win their adoption.[33]

Along with its interest in social institutions, the Baldwin administration was concerned with efficiency in government. The legislature, for example, approved a recompilation of the state laws in 1871, a task not done since 1857. Baldwin sought to raise the salaries of state officials, particularly those of judicial officers. The people, however, refused to approve a constitutional amendment authorizing the legislature to set salaries, thus leaving the low salaries set by the constitution in effect.

Baldwin maintained intact Crapo's policies on state finance. He praised the policy of "pay as you go," noted with pride that the sinking fund was adequate to provide payment of the state debt, and recommended tax reductions. He even made provision for financing the construction of a new state capitol so that it would be paid for upon completion.[34]

The Republicans in the legislature sessions of 1869 and 1871 also passed a variety of laws regulating economic activities. Two laws provided for salt and timber inspection, laws that enjoyed the support of the industries involved. In addition, the legislature established an insurance commission, as well as regulations providing more stringent capital requirements for insurance companies. The legislature also provided for regulation of savings banks. Finally, the legislature passed an act for the more effectual prevention of cruelty to animals.[35]

One of the major achievements of the Baldwin administration was securing black suffrage. Shortly after the Fifteenth Amendment was submitted to the states, Baldwin transmitted it to the legislature with a request for prompt ratification. Over strenuous Democratic objections, the amendment was ratified by a straight party vote in the overwhelmingly Republican legislature in March 1869. When the Fifteenth Amendment went into effect a year later, the white suffrage clause in the Michigan constitution was superseded, and "several hundred" Negroes reportedly voted in the spring elections of 1870. Michigan Republicans were still not satisfied. The rejection of the black suffrage amendment to the state constitution by the voters in 1868 was a "blot" on the state, and, in addition, the state constitution provided for legislative apportionment based wholly on the white population, and militia service was confined to whites only. Accordingly, Republicans in the legislature framed an amendment to the state constitution striking "white" in reference to suffrage, apportionment, and militia. Securing legislative approval at the end of March 1869, the amendment was submitted to the electorate for approval in November 1870. The amendment aroused surprisingly little public debate. The negrophobic Democratic *Free Press* concluded that since the Fifteenth Amendment was part of the United States Constitution, the amendment to the state constitution should be approved. While it was advocating approval of the amendment, the Republican press maintained a low profile on the issue. Although 186,277 voted for the gubernatorial candidates in the election of November 1870, only 104,277 voted on the amendment to strike "white" from the constitution. Of this total, 54,105 persons voted in favor of the amendment, while 50,598 opposed. The Lansing *Republican* claimed that "the stigma of reproach that rested upon the State is forever wiped out." It would be more accurate to say that persistent Republican efforts were finally successful in wringing a favorable vote for black suffrage from notably resistant Michiganians.[36]

The principal feature of the 1872 election nationally was the revolt and defection of the Liberal Republicans, who charged the Grant administration with both corruption and needless prolongation of a harsh reconstruction program in the South. For president the Liberal Republicans nominated Horace Greeley, whom Michigan Democrats accepted with poor grace as their nominee. On the state level, the Liberal Republicans seemingly made a much more acceptable choice as their gubernatorial candidate, Austin Blair, the popular Civil War governor who had been defeated by Zachariah Chandler in a Senatorial battle the year before. The election, however, demonstrated once again overwhelming popular support for the Republican Party in Michigan. Blair was beaten badly by John Bagley, the nominee of the regular Republicans.

Bagley had been born in New York in 1832 and attended district schools there until he moved with his parents to Constantine, Michigan. At the age of thirteen he began working in a country store. In 1847 he went to work in a Detroit tobacco factory, and in 1853 he established his own tobacco company, which prospered and brought him a fortune. He also became an organizer of a life insurance company and a stockholder and director of several banks. Politically, Bagley had been a Whig until the formation of the Republican Party. He held various city offices in Detroit until his election as governor in 1872 and was reelected in 1874.

The Bagley administration was directly affected by the panic of 1873, which also altered the direction of certain Republican policies at the state level. In an effort to stimulate the state's economy, the legislature authorized an expansion of the geological survey to seek out such natural resources as coal, salt, and gypsum in the Lower Peninsula. The decline in immigration and changes in the demand for labor as a result of the panic led Bagley to close the immigration office in New York City and to recommend abolition of the immigration commission in 1874.

Republicans also made significant alterations in land policy. The price of state lands was graduated to reflect increased values resulting from railroad construction. Bagley moved vigorously to stop trespassing and the cutting of timber on state lands. He was particularly disturbed over part-paid land, land bought at one-fourth down, stripped of its timber, and then allowed to revert to the state for nonpayment of taxes. In addition, he was concerned over the use of swamp lands to finance construction of roads and ditches, which he termed "a wasteful and extravagant expenditure of our swamp lands." He feared that the abundant swamp lands in the Upper Peninsula would be frittered away without plan. Accordingly, Governor Bagley suggested that such lands in the Upper Peninsula be used to subsidize construction of a railroad to connect Marquette with the Straits of Mackinac. Although the legislature approved and contracts were signed to build the railroad, the depression of 1873 prevented work on the project.[37]

The depression also forced the company that constructed the Portage Lake Canal into receivership. Unfortunately, the construction company claimed ownership of the canal, while Bagley refused to certify the completion of the canal until title rested with the state or federal government. The legal question of ownership remained unresolved at the end of Bagley's administration.

At Bagley's suggestion, the legislature established a fish commission in 1873 and authorized a fish hatchery. By the end of 1874 some 15 million fish had been hatched and placed in Michigan lakes. Prior to that time, the catch of fish had been decreasing yearly because of wholesale destruction of young fish by fishing methods then employed and because of "catching in season and out of season" without any regulation by the government. The governor urged that the attention of Michigan's Congressional representatives be directed to these questions, since the federal government had exclusive control over the Great Lakes.[38]

Bagley's most significant achievements were in the area of state regulation of business. He paid particular attention to railroads, which he claimed "are something more than mere private enterprises. They are not only a public convenience but a public necessity. They have, in large measure, taken the place of the highway known to the common law, and so far occupy the same relations to the public. By the law of necessity they must be made subservient to the public ends." At the governor's suggestion, the legislature created a railroad commission to enforce laws relating to railroads. The legislature gave the commissioner authority to set passenger rates (but not freight rates), even though, as the governor reported, competition made railroad rates as low in Michigan as anywhere in the Union. Subsequently, the commissioner drafted and the people ratified a constitutional amendment to maintain railroad competition. After the panic of 1873, when many railroads of the state could not pay interest on their bonds, the governor blamed such subsidiary enterprises as sleeping cars for sucking the life blood from railroads. He believed such enterprises should also be regulated.[39]

While the legislature had created an insurance bureau in 1871, which weeded out poor fire insurance companies, Bagley claimed additional regulation was needed for life insurance companies. Locally owned companies could not issue forfeitable policies; out-of-state companies did. Bagley suggested that all policies should be nonforfeitable, written in simple language, and devoid of "jokers." He also saw faults in banking laws. "Our banks of today," he admitted, "are well managed and in good hands, but this is good luck and not good laws." He repeatedly, though unsuccessfully, urged creation of a bureau of banking and reporting requirements similar to those of the National Banking Act.[40]

Bagley continued the vigorous Republican interest in education. "The door of every educational institution of the State," he proudly claimed, "from the log school-house to the University swings wide and free for all." He expressed particular concern for technical education. While most college students sought the learned professions, the state needed educated farmers, mechanics, architects, engineers, and chemists. Though he believed that the Agricultural College was well suited to offer such education, he was particularly pleased when the legislature of 1875 established a school of mines, a chair in architecture and design, and a chair in dental surgery at the university. He also thought that the graded and high schools should offer technical education.[41]

Governor Bagley was not at all satisfied with the state penal system, which consisted of three institutions: the state prison, the reform school for boys, and the Detroit House of Correction. The last was virtually an intermediate prison, receiving all women and a large proportion of the young men.[42] With these three institutions it should have been possible to classify prisoners, yet classification had not occurred. In addition, the capacity of the institutions was limited so that some persons were confined in jails after conviction. Because he believed work was an essential feature of reformation, Bagley thought that a jail was a terrible place for convicts, since it was not possible to provide work for its inmates. He reluctantly accepted the convict contract system because so few prison industries were feasible.[43]

Though he was unable to propose an alternative to the contract system, Bagley did develop an extensive program to improve the penal system. The first necessity was to rebuild and remodel the state prison; it was, except for "the walls and the shops," he noted, "all wants." By the end of his term the physical condition of the plant was much improved. In addition, rules governing the convicts had been revamped: stripes, the hallmark of convicts, were made less conspicuous; a good time rule, allowing reduction of sentence for good behavior, was initiated; and the convicts were given a portion of their small earnings from employment in prison industries. He urged that the members of the Board of Commissioners of Penal Institutions, which was authorized to examine and report suggestions for all penal and criminal laws, be provided compensation so they could perform their responsibilities effectively.

Bagley also made recommendations for the reform school. He believed it "lacks something, but I know not what it is." Perhaps, he suggested, it was too much a prison and too little a home and school. Two years later he was pleased that the reform school no longer had bars, iron doors, a fence, or corporal punishment. As a result, there were "no escapes, less destruction of property, and a better atmosphere."[44]

Bagley was also enthusiastic about adoption of his proposal for county agents. In essence social workers, the county agents were gubernatorial appointees who investigated the case of every child arrested for crime and advised the magistrate on disposition of the case, visited all children adopted or indentured from the public or reform school, and found homes for children. The work of these agents, stated Bagley, was of "inestimable value." These measures were not enough, however, so long as poorhouses continued to "feed" prisons with inmates. Thus, the governor urged a prohibition of the placement of any child under three in any poorhouse. Instead, the child should be sent to a private institution or, better yet, to private homes, with the county paying the cost of maintenance. With proper homes and acquisition of an employable skill, the prison population, he confidently predicted, would decrease dramatically.[45]

Governor Bagley held "to the firm belief that all insane and idiotic persons, and all deaf, dumb or blind children" were the wards of the state; and that it should exercise "for them, and over them, the same loving care, so far as possible, that a wise parent would [exercise] over his children." He contended that not only was this a humanitarian duty, but curing unfortunates and making them productive would save the state money in the long run. The asylum at Kalamazoo, he claimed, was "recognized as one of the best in the world." Yet he was disturbed at the practice of institutionalizing the insane in county poorhouses and jails; that practice, he felt, should be prohibited. With the completion of a new asylum the state would have sufficient capacity to take care of all the insane. The school for the deaf, dumb, and blind at Flint was expanded so that it housed nearly all the state's children who needed its care. Those children were instructed not only in the usual "schoolbook lore" but also in useful trades. The state public school at Coldwater, which the governor considered "the wisest of our state charities," opened in 1874. As a temporary home for "neglected and dependent children" from poorhouses, the school was expected to care for and to transform its inhabitants from "paupers to producers, from dependent to independent citizens." If so, the school was not a charity but an economy. From the opening in 1874 to 1876, the school received 412 children, most from poorhouses. Of these, 117 had been placed in private homes.[46]

Bagley drew a dark picture of poorhouses, which were a county responsibility. The public expense of caring for the poor of the state was $572,000 in 1875, of which $207,000 was spent for maintaining the poorhouses. The value of the paupers' labor at those institutions was estimated at $8,000. The increase in "tramps and able-bodied paupers," the squalid conditions of the poorhouses, among other things, induced the county superintendents of the poor at their 1876 annual meeting to adopt unanimously a resolution favoring district work houses. Bagley recommended legislation permitting formation of such districts.[47]

The Bagley administration addressed a number of other questions. In 1873, for example, the legislature created a state board of health, which had been recommended by the State Medical Society. Composed of "practical sensible men," the board published annual reports, largely statistical, which, it was hoped, would diffuse knowledge and lead to improvement in health conditions.[48] At the Governor's suggestion, the Military Law of 1862 was carefully amended, the result being the beginning of the modern Michigan National Guard. The legislature also passed a law regulating the sale of poisons and fixing standards for kerosene oil. The latter provision was expected to prevent kerosene explosion. On the other hand, sponsors failed to secure approval of a child labor law and a ten-hour day law. Agitation for the latter measure arose after an unsuccessful strike by Saginaw area saw mill workers to secure a ten-hour day.[49]

A particularly burning issue in the 1870s was prohibition. The only reconstruction governor to discuss the issue in his messages to the legislature ("at last the Governor of this State has spoken upon the liquor traffic"), Bagley condemned intemperance as "an evil that threatens our life, above and beyond all else.... Pauperism, crime, insanity, disease, and death are its direct results, and untold private griefs and miseries, want and wretchedness spring from its myriad planted seeds." Since the constitution forbade the state to license liquor-selling establishments, there was almost no regulation of the traffic in alcoholic beverages. Bagley despaired of outright prohibition. "There will always be drinking and drunkenness," he declared, but the state could diminish intemperance. His suggestion of taxing and regulating the traffic was adopted by the legislature in 1875. This law resulted in a reduction in the number of liquor-selling establishments, Bagley claimed, though he also observed that in certain counties local officials did not enforce the law. He recommended more stringent enforcement and institution of a process for removing officials who did not enforce the law.[50]

As had his two predecessors, Bagley sought to achieve efficiency in government. At his suggestion, the legislature sharply reduced the amount of state printing. He also made repeated pleas for better salaries for officials; his efforts failed when the people once more refused to remove the limits speci-fied in the constitution.

When Bagley first came to office, he found that laws regarding taxation seemed as "complete and perfect as they can well be made"; any defects, he claimed, lay in their enforcement. Later, he found a number of inequities. For example, he believed specific taxes (taxes specified rather than based on valuation) were grossly unfair. He estimated that property taxes in Michigan averaged $2 per $100 of valuation, while specific taxes cost the telegraph company $.23 per $100; street railways $.25 per $100, and the other rail-roads $.27 per $100. To correct another inequity, the legislature in 1873 passed a law providing for assessment and taxation of what were known as railroad lands. When a railroad questioned the constitutionality of the act, Bagley upheld the state's position. The federal district court found for the state, and the case was appealed to the supreme court at the end of his administration.[51]

Under Bagley the state remained on a strict "pay as you go" basis, and a sinking fund would provide adequate money to pay off the state debt by 1890. So sound was the state's credit that the treasurer was unable to pur-chase bonds before their redemption, even at a premium. In fact, Bagley predicted, the new state capitol, on which construction started in 1871, and which would cost over a million dollars, would be paid for when completed in 1879 despite the depression of 1873.

At the same time that Republicans under Bagley tried to battle the impact of the 1873 depression, they also had to battle a resurgent Democratic opposition. In the elections of 1874, though Republicans sought to make the "bloody shirt" and the money question the principal issues, Democrats raised certain state issues. They pointed to the surplus in the treasury and demanded lower taxes. Republicans replied that the surplus was a result of specific taxes mandated for particular purposes, such as debt reduction. Bagley pointed to Republican success in supporting the state's social institutions and promoting development. Nonetheless, financial panics hurt the party in power, and the election of 1874 was "fairly entitled to be called a political whirlwind." Republicans narrowly retained control of the legislature by a 54 to 46 margin in the house and 18 to 14 in the senate. Bagley barely squeaked through for reelection.[52]

The principal result of Democratic gains in the legislature was the over-throw of Zachariah Chandler, who sought reelection as United States Senator in 1875. Combining with a few dissident, violently anti-Chandler Republi-cans, the Democrats elected as Chandler's successor Issac Christiancy, an elderly justice of the supreme court, and a Republican of Democratic origins. After the Senatorial contest, however, Republicans and Democrats "join[ed] hands and circle[d] around together."[53] Democratic inroads in the legisla-ture did not change legislative policy.

Concurrent with the evidence of bipartisan harmony were signs of a conservative reaction by 1875. The legislative correspondent of the Detroit *Free Press* was critical of attempts by the legislature to extend regulation of railroads. The Lansing *Republican* cautioned against haste in bringing about tax reform and argued against treating railroad property as other real and personal property for tax purposes. Indeed, the newspaper was sharply critical of the "so-called 'reform' element" in the legislature, which wasted much time and prolonged the legislative session.[54] Such comments from that newspaper were particularly striking because it was the only time in the reconstruction era that the Lansing *Republican* made such sweeping criticisms of the legislature. It is not surprising that the Republican administration elected in 1876 pursued a conservative course. The end of the Bagley administration coincided not only with the end of the reconstruction era on the national level but also marked the end of a reform era in Michigan's political history.

Certain salient characteristics of Michigan politics during the reconstruction era seem clear. One is the transition from a state government that was limited in function to a government that became increasingly activist. Another is Republican dominance of the state government, along with its converse, Democratic impotence. Only in 1874, with the state prostrated by depression, did the Democrats make substantial gains. Two key elections, the elections of 1866 and 1872, when national reconstruction issues were clearly drawn, exhibited the inability of the Democrats to generate popular support. The failure of Austin Blair in 1872 to attract Republicans to the Democratic ticket was particularly striking. Republicans at the outset of the reconstruction era identified themselves as the saviors of the Union and linked the Democrats to the Southern disunionists. Republican efforts in Congress to nail down the results of the Civil War through various reconstruction acts received overwhelming support among the Michigan rank and file. Waving the "bloody shirt" was an effective Republican campaign tactic.

To equate Republican dominance with an activist state government, however, would be inaccurate. The only distinctively Republican policy was black suffrage. On other legislative questions, such as local aid to railroads, railroad regulation, and support for social institutions, Democrats and Republicans did not take partisan positions. Democrats and Republicans even in the closely divided legislature elected in 1874 did not split along party lines.[55]

Michigan government became increasingly active as recollections of ill-perceived and administered internal improvement and banking schemes of 1837 faded from memory. As immigration increased the population of the state, especially outside the Detroit area, and young persons reached voting age, new men came to office. The Republican Party claimed marked success in appealing to young people; the election of Thomas Ferry in 1871 as United States Senator, replacing the veteran Jacob Howard, was perceived as representing a triumph for younger men and outstate Michigan. So many new members were elected to the 1871 legislature that it was difficult to organize the body. In 1872 only five senators and but eighteen members of the house were reelected. With so much turnover among the legislators, it is not surprising that there was an "absence of imperious leadership" in the 1873 legislature. "The nearest to a combination," said the Lansing *Republican*, "was that including the members from Northern counties, who ardently desired a change in the Tax system." The Democratic gains in 1874, of course, insured a substantial turnover for the legislature in 1875.[56]

The increasingly activist state government, accordingly, is to be understood in the light of the fading memories of the disasters of 1837 and the election of younger men to the legislature. In addition, specific, practical needs, particularly those of the growing northern counties, dictated charges in governmental functions and operations.

In the reconstruction era two principal changes occurred in education. One was the final determination that the Agricultural College was not to be attached to the university. Support for the college came primarily from farmers and outstaters, whose strength increased as northern counties were settled. The other major educational change was the compulsory school law of 1871. This was defended on the practical ground that inhabitants of prison were largely uneducated. Proponents also urged that society needed an educated citizenry, but in the absence of a compulsory law parents might forbid school attendance by their children.[57]

One of the principal changes in the social institutions was expansion of facilities for the insane, for the deaf, dumb, and blind, and for homeless children, dictated by the increasing numbers of persons who needed institutionalization. In the institutions caring for children there was particular emphasis upon training for practical skills. Both Governors Baldwin and Bagley urged that a new prison be built because of overcrowding in existing facilities. Certain prison practices were instituted, such as the virtual abolition of the degrading striped uniform and a "good time" rule, as important in rehabilitating prisoners for productive lives. Attempts to reintroduce capital punishment were rejected on the grounds that the lack of capital punishment had not led to an increase in crime.

Significant changes in the relationship between state government and business also arose from immediate, practical concerns. Early in the reconstruction era the principal issue was local aid for construction of railroads; in the latter part of the era, after substantial construction had been completed, the emphasis was on regulation of railroad rates. The issue of taxation of railroad lands, a special interest of the northern counties, arose after railroads had been constructed and had been granted substantial amounts of land as a subsidy. The life insurance commission was created in 1873, no doubt in part because of the experience of many Michiganians in dealing with insurance companies after a series of disastrous fires in 1871. The establishment of the fish commission and the state fish hatchery were responses to problems arising from decreasing catches in the Great Lakes.

A number of other problems required attention. Threats to health had increased as a result of the growth in population. To meet this danger, the legislature provided for the state board of health, with its membership of "practical, sensible men," to gather data and statistics. The militia was decrepit and needed revitalizing, a task made possible by legislative enactment. The prohibition laws had not worked, and accordingly, were sharply modified.

The comment of the leading Democratic newspaper that Governor Bagley's message of 1875 was a "a matter of fact, business like document"[58] could well have applied to all gubernatorial messages during the reconstruction era. In Michigan the movement of the state government from a limited role to a far more activist role did not occur as the result of leadership by one person or group that planned and later implemented a program based on a consistent philosophy of government. Nor did the transition in Michigan government reflect a distinctively Republican position. Rather, Michigan's government became activist as memories of early statehood failures faded, as new men came into government, as population grew in northern counties, and as pressing problems required solution.

NOTES

1. "Since I have been acquainted at all with politics of Michigan," reported a party leader, "I have never known greater unanimity in the Republican ranks than today." Not a single federal officeholder in the state, he added, supported the President's policy. S. Y. Cutcheon to Zachariah Chandler, Ypsilanti, Michigan, May 29, 1866, Zachariah Chandler Papers, Library of Congress. Microfilm examined in Clarke Historical Library, Central Michigan University. Harriette M. Dilla, *The Politics of Michigan, 1865-1878* (New York, 1912) is the principal study of Michigan politics during the reconstruction era. Dilla closely follows the reconstruction views of William A. Dunning.

2. Ronald P. Formisano, *The Birth of Mass Political Parties: Michigan, 1827-1861* (Princeton, New Jersey, 1971), emphasizes the role of abolitionists, temperance men, anti-Catholic nativists, and moralists whose consonance before 1853 facilitated fusion efforts that resulted in the formation of the Republican party in 1854. See especially Chapters X and XI and p. 239. For an illustration of radical Republican historical theory, see the speech by Michigan Congressman John Longyear, *Congressional Globe*, 38th Cong., 1st sess., pp. 2013-14.

3. Crapo's views were part of a lengthy 4th of July oration, in which he dealt with issues of the Civil War and reconstruction. For the speech see Flint *Wolverine Citizen*, July 14, 1866. For background of the speech see my "A Fourth of July Portrait," *Detroit Historical Society Bulletin* 23 (Summer 1967):4-10.

4. This statement of Republican attitudes toward the Civil War and reconstruction closely follows my "Radical Republican Motivation: A Case History," *Journal of Negro History* 54 (April 1969):109-10.

5. The popular Civil War governor, Austin Blair, defected in 1872 and ran as the Liberal Republican-Democratic candidate for governor. His past services to the party did not shield him from vituperation, bitter reproach, and crushing defeat.

6. Madison Kuhn, "Tiffin, Morse, and the Reluctant Pioneer," *Michigan History* 50 (June 1966):113.

7. Willis F. Dunbar, "Frontiersmanship in Michigan," *Michigan History* 50 (June 1966):100.

8. George N. Fuller, ed., *Messages of the Governors of Michigan* (4 vols., Lansing, 1926), II:530.

9. The editor of the Lansing *Republican* attributed Michigan's lagging development in 1870 to the wildcat banks and rotten internal improvement schemes of 1837, which deterred immigration. "We *know* this, having heard it talked about in our boyhood at the East." Lansing *Republican*, November 3, 1870. S. D. Bingham, editor of the Lansing *Republican*, became chairman of the state central committee of the Republican party and was reputedly the "chief factotum" of Chandler. Bingham proclaimed that his paper was "the official organ of the Republican State Administration." Ibid., December 3, 1868. (The Negrophobic Detroit *Free Press* was the leading Democratic newspaper of the state.) For Bingham's role in the party see Henry A. Haigh, "Lansing in the Good Old Seventies," *Michigan History* 13 (1913):105. For the view that the 1837 railroad plans were not as disastrous as usually described in standard accounts see Robert J. Parks, *Democracy's Railroads: Public Enterprise in Jacksonian Michigan* (Port Washington, New York, 1972).

10. Fuller, *Messages of Governors*, III:192.

11. There are two major biographical studies of Crapo. Henry H. Crapo [II], *The Story of Henry Howland Crapo, 1804-1869* (Boston, 1933), is an account by a grandson, based on personal recollections and family papers. Martin D. Lewis, *Lumberman from Flint: The Michigan Career of Henry H. Crapo, 1855-1869* (Detroit, 1958), is a scholarly study with emphasis on Crapo's business career.

12. Despite his disclaimer of interest in the governorship, Crapo made a notebook that listed by county the principal political figures in the state and the delegates to the Republican convention with each of their leanings; Crapo Papers. Michigan Historical Collections, University of Michigan.

13. Fuller, *Messages of the Governors*, II:529-31.

14. In many localities, predicted one Republican newspaper, attitudes toward railroad aid would prove stronger than party affiliation. When the senate in a dramatic session barely sustained the governor's veto, the chambers were jammed with a lobby comprising "many of the very first businessmen of the State." The newspaper concluded that Governor Crapo had lost some of his friends. Grand Rapids *Daily Eagle*, March 4, 23, 1867. Crapo's veto message followed closely the reasoning of D. Bethume Duffield to Crapo, Detroit, January 21, 23, 1867, Crapo Papers; Duffield was a prominent Detroit Republican. Crapo's veto message is in Fuller, *Messages of the Governors*, II:597-608. The Crapo Papers have many letters and newspaper clippings relating to the railroad controversy, most of them supportive of Crapo's position. The Lansing *Republican* supported railroad assistance in 1867; the arguments cited appeared in editorials of January 14, 1869 and November 24, 1870. The conclusion that public opinion opposed railroad assistance rests upon the Crapo Papers, negative votes cast on the 1867 constitution, and the defeat of a proposed amendment to the constitution in 1871 to permit local assistance for railroad construction.

15. See, for example, Fuller, *Messages of the Governors*, II:569.

16. Ibid., p. 517.

17. At one time Crapo refrained from selling bonds to pay the bounties of soldiers because the securities market was depressed. He preferred the "odium of not paying the bounties to the soldiers to depreciating our state securities." Crapo, *Crapo*, p. 225.

18. A facsimile and text of the proclamation may be found in ibid., pp. 230-33. Henry H. Crapo to William W. Crapo, Flint, April 8, 1866, Crapo Papers.

19. For this question see Ronald P. Formisano, "The Edge of Caste: Colored Suffrage in Michigan, 1827-1861," *Michigan History* 56 (Spring 1972):19-41.

20. "The question of mere justice to the Negro is one of minor importance," claimed the Republican Detroit *Advertiser and Tribune*, July 3, 1865; "it is the Union which is in need of negro suffrage. A loyal majority in the South is absolutely necessary, and it can only be obtained by making the freedman a part of it."

21. Lansing *Republican*, March 26, 1868. A private expression of opinion was just as strong. After full discussion the Republican State Central Committee was "unanimous in the opinion that this issue was so vital, that the party must stand by it & if need be 'shoot all deserters.' Let ambitious Republicans beware. I do not believe the Republican organization will elect any man constable who turns his back on this fundamental principle. But 'I do not want to go to the polls with a d—n nigger' says one. They will." William A. Howard to Charles S. May, Detroit, February 20, 1868; May Papers, Burton Historical Collections, Detroit Public Library.

22. For the general topic of black suffrage in Michigan during the reconstruction era, see Willis F. Dunbar with William G. Slade, "The Black Man Gains the Vote: The Centennial of 'Impartial Suffrage' in Michigan," *Michigan History* 56 (Spring 1972):42-57. The statement about the reasons for defeat of the constitution are based on numerous manuscript references, particularly in the Blair Papers, Burton Historical Collections. Flint *Wolverine-Citizen*, April 11, 1868, has a good discussion on the defeat of the constitution. The only contemporary statement I have found supporting black suffrage on the grounds that it would help the local Republican party is a statement from Detroit in 1870 after adoption of the Fifteenth Amendment: "The colored vote is so large that it at least gives us a show and that being so different from anything heretofore, will help us." John Bagley to Henry Waldron, Detroit, August 26, 1870, Waldron Papers, Michigan State University.

23. The female college bill was defeated because legislators feared demands from existing state social institutions whose needs were unmet; Flint *Wolverine Citizen*, March 30, 1867. The Grand Rapids *Daily Eagle*, February 5, 9, March 19, 22, and 28, 1867 reported on the other measures. Marshall *Democratic Expounder*, January 17, 1867.

24. David S. Lang to Austin Blair, Marshall, January 28, 1868, Blair Papers; Lewis M. Miller, "Reminiscences of the Michigan Legislature of 1871," *Michigan Pioneer and Historical Collections* 32 (1903):422. A biographical sketch of Baldwin may be found in Fuller, *Messages of the Governors*, III:17-19.

25. Fuller, *Messages of the Governors,* III:87,140.

26. Ibid., pp. 82, 110. One newspaper acidly commented that bills providing for swamp land roads should be entitled "acts to feather the nests of a set of men who are too honest to steal money outright, and too sharp to fairly earn their bread by honest labor." Grand Rapids *Daily Eagle*, March 15, 1869.

27. October 20, 1870. A puzzling feature of this amendment is the lack of comment by the newspapers.

28. For railroad taxation see Detroit *Free Press*, April 7, 15, 1871; Marshall *Democratic Expounder*, March 2, 1871.

29. Grand Rapids *Daily Eagle*, April 6, 1869.

30. The Pontiac *Jacksonian* charged that Republicans were "cunningly endeavoring to debauch the youth" through education and that the purpose of compulsory education was to make the children Republicans; Marshall *Democratic Expounder*, April 27, 1871. In the House 51 Republicans and 17 Democrats voted for compulsory education; 11 Republicans and 6 Democrats opposed; Grand Rapids *Daily Eagle*, April 10, 1871.

31. Opposition to the Agricultural College reportedly stemmed from Detroit area residents who objected to the institutions's location in the north, and also because so much state money was deposited outside of Detroit and unavailable for loans to Detroit businessmen. Lansing *Republican*, February 25, March 18, 1869; The Battle Creek *Journal*, March 18, 1869; Madison Kuhn, *Michigan State: The First Hundred Years* (East Lansing, 1955), pp. 76-81.

32. Fuller, *Messages of the Governors*, III:72.

33. Baldwin's recommendations for social institutions may be found in his messages to the legislature; see particularly, ibid., pp. 72-81, 126-35.

34. The new state Capitol symbolized not only a more active state government but also reflected a sense of pride in a growing state. No longer would the citizens of Michigan be obliged "to apologize for the old rattle-trap that has so long been a humiliation if not a positive disgrace." Lansing *Republican*, March 23, 1871; see also Kalamazoo *Gazette*, February 17, 1871, Flint *Wolverine Citizen*, January 21, 1871.

35. Summaries of the legislative sessions of 1869 and 1871 may be found in Grand Rapids *Daily Eagle*, April 6, 1869; Flint *Wolverine Citizen*, April 15, 1871; Lansing *Republican*, April 20, 1871; Miller, "Reminiscences of the 1871 Legislature," pp. 441-47.

36. Discussion of the suffrage issue is based on Flint *Wolverine Citizen*, November 28, 1868; Battle Creek *Journal*, February 25, March 11, 1869; Grand Rapids *Daily Eagle*, March 1, 9, 1869; Lansing *Republican*, October 20, December 1, 1870, as well as the Dunbar and Slade article cited in note 22. In the 1870s Democrats in Detroit made serious efforts to secure black votes; David M. Katzman, *Before the Ghetto: Black Detroit in the Nineteenth Century* (Ann Arbor, 1972), pp. 250-55. Perhaps this is the explanation for the *Free Press's* tolerance of the Fifteenth Amendment.

37. Fuller, *Messages of the Governors*, III:219-20, 238-40, 260. An initial grant of land was made in 1873; a second grant, in 1875. Various sectional and economic issues were involved. The Republican Detroit *Post* opposed, while the Democratic Detroit *Free Press* favored the grant; the Escanaba *Tribune*, located in a town on the Chicago and Northwestern Railway, opposed the enterprise. One Upper Peninsula newspaper complained that the cost should not be borne solely by land grants; rather, the legislature should guarantee the bonds. But, warned the newspaper, if Lower Peninsula members were to defeat the measure, Upper Peninsula people "will have still greater cause to curse the political wisdom which brought about union of two sections which have no community of interest, into one government." Marquette *Mining Journal*, January 25, 1873, January 30, February 27, March 20, April 10, 1875. Detroit *Free Press*, March 18, 1875. At this time there was considerable agitation in the Upper Peninsula to join with northern Wisconsin and form a new state.

38. Fuller, *Messages of the Governors*, III:224, 267. The legislature also passed various conservation laws, particularly those limiting seasons for fishing and hunting in the 1860s and 1870s; Eugene T. Petersen, *The History of Wild Life Conservation in Michigan, 1859-1921* (Ann Arbor, 1963), especially Chapter I.

39. Fuller, *Messages of the Governors*, III:185-87, 219-20; Willis Dunbar, *All Aboard: A History of Railroads in Michigan* (Grand Rapids, 1969), pp. 250-52. From the comments of newspapers, railroad regulation does not appear to have been a partisan issue. See, for example, Detroit *Free Press*, April 15, 19, 1873 (a conservative approach), Lansing *Republican*, March 6, 1873 (favored regulation), the Democratic Kalamazoo *Gazette*, January 31, 1873 (favored regulation); Saginaw *Daily Courier*, March 15, 1873. Apparently the Granger movement did not play a significant role in Michigan politics. The first statewide organization meeting was held on April 15, 1873; at that time there were but twenty Granges organized in eight counties. Fred Trump, *The Grange in Michigan* (Grand Rapids, Michigan, 1963), p. 8.

40. Fuller, *Messages of the Governors*, III:156-57, 201, 262-64.

41. Ibid., 161-62, 205, 241, 243.

42. The Detroit House of Correction was an institution operated by the city of Detroit; even today it houses all female prisoners of the state. In 1873 the legislature authorized a state intermediate prison at Ionia, which was operative in 1877.

43. Fuller, *Messages of the Governors*, III:170-72. The problem of trying to provide meaningful employment for prisoners is illustrated by a complaint that convict labor received an average of 57¢ a day, which was much less than ordinary labor. Such wages, it was charged, constituted unfair competition. On the other hand, there were complaints that wagon-making by convicts constituted unfair competition for wagon-makers outside the prison. Saginaw *Daily Courier*, February 12, 1873; Flint *Wolverine Citizen*, February 15, 1873.

44. Fuller, *Messages of the Governors*, III:170-75. Bagley's message on prisons was "one of the most radical documents, to say the least, ever sent to the legislature." Yet it was approved by both Democratic and Republican newspapers; Marshall *Democratic Expounder*, February 20, 27, 1873; Lansing *Republican*, February 20, 1873; Flint *Wolverine Citizen*, February 15, 1873.

45. Fuller, *Messages of the Governors*, III:213, 249-50.

46. Ibid., pp. 162-64, 208, 244-47.

47. Ibid., p. 255.

48. R. C. Kedzie, "The Early History of the State Board of Health of Michigan," *Michigan Pioneer and Historical Collections* 32 (1903):361-80. In Massachusetts a similar board was justified, because "nothing is so economical as health and nothing is so wasteful as sickness"; ibid., p. 361.

49. Before the start of the 1873 season Saginaw millowners had agreed that the work day would be at least twelve hours; Saginaw *Daily Courier*, January 16, March 19, 1873; Marshall *Democratic Expounder,* May 1, 1873.

50. Manistee *Times*, January 20, 1875. Fuller, *Messages of the Governors*, III:228-30, 269-70. Most of the major newspapers of the state supported the governor's stand, though the Detroit *Free Press*, April 30, 1875, charged that taxes on liquor imposed by the legislators were too high.

51. Fuller, *Messages of the Governors*, III:165, 223, 261. The question of taxation of railroad lands (land grants to railroads to subsidize construction) was the "most important railroad question." Lansing *Republican*, March 6, May 1, 1873. By 1875 there were many proposals for reform of taxation, including railroad property, mortgages, and insurance premiums, as well as proposed changes in assessment and collection. The Lansing *Republican* cited Massachusetts, which had a special committee of three men to consider all questions about taxes and to make a report. The Lansing paper also opposed changing from a specific tax on railroads paid to the state to a direct tax based on the value of real and personal property paid to a local unit of government. Railroads, it argued, were not local, but of value to the state at large; hence, taxes should be paid to the state, rather than the political unit where the property was located. Further, railroad taxes should be based on use rather than simple value of the property. Ibid., March 23, 26, 1875.

52. The Republican platform and Bagley in a campaign speech cited the Republican record at the state level; the Democratic platform, however, concentrated on national issues. Lansing *Republican*, September 18, October 23, November 6, 1874. About 2 a.m. on the morning after the election, Bagley studied election returns at a newspaper office and said, "Well, boys, I'm beaten." But when the returns came in from the Upper Peninsula, he was elected. The UP had formerly been Democratic but in 1874 swung to the Republican column; William Livingston, *Republican Party* (2 vols., Detroit, 1908), I:282.

53. Lansing *Republican*, March 12, 1875. Anti-Chandler sentiment within the Republican party arose from his stalwart philosophy, which had alienated certain small pressure groups, such as prohibitionists, greenbackers, and Grangers. In addition, his use of patronage outraged some Republicans while disappointing others, Mary George, *Zachariah Chandler* (East Lansing, 1969), pp. 236-37.

54. Detroit *Free Press*, April 19, 1873; Lansing *Republican*, March 23, 26, April 20, 1875.

55. Lansing *Republican*, April 20, 1871, noted the lack of partisanship in the 1871 session. One newspaper summarized Bagley's 1873 message to the legislature as follows: "the governor treats the people of the State as children; and proposes to have them thoroughly cared for. They shall be well fed and well clothed. Their investments shall be jealously guarded. No one shall do their banking or their insurance save under the paternal supervision of the State. They shall not be permitted to waste their substance by any extravagance of which children should not be guilty. They must only fish and hunt when permitted." The Grand Rapids *Times*, quoted in the Kalamazoo *Gazette*, January 10, 1873. Such a criticism was rare. The Detroit *Free Press*, January 3, 1973, said legislators, were "impressed with most" of Governor Bagley's recommendations; the Democratic paper had previously praised Governor Baldwin; ibid., April 16, 1871.

56. Detroit *Free Press*, January 4, 1873; Lansing *Republican*, May 1, 1873.

57. The State Superintendent of Public Instruction argued that "Credulity and crime are in proportion to general ignorance, and the interest of the State as a Commonwealth is therefore dependent upon a thorough education of our children." Lansing *Republican*, January 30, 1873.

58. Detroit *Free Press*, January 8, 1875.

8

WISCONSIN

Shifting Strategies to Stay on Top

Richard N. Current

At the end of the Civil War the Republican or "Union" Party dominated Wisconsin politics. Republicans held the governorship and all the other state administrative posts, the three positions on the state supreme court, a large majority of the places in each house of the legislature, five of the six Congressional seats, and both of the United States Senatorships. For eight years the party continued to keep itself in power, though with a fluctuating share of the total vote. Then, in 1873, the Republicans faltered, losing the control of the state government that they had held since 1857. After that one loss, however, they promptly resumed their sway.

The Republicans' almost unbroken record of success during the reconstruction years was by no means automatic. It depended on the care with which the leaders maximized the party's strengths and minimized its weaknesses. Its greatest strengths were its appeals to patriotism (or sectionalism), idealism, and materialism. The leaders could identify the party with noble causes, with the war aims of union and freedom, and so long as their fellow partisans controlled the Presidency and Congress they could also promise the more solid benefits of the federal patronage and the federal pork barrel. To some extent, the party's weaknesses derived from its very strengths. Antislavery idealism, insofar as it carried over to the postwar movement for Negro rights, ran against the much stronger force of racism. The reform spirit, which animated the antislavery drive, also gave rise to demands for sumptuary laws against drinking and Sabbath-breaking, laws that would turn away foreign-born voters, who looked upon such legislation as a product of continuing nativism. Moreover, the reforming impulse directed itself against monoplies, against corporations in general and railroads in particular, and as a result of the Republicans' effectiveness in promoting federal aid to private enterprise,

144

especially through the financing of "internal improvements," the party exposed itself to charges of favoritism toward big business.

The leaders had to deal carefully, then, with the shifting cross currents of sectionalism, idealism, materialism, racism, nativism, and antimonopolism. Only by so doing could the politicians hold the party together and keep it on top. Holding it together required some effort, since the party was and had been from the beginning a congeries of rather disparate elements. It had originated in 1854—the first in any state to revive the name "Republican"—as a coalition consisting mainly of Whigs, but containing also Free-Soilers and other dissident Democrats. As it grew it incorporated all except a few of the Know-Nothings, and at the same time, by disavowing Know-Nothing aims and muting temperance and Sabbatarian cries, it managed to attract a number of immigrants, at least among some of the Protestant groups. Before the war it overcame centrifugal tendencies by emphasizing the one principle that all its various followers held in common, the principle of free soil, or opposition to the extension of slavery into the territories. During the war the party drew the support of additional Democrats, some as converts, others as fellow travelers, and it made use of a centripetal force even stronger than free-soilism, the force of a shared determination to win the war. Once the war had been won and slavery had been abolished, however, the leaders, if they were to remain in power, needed to find new issues that would unite the party, while continuing to avoid those that might divide it.

One possibility was to keep the war memories alive and thus maintain the identification of the Republican Party with patriotism and the opposition with treason. This could be done, in part, by making an issue of the veterans, backing them in peace as in war, and thus cultivating their support along with the support of their relatives and friends and of self-consciously loyal citizens in general.

Lucius Fairchild, the first three-term governor of Wisconsin (1866-72), early saw the possibility. Himself a veteran, one who had lost an arm at Gettysburg, Fairchild campaigned in 1865 as the Soldier's Friend. He got endorsements from his old comrades and promised generous benefits, including preference in political appointments, to all Wisconsin soldiers, and especially to the disabled. In his first inaugural the governor, his empty sleeve conspicuous, spoke of the nobility of sacrifice in the nation's cause. He referred to secession as treason and called for the hanging of Jefferson Davis as a traitor. In 1866 the Grand Army of the Republic's Madison department, a veterans' organization that Fairchild had helped to form, demanded that all leaders of the late Confederacy be condignly punished and that they be completely debarred from politics.

Once a colonel, now governor, Fairchild continued to view himself as still, at least potentially, a commander of troops against the traitorous foe. Again and again he referred to the veterans' "fears of another civil war" in case of a Democratic victory. "I confess to some little feeling of this kind," he wrote confidentially, in 1866, "and to a strong wish to prepare, so far as I am able as the governor of this state, to meet all enemies on their own terms." Publicly he insisted that only the maintenance of the Republicans in power would prevent a renewal of rebellion. Year after year he and his followers continued to identify the Republican Party with the Union army, as they did at an 1866 rally in Madison, where youthful party workers flaunted banners reading "We vote as we fought, against traitors," and "Boys in Blue, always true." As late as 1887 Fairchild was still waving the bloody shirt, and more dramatically than ever. That year, as commander in chief of the G. A. R., he delivered his famous "three palsies" speech, calling upon God to palsy the hand, brain, and tongue of President Grover Cleveland for having ordered the return of captured battle flags to various Southern states.[1]

If most of the men who had served the Union in war could be counted upon to support the Republican Party in peace, most of those who had evaded service could be expected to assist the Democrats. So, while encouraging the veterans to vote, the Republicans could further help themselves by taking the ballot away from men who, when drafted, had failed to report or who, after induction, had deserted. This would be as constitutional as it would be just, the state attorney general advised the legislature in 1866, confirming the opinion his predecessor had given the previous year. Accordingly, laws of 1866 and 1867 disfranchised draft-dodgers and deserters, provided for the publication of a list of their names, and required the posting of three copies of the list at every polling place. A "blue pamphlet" containing some 12,000 names was printed. Inclusion of a man's name was to be taken as *prima facie* evidence of his guilt and hence of his ineligibility to vote. Democrats protested that the laws violated the ancient Anglo-Saxon principle of no punishment without prior conviction, and the critics were by no means appeased when, in 1868, an amendment made it possible for a listed man to get his name removed by proving his innocence to the satisfaction of the attorney general. Even before the official pamphlet had been published, Governor Fairchild was already preparing partial lists to be used against Democrats in the Congressional elections of 1866. For a few years the pamphlet was of some value to the Republicans. Despite the zeal of Fairchild and certain of his fellow partisans, however, the disfranchising laws soon became dead letters.[2]

For Republicans, the question of taking the vote away from deserters was much less controversial than the question of giving it to blacks, whatever their war records. At the end of the war the issue of suffrage for Wisconsin Negroes was touchy indeed, despite their infinitesimal number and their willing service in the Union cause.

1. Notes to this chapter are to be found on pp. 164-166.

The wartime labor shortage had attracted additional Negroes to the state, and as early as 1862 a state senator introduced a bill to prohibit their in-migration. The next year, after President Lincoln, with his Emancipation Proclamation, had supposedly loosed the slaves upon the whole country, alarmed Wisconsinites showered the legislature with petitions for an exclusion act. During the 1860s the state's black population almost doubled, growing from 1,171 to 2,113. But this meant an increase to only about two-tenths of one percent of the whole population, which at the same time was rising from 775,881 to 1,054,670.

All together, 361 "colored troops" were credited to Wisconsin, though (according to the federal census superintendent in 1863) the total of "free colored males between the ages of 18 and 45" in the state was only 292. Thus Wisconsin appears to have provided a considerably larger number of black soldiers than its entire black male population of military age. The reason for the discrepancy is that many of the Negroes credited to the state were actu-ally recruited elsewhere. Still, there could be no question that Wisconsin's blacks had done their part. Understandably, they thought this entitled them to the ballot. "The record of the last four years is still before us," a conven-tion of the "colored citizens" of Wisconsin resolved on October 9, 1865; "white men and colored have fought side by side . . . our deeds upon the battle fields have been sealed in blood, and render us worthy of all the privileges that we ask of the voters."[3]

The next month the voters could decide on Negro suffrage in a referendum—the third such referendum to be held in accordance with the constitution of 1848. The wording of the constitutional provision was criti-cal, for upon the interpretation of the words was to depend the ultimate disposition of the matter. These were the words: "The legislature shall at any time have the power to admit colored persons to the right of suffrage but no such act of the legislature shall become law until the same shall have been submitted to the electors at the next general election succeeding the passage of the laws and shall have received in its favor *a majority of all the votes cast at such election*." In the 1849 election a suffrage bill was favored by 5,265 ballots and opposed by only 4,075, but a total of more than 31,000 votes were polled in the election itself. Fewer than a third of the voters had bothered to express themselves on the bill. Though it had received more affirmative than negative votes, it had not received in its favor a majority of all the votes cast at the election, and even its proponents therefore considered it as lost. In 1857 another suffrage bill was voted down by 40,915 to 23,074. Then, in 1865, the legislature passed a third such bill in response to a petition from 102 blacks.[4]

At their state convention that September, in Madison, the Republicans faced the question whether to endorse the suffrage proposal and make it a party issue in the fall election. A leading party organ, the *Wisconsin State Journal* of Madison, was urging the adoption of a platform of principles around which the "genuine earnest Union men" could rally, was reporting that a large majority approved the suffrage bill, and was citing in its favor the highest party authority, that of President Andrew Johnson, who had said "each state should be left to regulate the question of suffrage for itself." Yet, in fact, Johnson was unwilling for Wisconsin or other Northern states to be left to regulate the question in favor of the blacks. His agent in Wisconsin was Senator James R. Doolittle, a former Democrat (he had switched in 1856), the Senate's foremost wartime advocate of the "colonization" abroad of freed slaves, and an unctuous but effective orator. "All attempts to make the new issue of Negro suffrage a plank in the platform of the party," Doolittle told Fairchild, "is simply suicide." Presiding at the Madison convention, Doolittle managed to exclude from the platform any reference to Negro suffrage in Wisconsin.

Some of the Republicans, the former antislavery radicals, now the "friends of equal rights," denounced the "pernicious influence" of Doolittle and threatened to break away from the "Union" party. They called a second convention, to meet in Janesville and represent the "liberty-loving" people of the state. In Janesville the radicals found themselves a decided minority, however, and they concluded their rump session by endorsing the candidates who had been nominated in Madison.[5]

During the 1865 campaign the Democrats, who had an explicit antisuffrage plank in their platform, called upon Fairchild to debate the question with their gubernatorial candidate. Some of the Republican newspapers frankly advocated equal voting rights, and so did the radical politicians, prominent among them Sherman Booth and Byron Paine, the one the hero of the Joshua Glover slave rescue of 1854 and the other the attorney who had defended Booth and persuaded the state supreme court to defy federal authority and declare the fugitive-slave act of 1850 unconstitutional. But Fairchild hid behind his party's noncommittal platform and refused to speak out. His advisers cautioned him that Negro suffrage was distasteful to many party members and particularly to war veterans. "Nothing would please the copperheads more than to induce or compel you in some way to define your position," one of his friends counseled; ". . . the 'nigger' is the only card they have left." By his silence, however, Fairchild risked losing the support of radical voters. So, late in the campaign, he wrote letters to Booth and other radical politicians telling them he personally favored Negro suffrage and wished them to quote him whenever they met with like-minded Republicans.[6]

When the returns were in, the strategy of Fairchild seemed to have worked. He won by 10,000 votes and Negro suffrage lost by 9,000. The suffrage bill did much better in the Republican than in the Democratic counties, but nowhere did it do so well as Fairchild himself. Of the 38 counties he carried, only 24 had a majority for the bill. Of the remaining 19 counties, which his opponent carried, not one gave a majority for it. His fears regarding the veterans' antipathy to it appear to have been justified, if the separately counted soldier vote is taken as an indicator. By November 1865, only about 1,500 Wisconsin soldiers were still voting in the field. They went more than three to one (1,169 to 330) against the bill, while going for Fairchild in about the same proportion. The "suffrage question, if made an issue, would have carried us under," Doolittle assured him after the election.[7]

Despite the suffrage proposition's defeat, the radical Republicans were soon to have their way, and blacks were to be voting at the next election in Wisconsin. At the recent election a Milwaukeean named Ezekiel Gillespie had gone to the polls, along with Sherman Booth, and had offered his ballot even though he was unregistered, the Board of Registry having turned him away as a person of "mixed African blood." The election inspectors refused his ballot. Gillespie, with the aid of his lawyer, Byron Paine, then sued the inspectors, offered a demurrer before the county court, and promptly moved the case on to the state supreme court.

In Gillespie v. Palmer et al. (1866) Paine undertook to prove that Gillespie already had the right to vote in 1865 because the Negro suffrage measure had actually been approved at the 1849 election, in the very first referendum under the state constitution. The constitutional phrase "a majority of the votes cast at such election," Paine argued, must mean simply a majority of the votes cast on the specific issue. Otherwise, the measure could never be passed—even if all the voters should mark their ballots in its favor. These ballots could not add up to a "majority of all votes cast" at the election, for "all votes" would be the sum of those cast for the proposition, plus those cast on both sides for governor, plus those for lieutenant-governor, and so on. Surely, the framers of the constitution had not intended any such thing, nor had they meant to require more votes for passing a suffrage bill than for ratifying a suffrage amendment, which would require approval by merely "a majority of the voters voting thereon."

The three judges, all Republicans, accepted Paine's reasoning, literal and strained though much of it was. They ruled that despite the consensus to the contrary, which had prevailed for nearly seventeen years, Negroes had had the right to vote in Wisconsin since 1849, when a majority of voters casting ballots on the proposition—but only one-sixth of those voting in the election—had assented to a suffrage bill.[8]

The court's decision created "quite a commotion" in Milwaukee. Some Democrats threatened that any Negro attempting to vote in the upcoming local election would be mobbed. Yet the blacks were not intimidated, and though there was the "rare sight of negroes voting," the election on April 3, 1866 was one of the quietest the city had ever experienced. "Not a single fight occurred at any of the polls." Some of the black voters were immediately summoned, for the first time, for jury duty. In the Madison election also the Negro turnout was large. There was even a black candidate for mayor, William H. Noland, and he received 306 votes to 691 for his opponent. But Noland, a leader of the Madison black community, got no votes from his fellow blacks. All his votes came from Democrats who had announced his candidacy against his will and as a joke. In a dignified election-day statement he declared he was a "Union man" (that is, a Republican) and was himself voting the "straight Union ticket." "If any Democrat wishes to compliment me let him go and do likewise." In both Madison and Milwaukee nearly all the Negroes apparently voted straight Republican, except in some Milwaukee wards where Republicans put up no slates.

For Wisconsin Republicans, the Negro vote proved an asset only in marginal instances. It made the difference between defeat and victory, for example, in one of the closely contested Madison wards in 1866. But the Negro vote was too small to affect the outcome of most elections. Calculating the consequences of the possible defection of Johnson adherents, Republican politicians concluded, in May 1866, that the loss would be "more than balanced by the enfranchised colored vote." This conclusion depended, however, more on the smallness of the anticipated loss than on the largeness of the anticipated gain. After all, there were only a few hundred black adult males in the state.[9]

On balance, Negro suffrage at home was more a liability than an asset to Wisconsin Republicans. Their black support confirmed the charge of "niggerism" and helped the Democrats turn the widespread negrophobia to their own account. Democratic newspapers never tired of recalling supposed Negro "outrages" and describing Republican candidates as Negro lovers. The *Oshkosh Times* implied that Congressman Philetus Sawyer, for one, would stoop to almost anything for the "vote of a nigger" and accused him of neglecting whites to patronize blacks. If the party division had been closer, if the Republicans had been weaker, the added burden of race prejudice might have been too much for the party to bear.[10]

While bearing that burden, the party leaders also had to deal with the potentially disruptive issue of the postwar reconstruction of the South. In Wisconsin, as in other states, the party had adopted the name "Union" so as to encourage the affiliation of Democrats who backed the war effort. At the national convention of 1864 the Republicans had sealed the coalition by choosing the War Democrat Johnson as Lincoln's running mate. After Lincoln's assassination and Johnson's accession, the coalition could remain intact only so long as the Democrat in the White House could keep the loyalty of the Republicans in Congress and throughout the country.

At the outset Johnson seemed to be in a position to exert an especially strong hold on the Union Party in Wisconsin. His assistant postmaster general—whom he was to elevate to the head of the Post Office Department in July 1866—was Alexander W. Randall, a two-term governor of the state. Randall's friend Elisha W. Keyes was postmaster as well as mayor of Madison. Through his friendship with Randall he had a large share in the disposal of jobs in the nearly one thousand Wisconsin post offices. Associated with Keyes was Horace Rublee, chairman of the Republican (Union) state committee and co-owner and co-editor of the *Wisconsin State Journal*, a leading party organ. Together, Keyes and Rublee ran the Madison Regency, the most powerful Republican machine in the state. When Johnson took over, Keyes urged the people to "rally around" the new President as he tried to reunite the nation.

Johnson soon had on his side not only the Republican bosses of Wisconsin but also the state's senior Senator, the former Democrat James R. Doolittle. At the time of Lincoln's death Doolittle had been cooperating with Lincoln in his effort to reconstruct and readmit Louisiana on fairly quick and easy terms. Doolittle differed with his Senate colleague from Wisconsin, Timothy O. Howe, a former Whig, who was dissatisfied with Lincoln's policy and wished Lincoln "w'd tell the rebels" that the President could "only grant pardons" and that Congress alone could admit states. At first Doolittle feared that Johnson, as President, would deal too harshly with the defeated Southerners, but Doolittle soon convinced himself that Johnson's policy would be essentially the same as Lincoln's. Before long he felt that he and Johnson, along with Senator Preston King of New York, constituted a "trio whose hearts and heads" sympathized "more closely and more deeply than any other trio in America" (and King was shortly to commit suicide, leaving Doolittle and Johnson as twin spirits).[11]

The Wisconsin party's first big postwar test of unity and of support for the Johnson administration occurred at the September 1865 state convention. As chairman of the platform committee, Doolittle was ready with a set of resolutions applauding Johnson's program for speedily restoring the Southern states. He got his resolutions adopted after seeing the delegates turn down, by an overwhelming voice vote, an amendment calling for Negro suffrage in the South—a plank he thought would have driven "thousands of War Democrats" out of the party. To Johnson he boasted of his success, and the *Wisconsin State Journal* gave its approval to his work, but other party organs dissented, as did Senator Howe, and some of the radicals condemned Doolittle as a rebel sympathizer. Thus, despite the consensus he had maneuvered, the party already was developing strains.

After the 1865 election, Johnson's assistant postmaster general, Randall, predicted to a Wisconsin correspondent: "There is coming a 'big row' shortly which will and is clearing out the whole radical portion of our party and probably leading the Democratic element of the party to seek new alliances." A "big row" was indeed on the way, and some former Democrats were to desert the Wisconsin organization, but the radicals were by no means to be cleared out. The party itself was to be radicalized. Randall and the rest of Johnson's friends, not his opponents, would have to look for new alliances.[12]

When, during the winter of 1865-66, Johnson and the Congressional Republicans quarreled over reconstruction policy, only two members of the Wisconsin delegation took the side of the President. These two were Senator Doolittle and Congressman Charles W. Eldredge, the lone Democrat from the state. Senator Howe and the other five Congressmen supported the Republican program to postpone the seating of Senators and Representatives from the South, to extend the life and powers of the Freedmen's Bureau, and to confer civil rights upon Southern blacks.

At first, the Madison Regency tried to stay out of the fight. Keyes kept still and occupied himself with his duties as mayor of Madison. Rublee's *Wisconsin State Journal*, without taking a stand, gave equal space to the opposing speeches of Doolittle and Howe. But neutrality was no longer possible for Wisconsin Republicans after Johnson vetoed the Freedmen's Bureau bill and then the civil rights bill, thus ending all hopes for a compromise. The Republicans in the legislature, thoroughly aroused, telegraphed instructions to the state's Senators in Washington to vote for overriding the second veto. When Doolittle disregarded the instructions, the legislature formally requested him to resign. Now even the Madison Regency split. Keyes, after failing to "squelch" or even "tone down" the resignation demand, assured Doolittle he and the country were behind him. Keyes called a "Union meeting" and there spoke out in favor of Johnson's policy. Rublee, however, warned Doolittle that the great majority of Wisconsin Republicans were deeply alarmed by the President's course. The *Wisconsin State Journal* criticized the vetoes and endorsed Howe's position.[13]

Wisconsin politicians brought about something of a party realignment as they prepared for a trial of strength between Johnson's adherents and his opponents in the campaign of 1866. As two of his top lieutenants, Senator Doolittle and Postmaster-General Randall played leading roles in the National Union movement, through which its sponsors intended to bring together a great middle grouping of Republican and Democratic voters and thus elect to Congress a majority favorable to the President. But Randall and Doolittle failed to rouse much Republican support for the movement even in their home state. Keyes himself lay low for the time being. Only one really prominent Wisconsin Republican cooperated with the two Johnson leaders. That was Alexander Mitchell, banker, railroad magnate, and Milwaukee's richest man. "It requires no sacrifice from Democrats to support Johnson," another Republican for Johnson heard from a man in Appleton; "but, with Republicans, they must brace against the bulwark of previous political associations." Indeed, Democrats flocked to the President's standard with an enthusiasm that, to Doolittle, was gratifying and yet embarrassing, especially when he was flattered by Marcus M. Pomeroy, editor of the LaCrosse *Union and Democrat* and lately the most viciously anti-Lincoln Copperhead in the state, if not in the entire country. For a time, there were two parties claiming the magic name of "Union"—the National Union and the Republican Union. Soon the former became practically indistinguishable from the regular Democratic organization, and the latter reconstituted and retitled itself as simply the good old Republican Party.

During the 1866 campaign, however, party lines and party loyalties remained uncertain and confusing enough that Randall and Doolittle found it hard to make effective use of presidential patronage. Randall was quoted as saying that "only those sustaining the President should eat his bread and butter"—which led Johnson's foes to dub his followers the Bread and Butter party. The problem was to know who could be depended upon to sustain the President. Alexander Mitchell advised Doolittle that their side would "gain little strength by removing A and appointing B" unless B should actually prove a better Johnson man. "I do not see that the new appointees . . . are likely to be any better administration men than the old—if as good." Another difficulty lay in the jealousy between Republican and Democratic friends of the President. Democratic leaders feared that Doolittle and Randall, "because of old party associations," were "more likely to bestow the patronage at their disposal" upon Republicans than upon Democrats. Nevertheless, the patronage dispensers made a number of changes in Wisconsin. What effect these had, other than to exacerbate the anti-Johnson feeling of many Republicans, it would be hard to say.

The bitterness of the campaign solidified the Republican Party, bringing tightly together all its factions except the tiny group of die-hard Johnsonites. The proposed Fourteenth Amendment became a test not only of Republicanism but also of patriotism, of true Unionism. According to the *Milwaukee Sentinel* (which had lost its government printing contract because of its anti-Johnson stand) the "Rebels" were giving no sign that they had ceased to be "deadly enemies of the Union." They were refusing to ratify the amendment and they were adopting black codes which, for "atrocity," found "no equal in the annals of Russian serfdom." Condoning and encouraging the recalcitrant Southerners were Johnson and Doolittle. From one voter, who signed himself "Four-Fifths of Wisconsin," Doolittle received this bit of advice: ". . . you have turned traitor to your State and gone over to Johnson and the Rebels. . . you should come home and put a *ball* through your rotten head."

Such bitterness made for a sizable Republican turnout on election day. As the 1866 returns showed, the party had gained more from conversions than it had lost from defections. The five Republican Congressmen were reelected, along with the one Democrat, and the Republican majority in the state legislature was increased. Addressing the legislature early in 1867, Governor Fairchild took the result as a mandate for ratification of the Fourteenth Amendment: ". . . most of you are here today because your constituents knew that you deemed the amendment just and necessary." Both houses promptly ratified it.[14]

Wisconsin Republicans maintained their unity in supporting the passage of the Reconstruction Acts of 1867, the impeachment of Johnson, the presidential candidacy of Ulysses S. Grant, and the ratification of the Fifteenth Amendment. They ceased to consider Johnson's friend Doolittle even nominally a party member, and they did not count him among the seven Republican senators who broke ranks at the impeachment trial, though they blamed him (along with each of the seven) for the one not-guilty vote that proved decisive in bringing about the acquittal. When his Senatorial term ended, in 1869, they replaced him with Matthew H. Carpenter, a postwar convert from the Democratic faith, who had confirmed his Republicanism with his oratorical attacks on Doolittle during the 1866 campaign. Keyes having come out, after a two-year silence, for Grant and then for Carpenter, the new Senator used his influence with the new President to get him reappointed as Madison postmaster. Soon Keyes became the state Republican boss. With such a skillful organizer in command, with Carpenter and Howe cooperating in the Senate, with a harmonious delegation in the House, and with a sympathetic and obliging occupant of the presidency, the Wisconsin party seemed to be a highly efficient and fairly cohesive organization, despite the continued tension of personal rivalries within it.[15]

Nevertheless, while doing handsomely for Grant in the presidential election of 1868, the Republicans did much less well for their gubernatorial and legislative candidates in the state elections of 1867 and 1869. The party's majorities in the legislature shrank to ten in the assembly and only one in the senate. From the returns some of the Republican leaders drew the lesson that the bloody shirt and radical reconstruction no longer were adequate as campaign appeals. "Reconstruction is gone," Governor Fairchild opined. He thought the party ought to put less emphasis on abstract principles and more emphasis on material interests. "A material program founded on proposed advantages to the people," he believed, would be "ten times as strong as any other, and would set all other parties aside and make a new party for itself if necessary."

There was a material program that had long been immensely popular in Wisconsin, so popular that none of the state's politicians had ever dared oppose it, though they might disagree as to how and where it ought to be applied. That was the old Whig program of federal aid for internal improvements. As successors of the Whigs, the Republicans had endorsed such aid in their national platforms. Hence in Wisconsin the Republicans had a more persuasive claim than the Democrats to being true devotees of the policy. Much along that line remained to be done for the state after the war. There were harbors to be dredged and deepened at all the lake ports. There were canals to be dug and, most important, the ambitious Fox-Wisconsin waterway, connecting Lake Michigan and the Mississippi River, to be completed. Though the southern part of the state was already criss-crossed by rail lines, there were still railroads to be built in the north. Wisconsinites were practically unanimous in believing they must have better and cheaper transportation by land and water, if they were to market profitably their two most valuable products—wheat and lumber—and if they were to develop the state's economy as a whole. Few doubted that they must have federal assistance if they were to achieve these aims.

Wisconsin Republicans used the state's need for internal improvements to justify their demands for a radical reconstruction of the South. If the Southern states should be restored quickly and with little change, Senator Howe warned in 1866, the Southern representatives could join with northern Democrats to block the kind of economic legislation that the Wisconsinites desired. The *Wisconsin State Journal* presented figures to show that, under Johnson's plan of restoration, the South would offset the Northwest in Congressional power. As a matter of fact, the Northwest often ran into conflict with the Northeast, whose representatives generally had much less enthusiasm for improvement expenditures than for tariff protection. Whatever their differences on economic policy, however, the northwestern and northeastern Republicans had a common interest in opposing the early readmission of Southern Democrats, who could be expected to resist the appropriations and the tariffs alike.

From 1865 on, Wisconsin's Republican Congressmen kept busy introducing and pressing requests for surveys, land grants, and construction money in furtherance of plans for building railroads and canals and improving rivers and harbors. In the annual pork barrel, the river and harbor appropriation bill, the Wisconsin delegates usually got most of what they wanted, in exchange for their support of tariff measures. In the 1868 bill, however, they received only enough for the repair and maintenance of works already under way, the Northeastern Republicans taking the position that extravagance would be politically unwise in an election year. The Wisconsin Democrats then tried to claim for themselves the improvements cause. They contended that, once their party was in power in Washington, Congress would spend less on reconstructing the South and more on improving the North. They made the most of the fact that their presidential candidate, Horatio Seymour, was a director of the Green Bay and Mississippi Canal Company, the company that had charge of the Fox-Wisconsin waterway. Seymour's election, they said, would mean a President who would take a personal interest in the development of the state.[16]

All along, Governor Fairchild had advocated internal improvements in addition to veteran benefits. In 1869, when he was seeking a third term without the backing of the state machine, he made improvements the paramount issue and himself their foremost champion. He hoped to attract the support of railroad promoters, pine land speculators, and others in northwestern Wisconsin by keeping alive the St. Croix land grant, which was intended for the construction of a line from the Mississippi River to Lake Superior, and which was about to expire. At the same time he expected to win over the farmers along the Fox-Wisconsin route by providing a new stimulus to that project. "Give'em *hell* on *Improvements*, and you're all right in this section," a well-wisher advised him. He met with the governors of Iowa and Minnesota to arrange for bringing their combined pressure upon Congress, obtained a promise of $5,000 from his own legislature to pay for lobbying, visited Washington to use his persuasive powers on Congressmen, addressed a Portage gathering of enthusiasts from Wisconsin and neighboring states, and indeed talked about improvements at every opportunity. That year Wisconsin again got a fairly generous share of the river and harbor appropriations, and Fairchild secured his reelection without the assistance of Boss Keyes.[17]

By 1870 the advocates of a Fox-Wisconsin canal were convinced it would never be completed unless the federal government not only provided much more money but also assumed responsibility for the project. The twofold task of securing federal funds and arranging for a government purchase fell mainly upon Congressman Philetus Sawyer, of Oshkosh. His fellow townsmen long had dreamed of converting Oshkosh into a great inland seaport through the completion of the canal, and he himself had worked hard to get appropriations for that and for other Wisconsin improvements ever since going to Congress in 1865. As an influential member of the House committee on commerce, Sawyer took personal charge of the 1870 river and harbor bill, and he also helped in the passage of a measure authorizing the government to buy the Fox-Wisconsin works and rights from the Green Bay and Mississippi Canal Company. Oshkosh Democrats asserted that, as a friend of the Chicago and North Western Railroad, Sawyer secretly aimed to thwart the canal enterprise and, in the purchase bill, had consented to terms he knew the company would reject. Late in the campaign, by prearrangement, the company itself refuted the Democrats by announcing its acceptance of the government's terms. On election day the voters returned Sawyer to Congress with his largest majority yet.

"I am as usual getting up the River & Harbor bill, and that dont damage our prospects any," Sawyer wrote to Fairchild in 1872. So long as Sawyer remained in the House of Representatives, until 1875, he continued to see that his state and district got an undue share of federal largess. To what extent this contributed to Wisconsin's economic growth, it is hard to say. Much of the government's money seemed simply to disappear in the shifting sands of the rivers to be "improved," and the dream of a great ship canal was never to be realized. There can be no doubt, however, that the expenditures contributed mightily to the success of Wisconsin's Republican Party.[18]

By 1872 the party had recovered most of its former strength. It had made gains in 1870 and again in 1871, increasing its majorities in both houses of the legislature and bringing to the governorship another Republican, the wealthy businessman and former congressman Cadwallader C. Washburn, who won the office over Doolittle, by 1871 an out-and-out Democrat once more. The Wisconsin Democracy, despite its acquisition of Doolittle and Mitchell and other one-time Johnson Republican leaders, seemingly remained an almost hopeless minority party. As a contemporary observed, it was "like an ox in a blizzard turning his tail to the storm"; it "kept up its organization, fought on the defensive as well as it could, and faced the inevitable," that is, defeat. Yet it possessed one tremendous potential advantage, one that could transform defeat into victory if the circumstances were right. In the past the Democratic Party had been the favorite with most of the immigrants. It now needed only to regain its previous share of the ethnic vote.[19]

To both parties in Wisconsin, this vote was crucial. Wisconsin had, proportionally, the largest foreign-born population of any state east of the Mississippi. In comparison with other states it contained an especially high proportion of Germans (including Austrians and German-speaking Poles and Swiss), Scandinavians (mostly Norwegians), Hollanders, and Belgians; it also contained considerable numbers of Irish, British (English, Welsh, Scottish), and British Americans (both English-speaking and French-speaking). From the beginning the Roman Catholics—German, Irish, Dutch, Belgian, French Canadian—remained with few exceptions faithful to the Democratic Party. By 1860, however, the Republican Party had attracted most of the British and the Norwegians and some of the Protestant Germans. To keep its supremacy after the war, the party had to maintain if not increase its proportion of the foreign vote.[20]

In 1866 the Republicans tried to curry favor with the Irish by cheering them on in the Fenian movement. The Fenians claimed more than six thousand Wisconsin members, who contributed money and men for a proposed invasion of Canada. President Johnson, enforcing the neutrality laws, sent troops to stop the invasion and arrest its leaders. Wisconsin Republicans denounced Johnson for his interference, and his friends ridiculed his critics for their pretended "love for the Irish." To show the Republicans' insincerity, the Democratic *Appleton Crescent* raised the pointed question: "Why did not the Howe-Sawyerites repeal the damnable *Neutrality Laws* before they adjourned?" Apparently the Republicans beguiled few Irishmen for very long. Irish precincts, such as the townships of Erin in Washington County and Erin Prairie in St. Croix County, continued to give the Republicans at most 8 or 10 votes out of 200 or more.[21]

To the extent that they were associated with Negro suffrage in Wisconsin and radical reconstruction in the South, the Republicans repelled rather than attracted Catholic immigrants, Germans in particular. The most overwhelming majorities against the 1865 suffrage proposal came from the heavily German counties north and northwest of Milwaukee, while the largest majorities in its favor came from southeastern counties with the highest proportion of settlers with a New York or New England background. The semiofficial organ of the Wisconsin hierarchy, the German-language Milwaukee *Seebote*, continually deplored the Congressional program of reconstruction. The head of a Milwaukee seminary for priests, writing to his superiors in Munich, said the Republican Congressmen were "perhaps the most depraved" in the country's history, were fit to be "ashamed of their constant attacks on President Johnson," and were proceeding to "torment the South in an unnatural manner." On the other hand, native Protestant spokesmen, such as the Presbyterian and Congregational ministers, approved of granting civil rights to freedmen and called racial equality an expression of "universal truth."[22]

While antagonizing German Catholics, the Republicans could continue to hold the support of many German Protestants—freethinkers, evangelicals, and some Lutherans—so long as the party refrained from taking up the cause of sabbatarianism or temperance. Most of the German immigrants, whatever their religion, continued to enjoy and to insist upon their traditional "German Sunday" with its after-church drinking, dancing, and general *Gemuetlichkeit*. But pious sectarians of old American stock viewed such merry-making as a profanation of the Sabbath. The same Puritan ethic that prescribed emancipation and equal rights prescribed also temperance and a quiet Sunday—to be enforced by the government if necessary. During the war and immediately after it, the puritanical reformers concentrated their attention on saving the Union and freeing and elevating the slaves. For the time being, the state's strict liquor-control act, repealed in the early 1850s, was not revived. The prewar Sunday-closing law remained on the books but went unenforced.[23]

Before long, however, voices of moral reform began to be heard again. When the Wisconsin Conference of the Methodist Church met in Beaver Dam, in October 1867, the delegates adopted a "strong report" on the condition of the country. They rejoiced that "slavery as a system was no more, and reconstruction was progressing," one of the delegates later recalled. "But another gigantic evil began to loom in the moral heavens." A "large class of our foreign-born population," mostly Germans, were "turning the Christian Sabbath into a holiday for all kinds of sports and wickedness." A few years later the Bishop of the Wisconsin Episcopal Church expressed his alarm. He wrote an article describing the German Sunday as a custom that in the homeland was harmless enough, but in this country would degenerate into "immorality and vice." Meanwhile the temperance societies became busier and busier. At first the Good Templars stressed education rather than legislation, but in 1871 they began to petition for a strengthening of the liquor laws.

Risky though the drink issue was, the Republicans eventually took it up. In 1872 Governor Washburn recommended that the legislature consider the subject of liquor-control, and in response a Rock County representative, Alexander Graham, introduced a thoroughgoing bill. This would require a $2,000 bond from liquor licensees, would make them liable for damages caused directly or indirectly by the intoxication of customers, and would impose heavy penalties on those convicted of drunkenness. When the legislature passed and the governor signed the Graham Law, Germans understandably blamed the Republican Party. German leaders, among them the brewers Valentine Blatz and Joseph Schlitz, formed the Wisconsin Association for the Protection of Personal Liberty, accused the Republicans of having converted Wisconsin into a police state, and called upon liberty-loving citizens to vote for candidates pledging to repeal the liquor act.[24]

The party loyalty of German Republicans, already strained by the Graham Law, was further weakened as a result of the party split that developed from the Liberal Republican opposition to President Grant. Previously, in 1870, Wisconsin party leaders had turned the Franco-Prussian War to their own advantage; they had taken care that German voters should be "led to see that in the Franco-German War the Republicans have stood by the Germans & Fatherland while the Democrats have gone almost body & soul for the French." Now, in 1872, the anti-Grant Republicans were trying to deflect the German vote to the Liberal cause by showing that the Grant administration had, in fact, helped the French and hurt the Prussians. In the Senate, Carl Schurz of Missouri joined Charles Sumner of Massachusetts in charging that the administration, in a flagrant breach of neutrality, had sold government arms to E. Remington and Sons for resale to France. Schurz, formerly a Wisconsinite, still had a following among Wisconsin Germans. Senator Carpenter did his best to refute the charge. As chairman of an investigating committee, he issued what Sumner called a "whitewashing report."[25]

In Wisconsin the Liberal Republican movement was largely a Teutonic phenomenon. Milwaukee Germans organized (March 19, 1872) the first Liberal Republican club in the state. Germans rallied to the cause in such numbers that some leaders were a little embarrassed, and one spokesman made a point of denying that it was essentially a German affair. The most influential German-language paper of the Republicans, the Milwaukee *Herold*, switched from the regular party to the Liberal faction. To counter the Liberal appeal, the Grant Republicans subsidized a previously neutral German-language paper in Milwaukee and another in Madison, and they nominated German candidates for Congress in the two districts (out of the new total of eight) where the Democrats presented the greatest threat..

In the 1872 election the Liberal Republicans and the Democrats faced one serious handicap. Their presidential candidate, Horace Greeley, had a long record as a radical Republican and a moral reformer. Personally, he was a teetotaler, a contemptible "water-bibber," as Wisconsin Germans saw him. He had little charm for either disaffected Republicans or regular Democrats—like the one in Dane County who found it hard to "digest the Greeley dose, which with all its sugar coating" was "very nauseous" to him. On election day thousands of apathetic Liberals and Democrats stayed at home. Grant carried the state, though with a smaller majority than in 1868. Six of the eight

Republicans running for Congress were victorious, as were a majority of those running for the state legislature. The party had staved off the disaster that had threatened as a consequence of the liquor law and the German defections.[26]

But temperance remained an explosive issue, and the Republicans did nothing to defuse it. In the 1873 legislature they tightened instead of relaxing or repealing the Graham Law. As if this were not enough, the acting mayor of Madison began to enforce the old law against selling or giving away liquor on Sundays. To protest the "abridgment of their natural freedom," antitemperance leaders called a convention in Milwaukee, to which they invited all liberty-loving citizens, "without discrimination as to birthplace, party, or religious belief." Most of the delegates were Germans (they argued over the question whether the proceedings should be in English or in German), and prominent among them were saloon keepers, brewers, and distillers. These interests would be able, as Governor Washburn feared, to provide the Republicans' opponents with ample finances, with all the "sinews of war," in the state election of 1873.

When putting together the ticket for that election, the Republicans gave German voters additional reason for taking offense. The Republican leaders had intended, as usual, to name a German for the important position of state treasurer and a Norwegian for the much less prestigious job of immigration commissioner. But the Norwegians vehemently objected, insisting on the treasurer's post for one of their own, O. C. Johnson. To appease the Norwegians, the bosses put Johnson in the place of Henry Baetz, the incumbent treasurer and the party's most influential German politician. They left Baetz off the ticket altogether and placed a comparatively obscure German at the tail end of it.[27]

Thus, as the fateful election of 1873 approached, the Republicans confronted the prospect of losing the votes of Germans who considered themselves the victims of discrimination on ethnic grounds. But the Republicans also faced the danger of a much more massive defection on the part of farmers and businessmen, of whatever nationality, who were discontented for economic reasons. Resentment against big corporations, monopolies, and especially railroads had been festering for several years, and now the resentment was coming to a head.

In the northern half of Wisconsin, most of which remained quite thinly populated, the railroad was still welcome in the postwar years. From 1867 to 1872, the building of new lines in that area went on apace, more than doubling the state's total mileage. In the more thickly settled southern counties, however, the railroad had ceased to be the public's friend even before the beginning of the war. Here the predominant desire was not construction but control.

The railroad companies were becoming the biggest and most monopolistic of corporations. By 1868 two of them—the Chicago and North Western and the Milwaukee and St. Paul—owned or dominated every line of any importance in the state. That year the stockholders of the C. & N. W. elected to their board four directors of the M. & St. P., including the president, Alexander Mitchell, and the stockholders of the M. & St. P. elected the C. & N. W. president to theirs. For a time, Mitchell served as president of both companies. "Alexander Mitchell was in 1869 and 1870 the railroad king of the world, representing, with one possible exception, the greatest concentration of railroad mileage in existence." After 1870 he continued to direct the Milwaukee road and its subsidiaries. He also controlled, through ownership or lease, nearly all the grain elevators in Milwaukee, the Midwest's most important wheat market. Thus the one man held in his grasp practically the entire Wisconsin wheat trade.[28]

Generally, the two big Wisconsin railroad combinations avoided competing with one another, but from time to time the Milwaukee and St. Paul engaged in rate wars with the Illinois Central, which offered competition (across Illinois) on the "long haul" from the Mississippi River to Lake Michigan. The Milwaukee road kept its rates high, however, on the "short haul" from interior points to the lake. Both the Milwaukee and the North Western discriminated in favor of certain large shippers. The two also arranged a pool, each retaining half of its freight receipts and dividing the rest with the other. On September 15, 1873, just as the political campaign was getting under way, both companies raised their rates. Three days later the Panic of '73 began with the collapse of the country's foremost investment banking firm, Jay Cooke and Company, of Philadelphia. With the onset of the business depression, the Milwaukee wheat price dropped (it had been $1.41 a bushel in May; it was $0.95 by November).

Antimonopoly and antirailroad agitation in Wisconsin had first reached a peak in 1865-66. In those two years a total of twenty-one railroad regulation bills were introduced in the legislature, and in every year thereafter to 1873 one or more regulatory measures were proposed. Only two were passed. An 1867 law prohibited forever the consolidation of the Chicago and North Western with the Milwaukee and St. Paul, but the law did nothing to prevent the interlocking directorate or the pooling arrangement that the two companies soon set up. An 1871 amendment to the state constitution restricted the legislature's power to pass special chartering acts, of the kind which previously had conferred excessive privileges on railroad companies. The amendment required the legislature to frame a new general incorporation law, and the legislature did so, but this left the existing companies with all the privileges they had obtained earlier in their special charters.[29]

The antirailroad agitation that was to reach a new peak in 1873-74 came from businessmen as well as farmers, from wheat dealers as well as wheat growers. Exorbitant charges for transportation and storage cut into the profits of commission merchants, who bought the grain from farmers and shipped it to Milwaukee and stored it in elevators for later forwarding to eastern markets. One of these merchants, Francis H. West, as president of the Milwaukee Chamber of Commerce from 1871 to 1873, made himself the outstanding critic of Alexander Mitchell, the railroads, and their monopolistic practices. Meanwhile, the distressed farmers were joining the Patrons of Husbandry and discussing their common grievances at the meetings of their local Granges. In Wisconsin, where the order made its first appearance in 1871, it grew very slowly until 1873. Then the number of Granges suddenly increased from a few dozen to nearly three hundred.[30]

Throughout the years of agitation, each of the major parties had occupied a rather equivocal position in regard to big business and its alleged abuses. From 1865 on, the Republican governors, Fairchild and then Washburn, had repeatedly warned of the dangers of monopoly and called for state regulation of railroads. In his 1873 message Governor Washburn told the law-makers and the people once again that the "many vast and overshadowing corporations" were "justly a source of alarm." But Washburn himself was a very rich businessman, rapidly growing richer from flour-milling and other enterprises. Some other prominent Republicans also were wealthy, among them the millionaire lumberman Philetus Sawyer. "In every instance, and at all times," the *Oshkosh Times* contended in 1870, reviving the language of Jacksonian Democracy, "the votes cast by Mr. Sawyer have been against the productive interests of the country, and in favor of the capital which is continually aggregating and combining to depress and control labor, and establish a supremacy which will soon be seen in lines dividing the people into castes—making the poor dependent upon and subservient to the rich."[31]

Yet the Democrats could hardly make convincing their boast of being the party of the common man when their leadership included the greatest plutocrat of all, Alexander Mitchell, who was elected to Congress in 1871. He and other so-called "Bourbons" ran the Wisconsin Democracy. "You are represented as being the favorite candidate of the moneyed monopolies and corporations," the Bourbon James R. Doolittle heard from a party strategist, while running for governor in 1871. "I know there is a deeper and wider feeling on this subject than you are aware of." The "anti-monopolist mob" had much greater voting strength than the monopolists. Could not the Democratic candidate be as much of a "people's" man as the Republican?

In addition to the stigma of Bourbonism, the taint of treason still handicapped the Democratic Party. As late as 1871, one politician observed, many Wisconsinites continued to fear that, if the party should regain power in the state and nation, the Thirteenth, Fourteenth, and Fifteenth Amendments would "be abrogated if possible, the rights of the Negro be ignored and the public debt be repudiated." At the beginning of 1872 the Madison *Democrat* proposed that fellow partisans "abandon the name Democrat, and form a new party." For the election of 1873, they were to do just that.[32]

In 1873 the Grangers laid down a challenge to both of the major parties in Wisconsin. At a Watertown convention, in August, the Grangers denounced corruption in government and demanded state regulation of the railroads. Some delegates urged the formation of a third party. This was not done; indeed, the rules of the Patrons of Husbandry forbade the Granges, as such, to take part in political activity. But there was nothing to prevent the members from throwing their support to one set of candidates or another.

When the Republicans met for their regular convention, in September, they tried to identify their party with the farmers' cause. They renominated Washburn, the well-known advocate of railroad regulation. Keeping silent on temperance, they declared themselves in favor of honest government, the establishment of a state commission to regulate railroads, and the outlawing of the common railroad practice of awarding free passes to public officials.

Shrewdly, the Democrats and the Liberal Republicans, who had maintained their coalition since the 1872 campaign, avoided giving any party name to their 1873 convention. They labeled it a "People's Reform Convention," and they invited the attendance of "all Democrats, Liberal Republicans, and other electors of Wisconsin friendly to genuine reform." Many Grangers responded. The emerging platform condemned temperance legislation and committed the new party to enacting laws "for the restriction of the power of chartered corporations, for the regulation of railway tariffs, and for the protection of the people against systematic plunder and legalized robbery." The candidate for governor was William R. Taylor, president of the State Agricultural Society (and, incidentally, an active member of the Good Templars). The rest of the ticket included a German, an Irishman, and a Norwegian. Some of the candidates were Democrats and others Liberal Republicans, but only one (a former Congressman now running for attorney general) was a prominent politician. Supposedly, they were men of the people, not professional office seekers. The new organization came to be known as the Reform Party.[44]

Urging on Republican campaigners, Boss Keyes cautioned them that their opponents had gotten up "a plausible programme and ticket," even though in fact the "old Bourbon Democrats" were the "main spirit of the effort," the Reform convention had been "run and controlled in the interests of railroads," and the candidates were "wholly under the influence of these corporations." True enough, the Reformers had the financial support not only of the beer and liquor interests but also of Mitchell's and other railroad companies. The railroad men feared manufacturer Washburn more than they did farmer Taylor, but many of the farmers apparently could see little choice between the two as antimonopolists. On election day some 40,000 farmers, mostly Republicans, refrained from voting. Washburn, who had previously won by 10,000, now lost by 15,000, as the Reformers elected their entire state ticket and 59 assemblymen to 41 for the Republicans, though only 16 senators to 17. "You have been the victim of a situation created by the follies or worse of the party," a sympathizer wrote to Washburn. "Moreover, with a Granger who had the support of the railways, and a Good Templar who had

RICHARD N. CURRENT

the confidence of the whiskey and beer ring for an opponent, queer results might be looked for."[34]

Queer results could also be looked for when the legislature met in 1874. To carry out their platform promises, the Reformers would first have to agree among themselves in the assembly and then get the approval of Republicans in the senate. But the truly reform-minded members of the Reform coalition immediately ran against the opposition of the railroad-interested Bourbons. The anti-Mitchell grain dealer Francis West, who had been elected to the assembly as a Liberal Republican, introduced a bill for the drastic reduction of elevator charges and another for the drastic reduction of freight rates. Both were defeated through Mitchell's influence. The Republicans sponsored and the legislature finally adopted a much less stringent measure, the Potter Law, which provided for a railroad commission with only limited authority to make rate changes. On the temperance question, the Republicans and the Reformers compromised. The Graham Act was not eliminated, but was so amended as to be made innocuous.

Politically, the Republicans gained more from the 1874 session than their opponents did. The Reform coalition soon was shattered by conflicts over the enforcement of the Potter Law. For a time, Mitchell and the railroads gave their support to the Republicans, who cooperated with the Bourbon Democrats in repealing the law in 1876. In the 1874 election, the Republicans recovered control of the legislature and, in the 1875 election, the governorship. By 1877, with economic recovery at hand, the Republican Party was as securely in command of Wisconsin politics as it had ever been. Not until 1890, when ethnic and economic discontent again peaked simultaneously, was the party to suffer another overturn comparable to that of 1873.[35]

NOTES

1. Sam Ross, *The Empty Sleeve: A Biography of Lucius Fairchild* (Madison, 1964), pp. v, 66-76, 79-94; Mary R. Dearing, *Veterans in Politics: The Story of the G. A. R.* (Baton Rouge, 1952), pp. 94, 104-05, 140-41, 147, 180; Karen J. Wise, "Wisconsin and the Fourteenth Amendment, 1865-1867" (master's thesis, University of Wisconsin, 1966), 69-70.

2. *Chicago Tribune*, January 19, 1866; *List of Persons, Residents of the State of Wisconsin, Reported as Deserters from the Military and Naval Service of the United States* (Madison, 1868), pp. 3-6 and passim; Alfons J. Beitzinger, *Edward G. Ryan, Lion of the Law* (Madison, 1960), 82-83; Ross, *Empty Sleeve*, pp. 93-94.

3. *Milwaukee Sentinel*, June 9, 12, 1862, October 9, 1865; Francis A. Walker, *Ninth Census—Volume I: The Statistics of the United States . . . (June 1, 1870)* (Washington, 1872), pp. ix-xii, 334; Edward Noyes, "The Negro in Wisconsin's Civil War Effort," *Lincoln Herald* 69 (Summer 1967): 70-71.

4. *Milwaukee Sentinel*, March 29, November 8, 21, December 24, 1849; Leslie H. Fishel, Jr., "Wisconsin and Negro Suffrage," *Wisconsin Magazine of History* 46 (Spring 1963): 184, 189-90. Italics have been added in the quotation of the constitutional provision.

5. Wise, "Wisconsin and the Fourteenth Amendment," p. 408; Fishel, "Wisconsin and Negro Suffrage," pp. 190-92.

6. Wise, "Wisconsin and the Fourteenth Amendment," pp. 11-13; Ross, *Empty Sleeve*, pp. 72-73; Dearing, *Veterans in Politics*, p. 66.

7. Fishel, "Wisconsin and Negro Suffrage," p. 193; Ross, *Empty Sleeve*, pp. 73-75; Wise, "Wisconsin and the Fourteenth Amendment," p. 14. Returns by counties are given in a manuscript "Tabular Statement" of votes polled in 1865, in Secretary of State, Elections and Records, in the State Historical Society of Wisconsin.

8. William J. Vollmar, "The Negro in a Midwest Frontier City: Milwaukee, 1835-1870" (master's thesis, Marquette University, 1968), pp. 76-82; Fishel, "Wisconsin and Negro Suffrage," pp. 194-95.

9. *Milwaukee Sentinel*, March 31, April 4, 5, 7, 10, May 29, 1866. David Montgomery, *Beyond Equality: Labor and the Radical Republicans, 1862-1872* (New York, 1967), states on page 83: "During the elections of 1866, Negro candidates were elected for the first time to state offices in both Wisconsin and Massachusetts." In fact, no Negro was elected to state office in Wisconsin in 1866 or for many years after that.

10. Richard N. Current, *Pine Logs and Politics: A Life of Philetus Sawyer, 1816-1900* (Madison, 1950), p. 58.

11. Richard W. Hantke, "Elisha W. Keyes and the Radical Republicans," *Wisconsin Magazine of History* 35 (Spring 1952):203-08; Biagino M. Marone, "Senator James Rood Doolittle and the Struggle Against Radicalism, 1857-1866" (master's thesis, Marquette University, 1955), pp. 33-35; Howard K. Beale, *The Critical Year: A Study of Andrew Johnson and Reconstruction* (New York, 1930), p. 36; John T. Morse, Jr., ed., *Diary of Gideon Welles* (3 vols., Boston, 1911), 2:385-86.

12. Marone, "Senator James Rood Doolittle," pp. 35-44; Wise, "Wisconsin and the Fourteenth Amendment," p. 14.

13. Hantke, "Elisha W. Keyes," pp. 204-05; Wise, "Wisconsin and the Fourteenth Amendment," pp. 20-22.

14. Hantke, "Elisha W. Keyes," pp. 205-06; Marone, "Senator James Rood Doolittle," pp. 63-66, 91, 100, 136; Wise, "Wisconsin and the Fourteenth Amendment," pp. 41-43, 52-53, 72, 84-85; James R. Sellers, "James R. Doolittle," *Wisconsin Magazine of History* 18 (June 1934): 27-28.

15. Hantke, "Elisha W. Keyes," pp. 207-08; Alexander M. Thomson, *A Political History of Wisconsin* (Milwaukee, 1900), pp. 166-69, 171-73, 185, 188; E. Bruce Thompson, *Matthew Hale Carpenter, Webster of the West* (Madison, 1954), pp. 106-18; William J. Gillette, *The Right to Vote: Politics and the Passage of the Fifteenth Amendment* (Baltimore, 1965), p. 145.

16. Helen J. and Harry Williams, "Wisconsin Republicans and Reconstruction, 1865-70," *Wisconsin Magazine of History* 23 (September 1939):17-39. That article is based on Helen Jenson's more descriptively titled "Internal Improvements and Wisconsin Republicanism 1865-1873" (master's thesis, University of Wisconsin, 1937).

17. Ross, *Empty Sleeve*, pp. 103-22.

18. Current, *Pine Logs and Politics*, pp. 50-54, 64-82.

19. The quotation is from Thomson, *Political History of Wisconsin*, p. 286.

20. On Wisconsin's ethnic vote as of 1860, see Joseph Schafer, "Who Elected Lincoln?" *American Historical Review* 47 (October 1941):51-63. On the importance of the German Lutheran vote to the Republicans after the war see Paul Kleppner, *The Cross of Culture: A Social Analysis of Midwestern Politics, 1850-1900* (New York, 1970), pp. 110-12.

21. M. Justille McDonald, *History of the Irish in Wisconsin in the Nineteenth Century* (Washington, 1954), pp. 142-49, 152-58.

22. The Rev. Joseph Salzmann to Ludwig Ignatz Lebling, July 31, 1867, edited and translated by Peter Leo Johnson, in *The Salesianum* 43 (April 1947):65-69; Wise, "Wisconsin and the Fourteenth Amendment," p. 58, referring to resolutions adopted by a Presbyterian and Congregational conference in October 1866.

23. On the clash of cultures see Joseph Schafer, "The Yankee and the Teuton in Wisconsin" and "Prohibition in Early Wisconsin," *Wisconsin Magazine of History* 7 (December 1923):148-71 and 8 (March 1925):281-99.

24. P. S. Bennett, *History of Methodism in Wisconsin* (Cincinnati, 1890), p. 224; Herman J. Deutsch, "Yankee-Teuton Rivalry in Wisconsin Politics in the Seventies,"

Wisconsin Magazine of History 14 (March 1931):403-04; Joanne J. Brownsword, "Good Templars in Wisconsin, 1854-1880" (master's thesis, University of Wisconsin, 1960), pp. 87-89.

25. Current, *Pine Logs and Politics*, p. 67; Thompson, *Carpenter*, pp. 158-75.

26. Herman J. Deutsch, "Disintegrating Forces in Wisconsin Politics of the Early Seventies: The Liberal Republican Movement," *Wisconsin Magazine of History* 15 (December 1931):169-72, 174-79; Graham A. Cosmas, "The Democracy in Search of Issues: The Wisconsin Reform Party, 1873-1877," ibid. 46 (Winter 1962-63):93-97.

27. Deutsch, "Yankee-Teuton Rivalry in Wisconsin Politics," pp. 265-68, 273, 276, 412-13; Brownsword, "Good Templars in Wisconsin," p. 92.

28. Frederick Merk, *Economic History of Wisconsin during the Civil War Decade* (Madison, 1916), pp. 292-99 (the quotation is from Merk, p. 298); Herbert W. Rice, "Early History of the Chicago, Milwaukee and St. Paul Railway Company" (doctoral dissertation, University of Iowa, 1938), pp. 255-56; Dale E. Treleven, "Railroads, Elevators, and Grain Dealers: The Genesis of Anti-Monopolism in Milwaukee," *Wisconsin Magazine of History* 52 (Spring 1969):205-08, 213-14.

29. Merk, *Economic History*, pp. 306, 325-28, 342; Rice, "Chicago, Milwaukee and St. Paul," pp. 257-58, 268-69; Chester C. Brown, "A Comparative Study of Constitutional Development in the Old Northwest, 1847-1875" (master's thesis, University of Wisconsin, 1937), pp. 152-54.

30. Treleven, "Railroads, Elevators, and Grain Dealers," pp. 209-11; Solon J. Buck, *The Granger Movement* (Cambridge, Mass., 1913), pp. 54, 58-59.

31. Brown, "Constitutional Development of the Old Northwest," p. 137-40; C. W. Butterfield, "History of Wisconsin," in *History of Sauk County, Wisconsin* (Chicago, 1880), p. 98; Current, *Pine Logs and Politics*, p. 71.

32. Horace S. Merrill, *Bourbon Democracy of the Middle West, 1865-1896* (Baton Rouge, 1953), pp. 69-71.

33. Earle D. Ross, *The Liberal Republican Movement* (Ithaca, N.Y., 1919), pp. 207-09; Cosmas, "Democracy in Search of Issues," pp. 98-99.

34. Merrill, *Bourbon Democracy*, pp. 85-90; Cosmas, "Democracy in Search of Issues," p. 100; Herman J. Deutsch, "Disintegrating Forces in Wisconsin Politics in the Early Seventies: The Ground Swell of 1873," *Wisconsin Magazine of History* 15 (March 1932):295-96; Frank N. Elliott, "The Causes and the Growth of Railroad Regulation in Wisconsin, 1848-1876" (doctoral dissertation, University of Wisconsin, 1956), pp. 286-93. In 1873 the Wisconsin Republicans bore some of the odium of national corruption, since the scandals of the Grant administration were coming to light, and Senator Carpenter brazenly defended the Credit Mobilier and the Salary Grab. Thompson, *Carpenter*, pp. 192-205.

35. Treleven, "Railroads, Elevators, and Grain Dealers," pp. 215-19; Cosmas, "Democracy in Search of Issues," pp. 101-08; Current, *Pine Logs and Politics*, pp. 236-55.

9

IOWA

"Bright Radical Star"

Robert R. Dykstra

The political history of the Hawkeye State is unique in at least one respect. On November 3, 1868, Iowans trooped to the polls and, obeying their state's Republican party leadership, ratified an amendment to the Iowa constitution that struck the word "white" from the article on suffrage. They thereby provided the nation's first and only grass-roots victory for black political equality where the ballot offered voters a clear alternative to uncompromising racism.[1]

The proposed admission of blacks to state electorates provoked the racist outrage of thousands throughout the North in the immediate aftermath of the Civil War. It inspired the resurgence of chastened Democratic parties in the face of seriously fractured Republican solidarity and in some quarters demolished nascent Republican efforts to impose broad programs of social reform, bringing to an end the Grand Old Party's early progressive phase, signaling its emergence as the champion of corporate business and the social status quo.[2] With respect to Iowa, therefore, three questions offer themselves for analysis: How is Iowans' progressivism on black suffrage in the sixties to be accounted for? What was the relationship of this volatile issue to Republican Party solidarity? And in what discernible ways did the issue relate to other reform questions of the 1860s and 1870s?

I

The racism of Iowa's founding fathers is a matter of record. In the constitutional conventions of 1844 and 1846 they restrained themselves from an

1. Notes to this chapter are to be found on pp. 189-193.

outright prohibition on black immigration only because they feared that an exclusion law would jeopardize the territory's admission to statehood. They were forced to rest content with barring black service in the militia, black office-holding, and black voting. Statehood once achieved, an exclusion law won passage in the legislative session of 1851, though it was never enforced.[3]

The emergence of Iowa's Republican Party dates from the gubernatorial triumph of James W. Grimes, who in 1854 ran successfully on a Whig ticket that among other things pledged an end to the state's constitutional restraints on banking.[4] Within two years Grimes's coalition had become a Republican organization, and it moved to redeem its pledge. Called primarily to reverse the antiquated prohibition of banks,[5] the Republican-dominated constitutional convention of 1857 also found itself required to deal with the issue of black political equality. It tabled an exclusion proposition and agreed to permit blacks to testify in court; it excluded them from sitting in the state legislature, from serving in the militia, from being taken into account when apportioning the legislature, and from being counted in state census enumerations. It shied from granting black suffrage, but after much debate agreed to submit the issue to voters as a referendum separate from that concurrently asking approval of the new constitution.[6] The proposal was burdened, however, with a most extraordinary handicap: it would pass only if the votes in favor of black suffrage exceeded half the whole number of votes cast for and against the constitution. This meant that anyone casting a ballot on the new constitution could then vote against black suffrage simply by casting no vote at all.[7]

While the constitution succeeded at the polls by a slim margin, black suffrage mustered a mere 10.4 percent. Only one county in the state, Mitchell, recorded a majority for the amendment, granting it a margin of less than 3 points. Of the fourteen counties giving at least 20 percent of their vote to the controversial amendment, only one of them lay in the southern half of the state, where voters of Southern and Border-state birth undoubtedly had their greatest numerical influence. In fact, counties in the northern half of Iowa averaged 10.3 percentage points more support to franchise extension than southern counties. The smallest average percentage in favor of black suffrage (5.2) was returned by the counties of Iowa's southwestern quarter, which abuts Missouri, then of course a slave state.[8]

The events of the next decade, however, dramatically reversed this racist decision. By early 1866 Iowans of both parties were equating "Radical" Republicanism with support for impartial suffrage in Iowa as well as in the defeated but unrepentant South. In this paper the same general equation pertains: the terms "radical" or "Radical Republican" will indicate adherence to the doctrine of unqualified suffrage for black male residents of the Hawkeye State.

The causal ingredients of Iowa's ultimate racial progressivism resist easy identification. Not that causal observations have been lacking. But in addressing them we cannot consider Iowa in a vacuum, since the state's position relative to other states—particularly those that stood by the Union during the Civil War—is what is at issue. In selecting states for comparison it seems reasonable to exclude the Border states and the states of the trans-Missouri West, where in both instances regional social and political circumstances appear so dissimilar as to confound comparability with Iowa. Let our sample therefore consist of the six New England states, the three Middle Atlantic states, and the five states of the Old Northwest plus Minnesota. While all fifteen were, like Iowa, unequivocally Unionist during the rebellion, only five of them—Maine, New Hampshire, Vermont, Massachusetts, and Rhode Island—allowed impartial male suffrage as of 1865. Several of the others held at least one unsuccessful referendum on the black suffrage question in the sixties.

"Generally," notes William Gillette, "the states with the smallest number of Negroes were those most disposed to be broad in sympathy [with black political equality] and liberal in outlook."[9] The first column of Table 1 therefore lists, in reverse order of magnitude, the percentage of blacks in each sample state's total population in 1860. While Iowa indeed ranks very close to the top, it is at once apparent that blacks were more than a tiny minority in *no* state in the sample. It would seem difficult, then, to make a case for Iowa's racial progressivism based—at the most—on a demographic difference of only 3.61 percentage points. Surely variations in Northern states' racial attitudes, insofar as they were a product of resident black populations, can hardly have hinged on such modest increments and declensions as displayed in Table 1.

Jacque Voegeli offers a second generalization capable of simple comparative examination: "In states such as Iowa where Republicans were distinctly in the majority [during the Civil War] they tended to be more radical than they were in closely divided states such as Illinois and Ohio."[10] The second column of Table 1 addresses this variable, distributing the states of the sample according to average Republican voting strength during the war. In this instance the relative positions of the states would seem to have more utility, an average of at least 57 or 58 percent plausibly identifying a "safe" Republican state in which postwar voter reprisals for GOP radicalism could have been considered a fairly minimal threat. Iowa and Minnesota rank with five New England states as safely Republican. These New England states already allowed universal manhood suffrage; both Iowa and Minnesota, interestingly enough, joined them in this uncommon attribute in 1868. Minnesotans that year approved black suffrage, after two previous and relatively close referendum defeats, when its Republican leadership submitted the constitutional

ROBERT R. DYKSTRA

TABLE 1.
RANK ORDERINGS OF NORTHERN STATES ON VARIABLES
POSSIBLY RELATED TO DEGREE OF POST-CIVIL WAR RADICALISM

Black population as percent of total population (1860)		Average Republican electoral strength (1860-64)		Per cent of military population furnished to Union armed forces[a]	
Minn.	0.15	Vt.	78.0	Ind.	57.0
Wisc.	0.15	Mass.	66.6	Ill.	56.6
N.H.	0.15	R.I.	65.4	Conn.	50.1
Iowa	0.16	Minn.	60.5	Ohio	49.8
Maine	0.21	Iowa	59.1	Iowa	48.8
Vt.	0.22	Maine	58.8	N.H.	47.2
Ill.	0.44	Ohio	55.2	Mich.	46.7
Mass.	0.77	Wisc.	55.0	Wisc.	46.4
Ind.	0.84	Mich.	54.6	N.Y.	46.1
Mich.	0.90	N.Y.	53.3	Minn.	45.0
N.Y.	1.26	Conn.	52.9	Maine	44.7
Ohio	1.56	N.H.	52.9	Vt.	44.5
Conn.	1.87	Penn.	52.4	Mass.	44.4
Penn.	1.95	Ill.	52.1	R.I.	43.8
R.I.	2.26	Ind.	50.9	Penn.	41.2
N.J.	3.77	N.J.	45.4	N.J.	39.7

[a]Specifically, white males furnished to the Union army and navy (three years' standard) as a percentage of white males ages 18-45 in 1860.

question to voters as "an amendment of Section 1, Article 7"—that is, without any direct reference to suffrage. This was the nation's only other, albeit somewhat less than straightforward, referendum victory for black suffrage in the sixties.[11] It would appear, in short, that Voegeli's observation has considerable merit, though a comprehensive test of it awaits some strategy for independently assessing radicalism in all Northern states.

That question aside, the spectacular turnabout in public sentiment in Iowa between the suffrage referenda of 1857 and 1868 tempts one to seek a rather more direct influence of the intervening Civil War. The closest approximation to a causal variable, to my knowledge, is that offered by a political scientist: " . . . Iowa contributed more men per capita to the Union army in the Civil War than any other state."[12] This statement, however, is incorrect. With only 11.3 percent of its 1860 population in uniform, according to final War Department figures, Iowa was outclassed by over half the states in the sample, including all other midwestern states.[13] Yet, as the military historian William Fox notes, in any statement about states' relative manpower contributions to the Union war effort the official data

require modification in order that the statement may be complete and fair. The figures for the number of men furnished . . . favor certain States whose troops contained a larger proportion of three months' men or regiments with other short terms of enlistment. Some States, also, furnished money in commutation for soldiers, and . . . it may be deemed that money was not a complete offset for men. Then, again, the military population, as enumerated in the census of 1860, embraced white males only, while the troops credited . . . to the various States include the colored soldiers from those States; and although these colored troops were, in some States, a serious drain upon the agricultural resources of the community, they formed no part of the military population in question, and might be considered as unfairly influencing the comparative percentages.

To forestall discussion on such points, and to arrive accurately at the percentage of its able-bodied whites which each State sent to the war, it becomes necessary to base a percentage on the white troops alone (including sailors), and, further, to reduce their number to the common standard of a three years' enlistment; also, to throw out the item of commutation.[14]

In compliance with these strictures, I have listed in order of magnitude the relative manpower contributions of the sample states as the third column of Table 1.[15] Iowa, it can be seen, was outranked by only four other states in the sample. Yet those four states can hardly be deemed progressive on black suffrage; the voters of three of them, in fact, specifically rejected political equality for blacks. And, as in the case of column one of Table 1, it might be asked if the spread from top to bottom, a distribution purposefully narrowed by federal conscription policy, really allows for much causal explanation according to ranking.

Do these manpower data possibly mask some more dynamic factor, such as relative mortality among the various states' Union soldiery? Table 2 treats this possibility.[16] It shows that, in addition to suffering substantially on Southern battlefields, the men and boys of Iowa regiments died from disease in a proportion unequalled by troops from any other sample state. This was, no doubt, a result of their having been employed almost exclusively in the western theater of operations; whereas northern Virginia was the Civil War's great killing ground, it was the lower Mississippi Valley that proved so lethal in other respects. However it is computed, a larger proportion of Iowans in uniform met death than did men from most Northern states. But yet again the percentage-point spread seems too narrow to support generalizations about differing political behavior. Moreover, Indiana and Michigan, positioned close to Iowa in the rankings, by no stretch of the imagination could be considered as racially progressive as the Hawkeye State.

In postwar Iowa, true enough, the price of union was no mere abstraction. The South had exacted a frightful payment in agony and blood and domestic tragedy in the name of a cruel cause. To most Iowans, those who preached immediate sectional reconciliation were either traitors or fools. Such an experience, such attitudes, they shared with the citizens of all states that had

TABLE 2.
RANK ORDERINGS OF NORTHERN STATES
ACCORDING TO MORTALITY AMONG WHITE UNION SOLDIERS FURNISHED

Percent killed or died of wounds[a]		Percent died of disease[a]		Total mortality (all causes) as percent of total furnished[a]		Total mortality (all causes) as percent of military population[b]	
Penn.	7.1	Iowa	12.5	Vt.	19.8	Ind.	10.0
Vt.	6.8	Ind.	11.1	Mich.	19.3	Iowa	9.3
N.H.	6.5	Mich.	10.8	Iowa	19.0	Ill.	9.3
Maine	6.4	Maine	10.5	Maine	18.9	Mich.	9.0
Mass.	6.2	Wisc.	10.1	Ind.	17.7	Vt.	8.6
Mich.	5.8	Ill.	10.0	N.H.	16.7	Wisc.	7.7
N.J.	5.8	Vt.	9.8	Wisc.	16.6	Ohio	7.7
N.Y.	5.7	Minn.	9.0	Ill.	16.5	Maine	7.7
Iowa	5.2	Ohio	8.6	Ohio	15.7	N.H.	7.7
Wisc.	5.1	N.H.	8.3	Penn.	15.4	Minn.	6.3
Ohio	5.1	N.Y.	5.9	Mass.	14.1	Penn.	6.0
Ind.	4.8	Conn.	5.6	Minn.	13.9	N.Y.	5.8
Ill.	4.7	Mass.	5.6	N.Y.	13.8	Conn.	5.7
Conn.	4.3	Penn.	5.5	N.J.	12.9	Mass.	5.4
Minn.	3.4	N.J.	5.4	Conn.	11.8	N.J.	4.3
R.I.	3.3	R.I.	4.7	R.I.	9.6	R.I.	3.7

[a]Military contributions calculated on a three years' standard.

[b]Specifically, white males furnished to the Union army (three years' standard) as a percentage of white males ages 18-45 in 1860.

suffered from the war in something of the same degree. But in addition to this, what Iowans may have possessed in some relatively uncommon measure was a Republican leadership peculiarly confident in their hold upon the state. These men could with more tolerance than elsewhere indulge the racial equalitarianism of the party's left wing. They could afford the political luxury of an incautious moral commitment. And when, in consequence, the going got rough, they would not lose heart.

II

In Iowa the black suffrage issue emerged, as it did in several Northern states, in the spring of 1865. The last Confederate forces had not yet surrendered when the abolitionist editor of the Davenport *Gazette*, Edward Russell, urged the forthcoming Republican state convention to declare emphatically in favor of a constitutional revision to undo the wrong done in 1857. The initial response around the state was cool, many GOP spokesmen fearing what was just then becoming a Republican problem all over the nation: defections by antislavery but also anti-Negro Republican voters. Better a noncontroversial pronouncement that might satisfy equalitarians without alienating racists.

At the June 14 convention, held in Des Moines, the cautious platform committee reported a suffrage plank, the so-called Fourth Resolution. This proposition asserted that "the elective franchise should be based upon loyalty to the Constitution of the union, recognizing and affirming equality of all men before the law." Whereupon by parliamentary maneuver Davenport's Edward Russell forced his fellow delegates to a direct vote on the real issue involved, offering an amendment to the Fourth Resolution that placed the party "in favor of amending the Constitution of our State by striking out the word 'white' in the article on suffrage." The assembled Republicans, "being unwilling to stand committed even in *appearance* against the principle of negro suffrage," as the editor of the Des Moines *Register* put it, granted the amendment a surprising 67.9 percent majority, "and the universal expression of the delegates after the adjournment was that inasmuch as the issue must be squarely met, it might as well be met this year as next." Iowa's incumbent governor, William M. Stone, standing for reelection, had little choice but to declare himself in favor of black suffrage.[17]

The full significance of the Fourth Resolution was not lost on the hitherto dispirited Democrats. "It is perfectly idle for us to run a ticket if we can[']t get some votes off of the Republicans," a local party man wrote the state's Democratic chairman, "and I think the only chance we have is upon the question of Negro suffrage." On July 12 a faction of the party's state central committee caucused in Davenport and, eschewing the Democratic label, issued a nonpartisan call for all those opposed to black suffrage to gather in Des Moines in August to nominate a white-supremacy ticket.[18]

This Democratic stratagem fooled hardly anybody. Many conservative Republicans preferred their own approach. In some places they tried to get GOP county conventions to nominate white supremacists for the legislature and to repudiate the Fourth Resolution.[19] They had more success with an alternative tactic: promoting nonpartisan county assemblies at which veterans were given prominence. Iowans of both parties held to a conviction that returned soldiers, having seen American blacks at their most debased while campaigning through the South, were particularly hostile to racial equality of any kind. These assemblies elected delegates to a "Soldiers' Convention" that met in Des Moines on August 23 and nominated a Union Anti-Negro Suffrage Ticket headed by General Thomas Hart Benton, Jr., a nephew of the late United States Senator from Missouri. On the same day the Democrats also met in Des Moines as scheduled, passed a similar set of resolutions, and endorsed the Soldiers' Ticket, as the antisuffrage slate soon came to be called.[20]

How did the Republican faithful across Iowa react to this continued escalation of the black suffrage question? Did an increasing number retreat from the controversial Fourth Resolution as opposition to it grew steadily more serious? Did a split in Republican ranks take some discernible shape?

The closest approximation of Republican opinion at large, and thus the best source for any systematic response to the questions posed, is Republican editorial opinion during the 1865 campaign..Of the eighty-three Iowa newspapers claiming a Republican "political cast" in 1865,[21] relatively complete files of over half for the period under review repose in the collections of the State Historical Society of Iowa and the Iowa Historical Museum and Archives.[22] Since most were weekly publications, I insured comparability with the relatively few GOP urban dailies by using only the weekly editions of those daily papers. This sample of forty-two weekly newspapers represented a majority of the sixty-four counties in which Republican newspapers were printed in 1865.

I divided the second half of 1865 into four periods reflecting distinct phases of the political campaign of that year:

I) June 14-July 15: following the Republican convention but before the call for an organized opposition keyed to black suffrage.

II) July 15-August 22: following the emergence of opposition but before the Soldiers' Convention.

III) August 23-October 9: following formation of the Soldiers' Ticket but before the election.

IV) October 10-November 10: the immediate aftermath of the election. For each period I characterized the coverage given by each newspaper to the black suffrage issue—including material on the national issue of freedmen's voting in the South—according to the following simple scale ranking attitudes from most to least progressive:[23]

a) *Ultra radical*: Demanded immediate black enfranchisement on grounds of justice and natural rights. Strong moral tone employed.

b) *Radical*: Endorsed black suffrage on mixed grounds, with some reference to principle but with emphasis on the pragmatic instrumentation of a larger Republican policy exemplified by the proposed Fourteenth Amendment to the Constitution. One editor expressed this viewpoint in the following words:

> Aside from the simple matter of justice—and justice is always safe—self defence from Southern barbarism compels us to insist, firmly, inflexibly and to the bitter end and through all opposition, that the colored men of the South shall vote or cease to be represented in Congress. As it now stands and [with] the old three-fifths clause turned into five-fifths, thirty members representing nobody, will take their seats in the House from the South, overcoming that number from the North. We must crush this new scoundrelism; and the preliminary part of the fight is to make ready at home by cleaning our own skirts, and not have the rebels and their allies the copperheads throwing in our teeth the old adage—"Pull the beam out of your own eye!"[24]

Whatever the variation on this theme, loyalty to the Union was considered the only legitimate test for admission to the franchise in Iowa or in the South.

c) *Neutral*: Totally avoided the black suffrage question, discussed it only as an issue between the federal government and the South, limited discussion of the Iowa case to explaining constitutional procedures involved, or carefully balanced the arguments of the Iowa case without taking a stand.

d) *Conservative:* Grudgingly accepted the suffrage proposal out of party loyalty, with profound regret for the question's "premature" presentation to the public. In any case, expressed a preference that suffrage be granted only to black war veterans and those able to pass a literacy test.

e) *Ultra conservative:* Endorsed the Soldiers' Ticket.

Figure 1 displays the results of the analysis. Each circle represents an editorial position on black suffrage for a given period, the enclosed figure showing the number of weeklies whose news stories and editorial comment were judged as averaging on that position. The arrows, with associated numerals, illustrate the type and frequency of editorial position changes from period to period.

It is immediately apparent that the "radical" and "neutral" positions were in every period the most popular with Republican editors, although a good deal of jockeying into and out of these positions occurred. It is also apparent that the greatest erosion, as opposition to black suffrage crystalized, was suffered by the "ultra radical" cluster, which declined from nine adherents in Period I to a single adherent in Period II, recovering only partially in the election's aftermath. As for the "radical" position, its constituents peaked in Period II, mainly because of an influx from the "ultra" position; it then declined through the last two periods. The only consistent gainer was the "neutral" position, which proved increasingly attractive as the attack on suffrage mounted. Escalation of the opposition *did* have a measurably destructive effect on Republican editorial enthusiasm in support of black suffrage. Nearly a third of the newspapers in the sample dropped to a less progressive attitude in moving from Period I to Period II, and a third also descended in the transition to Period III. In the six weeks preceding the election, in fact, less than a third of the sample espoused a radical—that is, a wholly favorable—position on black suffrage. Almost half held to a cautious neutrality, while conservatism, with its near repudiation of the GOP suffrage resolution, embraced over one-fifth. The period after August 23, then, found Republican morale at its lowest point, black suffrage having become much more controversial, apparently, than many editors had imagined back in mid-June.

On the eve of the election, however, the Republican state chairman was finally able to offer assurances that there was little cause for alarm. "I have reports from nearly all the counties in the state," he wrote a concerned party

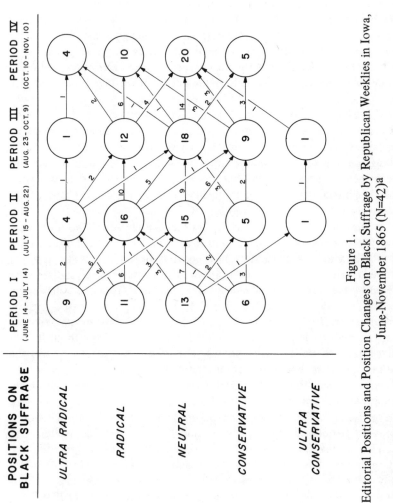

Figure 1.
Editorial Positions and Position Changes on Black Suffrage by Republican Weeklies in Iowa,
June-November 1865 (N=42)[a]

[a]Columns do not total 42 because for each period all issues were missing for at least one newspaper in the sample.

leader, "and they are much more favorable than I anticipated. Our majority will be about 20,000."[25] On October 10, election day, this prediction proved entirley accurate—with the important exception of Governor Stone, who ran some 2,000 votes behind the rest of the ticket, an event to be accounted for less by Stone's stand on black suffrage than by lingering resentments over certain of his war-time policies as governor.[26] Stone defeated Benton by a comfortable 56.4 percent; his running mate, Lieutenant Governor-elect Benjamin F. Gue, won by 58.0 percent, a somewhat better measure of the Republican vote. But even Gue's margin was down 6.3 percentage points from the enormous majority given to the top of the Republican state ticket in 1864, a drop that without doubt reflected some defection of conservative Republicans to the Soldiers' Ticket. Far more important, however, was the sheer numerical decline in Republican ballots since the previous election, a figure exceeding 17,000 that seems too large to be explained either by losses to the opposition or by an expected drop-off in the total vote between a presidential election and a subsequent off-year election. Assuming that the rise in nonvoters overwhelmingly represented unhappy Republicans, and assuming that very few Democrats switched to the GOP, it may have been that perhaps 20,000 men who had voted Republican in 1864 refused to support the ticket in 1865. Relatively few could stomach the "copperhead" alternative; the vast majority apparently did not vote at all.[27] Their future relationship to the Grand Old Party remained in doubt.

Figure 1 shows, however, that Republican editorial courage rallied a bit in the immediate wake of the election. For the first time fewer newspapers dropped to a more conservative stance (six) than rose to a more progressive position (eleven). Though some editors refused to see in Benton's defeat a popular endorsement of black suffrage, the conclusion offered by a Sioux City editor probably best reflected that with which most Republican spokes-men and party figures would have agreed. No friend of the Fourth Resolution (he registered as "conservative" in Period I, then refused even to discuss the issue in Periods II and III), this observer bespoke an assurance that the outcome was all to the good:

Stone has been elected upon the "negro suffrage" platform, by a large majority, and therefore we may regard the popular opinion of the State as expressed in favor of the extension of the rights of citizenship to the black man. Had not this have been the issue—and there was no occasion for it—Stone's majority would have been at least one half larger than it is, and perhaps double. But the contest is passed the victory won, notwithstanding the side issues; and today the Republican party is stronger than it would have been had the "negro suffrage" clause been left out of the platform. We are now out of the woods, let all crow who feel like it.[28]

The ultimate fate of black suffrage would now be decided by means of a three-phase scenario dictated by the requirements of the constitution-amending process in Iowa: passage of amending legislation by two successive sessions of the General Assembly, which met biennially, followed by a favorable referendum vote. Victory, at its earliest, would come in the autumn of 1868. The proposal soon confronted its first test.

The legislators of 1866, responding to Governor Stone's formal request for action enabling a black suffrage amendment to go before the people, passed a joint resolution eliminating the word "white" from the suffrage article. In the most crucial house roll call, four Republicans—two of them having been elected as conservative independents—joined the Democrats and voted against extending the franchise. The most critical senate vote was on adopting a committee minority report that would have restricted nonwhite suffrage to Union war veterans and those able to read and write. Seventeen Republicans voted in favor of this conservative option; ironically, only the opposition of diehards who were against *any* black suffrage kept this measure from passing. Following its defeat, the black suffrage resolution passed with the defection of only four senate Republicans.[29]

The General Assembly's joint resolution also proposed removal of all other racist discriminations from the constitution except that excluding nonwhites from membership in the legislature. This was by no means an oversight. Representative Alonzo Abernethy of Fayette County offered a rectifying resolution, which went to the Committee on Constitutional Amendments. The committee refused to recommend it. Abernethy once again brought up the matter on the house floor, and a week later the committee's recommendations *did* include the matter of legislative qualifications. But of the six specifications voted upon, it was the only one to fail. It did so because thirty-two Republicans joined the Democrats in opposition.[30] Black suffrage was as far as a third of the GOP house contingent would go; black membership in the General Assembly was too much to ask.

This roll call to eliminate the ban on nonwhite legislators permits some insight into the ideological nature of Republicans in the house. With the exception of the ten house Republicans who cannot be classified because of failure to vote on the question of black legislators, we can conveniently separate those we might term "ultra radical," who favored eliminating *all* racist distinctions in the organic law of the state, from others who, no matter how they might stand on black suffrage, wished to keep the General Assembly lily-white. Did the two groups differ in any appreciable way with respect to backgrounds and attitudes on other important questions?

Table 3 compares the ultra radicals with other classifiable Republicans in the 1866 house, employing a number of personal and political characteristics, as well as their responses to three key roll calls that reveal attitudes toward women's suffrage, temperance, and business regulation.[31] In dealing with

TABLE 3.
CHARACTERISTICS OF ULTRA RADICALS AND OTHER REPUBLICANS
IN THE IOWA HOUSE OF REPRESENTATIVES, 1866

	Ultra Radicals (N=41)		Other Republicans (N=32)[a]	
	N	%	N	%
Birthplace				
New England	8	19.5	6	18.8
Middle Atlantic States	13	31.7	7	21.9
Middle West	14	34.1	11	34.4
South	3	7.3	4	12.5
United Kingdom	2	4.9	2	6.3
Ireland	–	–	2	6.3
Germany	1	2.4	–	–
Age 45 or older	6	14.6	8	25.0
Moved to Iowa 1850 or before	9	21.9	13	40.6
Civil War veteran	18	43.9	15	46.9
Occupation				
Farmer	13	31.7	14	43.8
Lawyer	10	24.4	9	28.1
Merchant	6	14.6	5	15.6
Religion				
Methodist	7	17.1	9	28.1
Presbyterian	6	14.6	5	15.6
Baptist	8	19.5	1	3.1
Episcopalian	3	7.3	1	3.1
Congregationalist	1	2.4	2	6.3
Quaker	–	–	1	3.1
United Brethren	1	2.4	–	–
Universalist	1	2.4	–	–
Nondenominational Protestant	6	14.6	6	18.8
"Liberal"/"doubtful"/"none"/				
no entry	8	19.5	7	21.9
Constituency gave at least 15%				
support to black suffrage, 1857	21	51.2	1	3.1
Attitude on selected issues				
Women's suffrage				
For	7	17.1	8	25.0
Against	19	46.3	18	56.3
Liberalized prohibitory law				
For	7	17.1	16	50.0
Against	27	65.9	12	37.5
Threshing machine safety				
standards				
For	25	61.0	17	41.5
Against	7	17.1	9	28.1

[a]Excluding ten unclassifiable Republicans.

such relatively small numbers, of course, we must treat percentage relationships with caution. In three categories, nevertheless, the differences exceed 30 percentage points. Comparison suggests that the ultra radicals were much more likely (by 48.1 points) to be from constituencies that supported black suffrage by at least 15 percent in the 1857 referendum, a finding that should occasion no surprise. And the ultra radicals were very much more against (48.4 points), and other Republicans emphatically for (32.9 points), liberalizing the state's prohibitory law. This lends credence to the notion that black equality, like temperance, was an uncompromising moral position based primarily on particular religious convictions. Yet in only one religious category do ultra radicals differ to any extent at all from their opposites: a 16.4-point difference in Baptist members that does not seem qualitatively significant. The question remains open.

The remaining political events of 1866 resolved any lingering doubts about the ideological role of black suffrage within Iowa Republicanism. June's annual GOP convention featured a determination to excise all intraparty disunity on the question. Delegates approved the platform before selecting candidates, thus minimizing the possibility of a nominee later repudiating the suffrage plank. A committee privately fashioned a compromise acceptable to delegates from southern Iowa, among whom, as the *Register* reported, "great anxiety was manifested relative to the tone of the Resolutions which should be adopted . . . and while they asked no deviation from the line of policy which was ratified at the polls last fall, they asked that no new test should be introduced into the Resolutions this year."

Adopted in an enthusiastic display of unanimity, the 1866 suffrage plank simply asserted that the "first and highest duty of our free government is to secure all its citizens, regardless of race, religion, or color, equality before the law, equal protection from it, equal responsibility to it, and to all that have proved their loyalty by their acts, an equal voice in making it." Most of the words were those of Major Henry O'Connor of Muscatine, an old Free-Soiler and one of the Fourth Resolution's strongest supporters in the 1865 convention, but who this year recognized the political utility of a less specific statement. The phrase about proofs of loyalty was not his, however, and from the convention floor he apparently objected to a possible construction that the franchise belonged only to black war veterans. He seems to have been shouted down.[32]

Actually, of course, the added touch reinforced the plank's attractiveness. It could appeal to GOP conservatives who still hoped for a qualified extension of the suffrage to blacks. On the other hand, while clearly referring to the late war, the phrase could satisfy those radicals who saw it as acknowledging that the whole black population of Iowa had vicariously proved itself through its sponsorship of a soldiery. It could also, finally, serve as an endorsement of Congressional Republicans' policy toward the South. The lavish praise heaped on it by the ultra-radical editor Edward Russell simply reinforces the conspiratorial ambience surrounding its lack of specificity. Yet, in light of the general retreat from black suffrage apparent in other Northern states that year, any endorsement, however ambivalent, was remarkable. "Iowa Republicans alone," writes Leslie Fishel of 1866, "came out strongly for enfranchisment."[33]

TABLE 4.
THE POPULAR VOTE IN FOUR IOWA ELECTIONS

	Republican	Opposition	Not Voting[a]
Secretary of State (1864)	90,033	49,943	27,843 (16.6%)
Lieutenant Governor (1865)	72,834	52,755	44,933 (26.3%)
Secretary of State (1866)	91,227	55,815	30,933 (17.4%)
Governor (1867)	90,228	62,803	37,459 (19.7%)

[a]The percentages of this column are derived from the estimated total of eligible voters for each election year. They have, therefore, no statistical relationship to the dichotomous party percentages mentioned in the text and used in the computations.

Reconstruction policy was the main issue that autumn, though the politics of 1866 were in part a replay of the previous year. Convinced that with more time to campaign he could have won on the Soldiers' Ticket, General Benton helped organize a so-called Conservative Republican convention. This body assembled, nominated racist candidates, and approved a platform, penned by Benton himself, opposing impartial suffrage. What was new was its applause of President Johnson's permissive program for the South. Iowa's Democrats, once again offering no slate of their own, endorsed the Conservative nominees.[34]

This time the fusionists reaped disaster (see Table 4). Assuming that the decline in nonvoters can be attributed mainly to Republicans and that few Democrats switched to the GOP, then perhaps 13,000, or roughly 65 percent, of those who had voted Republican in 1864 but sat out 1865 now, in October 1866, came back to the aid of their party. We cannot know what impelled them. We can guess that it was Andrew Johnson, whose break with the Radical Republicans in Congress had characterized the intervening year. Racists these Iowans might be, but they would not acquiesce, any more than their more enlightened Republican compatriots, in a Johnsonian attitude of forgive and forget. In all, it was a remarkable display, a GOP resurgence all across the state. The Republican candidate for secretary of state, Colonel Ed Wright, won a resounding 62.0 percent. His opponent at the top of the Conservative Ticket took only eight counties, three of them by margins of less than five votes each. All eight Conservative counties had been carried the year before by Benton, seven by larger majorities. Benton's other ten counties now went Republican. That the Conservative vote of 1866 was a diminished Soldier's Ticket vote of 1865 is an impression reinforced by a Pearsonian correlation coefficient of .87 between county-level support for Stone and Wright.

Years later, without benefit of computer, Benjamin Gue concluded that among other things the 1866 election "clearly demonstrated the fact that the people of Iowa, by a large majority, were determined to remove from the organic laws of the State . . . all race discriminations which in early years were enacted against persons of African descent." His colleagues within middle levels of the Republican elite must have agreed with Gue; at least they collectively acted as if they did. There seemed little need for them to equivocate further. The GOP platforms of 1867 and 1868—adopted in both instances without important convention dissent—specified that amending the Iowa constitution so as to "secure the rights of the ballot . . . to all men, irrespective of color, race, or religion" was now to be considered "a cardinal principle of our political faith." And in both years the assembled delegates enthusiastically nominated Henry O'Connor for attorney general, an honor understood to be a full vindication of O'Connor's fight for black suffrage in the conventions of 'sixty-five and 'sixty-six.[35]

Had black suffrage already become a test of party loyalty, months before October 1866, in the topmost echelons of the Iowa GOP? The evidence is equivocal. During the 1865 campaign Iowa's Congressman John A. Kasson had urged—as had many less prominent conservatives and moderates—that full acceptance of the Fourth Resolution not be so construed. Himself most unenthusiastic about black suffrage either in Iowa or the South, Kasson soon found himself purged from the state's delegation in Congress. But what cost him renomination was his pro-Johnson Congressional behavior, making him the odd man out in an otherwise solidly Radical Iowa representation.[36] A second member of that delegation, J. B. Grinnell, also failed of renomination in 1866, but apparently for reasons other than his opposition to the Fourth Resolution at the 1865 convention.[37] As for U.S. Senator James W. Grimes, this venerated father of Iowa Republicanism had endeavored to remain silent on the black suffrage plank in 1865, but was finally forced to confess his strong displeasure with it. Seven months later, however, he accepted the pragmatic connection between Radical Reconstruction and black suffrage in the North,[38] and did not fall out with the Iowa GOP until his famous negative vote at the Johnson impeachment trial.

Yet hardly was the 1865 campaign won than the question of his soundness on black suffrage *was* employed against a high party figure. In the contest between U.S. Interior Secretary James Harlan and ex-governor Samuel J. Kirkwood for the regular Republican nomination to the U.S. Senate, gossip (much of it no doubt inspired by Harlan's friends) circulated that Kirkwood opposed the Fourth Resolution, had shirked the suffrage issue during the late campaign, and once elected to the Senate might openly espouse a Johnsonian viewpoint. Kirkwood lost in the legislative balloting, but that these allegations were central to his defeat is doubtful. And though this fight touched off a protracted power struggle between the James Harlan and Grenville M. Dodge factions within the higher circles of Iowa Republicanism, it was, as Leland Sage has noted, mainly a question of spoils, both cliques being impeccably radical.[39]

In the immediate aftermath of the 1866 debacle a Muscatine correspondent warned the state Democratic party chairman that "there is a well

defined and clear determination among democrats to fight our battles hereafter under the old Democratic banner and *nothing else.*" Fusion, he concluded, had not worked because the conservative element of the Iowa GOP
was not numerically strong enough to be worth trifling with. In response to
such advice from many quarters, the Democrats in 1867, for the first time in
three years, fielded their own slate of candidates. And while their platform
denounced black suffrage (plank 2), it made opposition to the protective
tariff and the tax-exempt status of federal bonds (planks 3 and 4) the key
questions with respect to national affairs. But advocating repeal of Iowa's
prohibitory law and the enactment of "a well regulated license law in lieu
thereof" (plank 5) reactivated a party position on which the Iowa Democracy
would campaign annually until well into the twentieth century. While by no
means conceding the black suffrage question, it brought another divisive issue
effectively into play.[40]

The finer points of this Democratic tactic, and its effect on Republican
unity, constitute another story. Let it be noted here only that the GOP
gubernatorial nominee, Colonel Samuel Merrill, won election by 59.0 percent,
a slight falling off from Wright's 1866 support, though a correlation of .89
between the two votes suggests little in the way of major realignments among
Republicans at large. Still, as Table 4 indicates, prohibition portended
trouble. The proportion of those not voting rose slightly, and one apparent
result was a Republican decline, in absolute strength, of a thousand votes.
"The Election Lesson," as one worried Republican editor concluded, no
longer hinged on black suffrage (which he did not mention), but rather on
"premonitions of weakness growing out of distractions" better left to philanthropists and other nonpartisan reformers. "The temperance issue has lost us
five or six legislators in Iowa this fall," he warned, "and thus we are playing
into the hands of the enemy." As the new General Assembly convened in
January 1868 close observers echoed this disquietude. The GOP leadership's
problem was, said one, to avoid jeopardizing "the paramount question of
reconstruction[;] & yet something is necessary to quiet the stormy feelings of
the temperance men on one side & the license men on the other . . . within
the Republican party."[41]

Divided they might be on liquor, but Republican assemblymen toed the
line on black suffrage with remarkable unity. The suffrage measure passed the
house with only one Republican dissent, that of the representative from
Fremont County in the extreme southwest corner of the state, a normally
Democratic county in the late 1860s despite its very Republican name. Even
conservative John Kasson, elected to the Iowa house by a portion of his old
Congressional constituency, found it in himself to join the majority. A resolution that would also have eliminated the ban on nonwhite legislators passed
the house with much more cohesive GOP support than its champions had
been able to muster in 1866. Table 5 displays the markedly progressive shift

TABLE 5.
IDEOLOGICAL POSITIONS OF REPUBLICANS IN THE
IOWA HOUSE OF REPRESENTATIVES, 1866 AND 1868

	1866 (N=83)		1868 (N=78)	
	N	%	N	%
Ultra radical [a]	41	49.4	66	84.6
Radical [b]	28	33.7	2	2.6
Conservative[c]	4	4.8	1	1.3
Unclassifiable [d]	10	12.0	9	11.5

[a]Voted "yes" on question of black legislators.
[b]Voted "no" on question of black legislators, "yes" on black suffrage.
[c]Voted "no" on black suffrage.
[d]Did not vote on question of black legislators.

of house Republican attitudes in the two-year interim. The number of unclassifiable Republicans remains virtually constant, but the middling radical position is all but eliminated by the new consensus. Only a dozen Republicans sat in both sessions. All twelve, however, registered as ultra radical in 1868, though two had been only moderate radicals in the earlier assembly and one had been a conservative.[42] While the black legislators measure died in a senate committee, the black suffrage amendment passed the senate with no Republican opposition at all. Even one *Democratic* senator felt the will of the whole people of Iowa more impressive than that of his ultra-conservative Dubuque County constituency, and cast an absolutely unprecedented pro-suffrage vote.[43]

Having passed two consecutive General Assemblies, the black suffrage amendment finally went to Iowa's voters for approval in November 1868. With the popular General Grant heading the GOP ticket that fall, the Iowa leadership felt little anxiety about the impending presidential race. Their strategy with respect to black suffrage was simply to hold otherwise loyal Republicans in line. In mid-September the party's state chairman was able to assure Grenville Dodge that "Things look bully for Grant & Colfax," and his executive secretary informed national headquarters that black suffrage would probably carry by a small majority.[44] Republican editors now made a special effort to rally a substantial vote for the amendment. Their theme was that, as one of them forcefully if somewhat clumsily phrased it, "A vote for Grant and Colfax in Iowa, is *not a true, honest, Republican, vote*, unless it contain[s] the clause striking the word 'White' from the Constitution."[45] Decisive emphasis came in the final hour of the campaign, a report that Grant himself had said that he "hoped the people of Iowa, whose soldiers achieved such immortal renown in the field, would be the first State to carry impartial suffrage unfalteringly. It had gone down in other States, but he trusted that Iowa, the bright Radical star, would proclaim by its action in November that the North is consistent with itself, and willing to voluntarily accept what its Congress had made a necessity in the South."[46]

TABLE 6.
PEARSONIAN CORRELATIONS AMONG REPUBLICAN PARTY
AND BLACK SUFFRAGE VOTES IN IOWA COUNTIES, 1857-68

	Grant (1868)	Merrill (1867)	Wright (1866)	Stone (1865)	Black suffrage (1857)
Black suffrage (1868)	.91	.82	.82	.79	.64
Grant		.88	.85	.77	.56
Merrill (1867)			.89	.81	.59
Wright (1866)				.87	.51
Stone (1865)					.62

In the balloting Grant indeed carried Iowa handily, winning 61.9 percent of the popular vote and all but six counties.[47] As anticipated, black suffrage lagged behind, its majority of 56.5 percent slim enough to lose fourteen counties in addition to those it and Grant lost in common. Yet Grant's support and support for the amendment correlate at .91, indicating that the effort to make black suffrage part of a GOP "straight ticket" succeeded exceptionally well. Or, to put it another way, Grant's coattails proved long enough to carry the burden assigned them. None of the counties carried by Grant's Democratic opponent approved black suffrage, and in the fifteen counties carried or tied by Grant but in which the amendment failed, the General's majorities were simply too small to lift black suffrage above 50 percent.

But Grant need not be given all the glory, as Table 6 indicates. The .64 correlation between the black suffrage referendum of 1857 and that of 1868 reveals that the basic configuration of the prosuffrage vote had congealed before the Civil War. Stone's 1865 election brought the suffrage vote closer to its final form, his support correlating .79 with that for the 1868 referendum and winning what would turn out to be an almost identical percentage of the popular vote, 56.4 as compared to the amendment's 56.5. What occurred between the 1857 and 1868 referenda was a massive shift all across Iowa, wherein the prosuffrage percentage in *every* county rose dramatically, the altitude of its final approval very much related to how progressive its vote had been in 1865 and, to a lesser extent, in 1857. So-called multiple regression analysis, employing only the votes of the eighty counties for which 1857 returns exist, reveals that Stone's support is nearly four times more useful than the 1857 support in predicting the configuration of the suffrage vote in 1868. Together, however, the two votes predict fully 72 percent of that final configuration. Thus the influence of Grant's coattails—as well as any independent effect of the Wright and Merrill elections—could not have been more than 28 percent.[48]

Principle or merely "policy"? How much of this Republican triumph reflected a genuine respect for the doctrine of racial quality? It is easy to be cynical, to point out that Republican campaign spokesmen, even the most progressive such as Ed Russell, universally denied they favored interracial "social" equality, a disclaimer any nineteenth-century scholar will recognize as the standard response of almost all racial progressives—everywhere—to the ubiquitous specter of miscegenation. Whether in individual cases these were truly honest denials, or whether political compromises with a profoundly racist society at large, to give them any weight at all is to make meaningless any distinction between the relatively enlightened and the unenlightened, leaving the larger question unanswerable.

More serious evidence against authentic equalitarianism is the initial failure of the effort to eliminate the word "white" from the constitutional article on make-up of the state's General Assembly. It was not, after all, until 1880 that this last discriminatory clause in the organic law of Iowa was overthrown. But it *was* overthrown, the main problem of its enemies being to get it brought before the people as a referendum. Once Iowa's voters had a chance to pass judgment on this egregious racist survival they disapproved it by a solid 63.5 percent.[49]

Perhaps the best evidence on the side of principle is Iowans' unique hostility to racial segregation in the postwar years. The popularly elected, Republican-controlled Iowa Supreme Court ruled against "separate but equal" public schools in 1868 and again in 1875. It did the same for public accommodations, specifically in the case of a segregated Mississippi River steamboat, in 1873. As legal historian Robert Kaczorowski observes: "What is interesting about these cases is their twentieth century definition of equal rights . . . in an era when separate but equal was not generally regarded to be a denial of the civil rights of Blacks. . . . Thus Iowa, at least the Iowa Supreme Court, took a position far in advance of most other states during that period by ordering the integration of these facilities."[50]

There seems, in short, no reason to ascribe the entire victory in the black suffrage campaign of 1865-68 to the pragmatics of Congressional reconstruction. Careful investigation, already underway, of grass-roots voting in the referenda of 1857, 1868, and 1880 should provide further enlightenment. I must admit that at present my own preference in the way of a summary description of Iowans' majority attitude in 1868 is that unintentionally offered by a state official a half-century later. To him the only defect of the original 1857 constitution was its *"unpatriotic* discrimination against the black race" (italics mine).[51] No radical Republican could have put it in terms more appropriate for the Iowa generation that fought the Civil War.

III

Was this Republican progressivism reflected in spheres other than black political equality? Was the reconstruction era characterized by some version of a reform program with which the Iowa GOP sought to hold its popular majorities?

One scans in vain the party's campaign platforms of 1860-76 for pronouncements on such questions as municipal and educational reform, mine safety, prison reform, health, sanitation, ecology. And while Republican governors' messages that opened all sessions of the General Assembly contain much recommended legislation of an advanced character, it is doubtful whether these gubernatorial remarks can be considered a party program. "Constitutionally," as Mildred Throne notes, "the Governor of Iowa does not have much power. Politically, his power varies with the individual; if he is adept at playing politics and is a member of the inner ring of the party, his influence can be very great."[52] But the three governors of the period—Stone, Merrill, and C. C. Carpenter—were simply the first of a dignified procession of decent and well-liked men who had come out of the war with high military rank. None was politically adept, none was personally powerful within the state's Republican hierarchy. Their biennial messages were viewed simply as their personal opinions of what the assembly would or should consider.

And yet, despite the absence of what could pass for a formal program, a close examination of two areas—labor and social legislation—suggests that in the 1860s and 1870s the Republican Party of Iowa was indeed a progressive instrument. Iowa's first employers' liability law was approved in 1862, the first regulation of dangerous machinery in 1866, the first mine labor law in 1872. Important wage legislation dates from the early seventies, and the regulation of child labor from 1874.[53] Similarly, in the social domain the most important advances in legislation between 1851 and the Progressive era occurred during and immediately after the Civil War. Certain statutes exempting soldiers' dependents (and later their widows and orphans) from the Elizabethan mercies of the ordinary welfare laws, in the considered opinion of their student, "represent the first real, humane thought given to the subject of poor relief in the history of Iowa." The General Assembly in 1866 established state control of three homes for soldiers' orphans, ten years later opening them to other children. In 1868 the same legislature that gave second approval to black suffrage also was particularly responsive to the needs of the handicapped. It authorized public funds for care of the severely retarded, a second state mental hospital, and a new school for the deaf. In addition, it liberated persons other than veterans' dependents from exclusively indoor relief, and introduced free medical care for the indigent. In 1873 blacks and married women, heretofore excluded from welfare, were brought under the appropriate laws.[54]

Since the Republican Party's control of the General Assembly never fell below 65.7 percent between 1862 and 1876—except for the 1874 session, when the party had to share the house with a coalition Anti-Monopoly Party—these important advances may appropriately be considered a Republican triumph, a product, we should suppose, of some general feeling among GOP assemblymen that a mandate had been laid upon them to bring institutions into congruence with nineteenth-century realities.

A few last questions remain. Since the Iowa GOP emerged from each phase of the fight over black suffrage with its popular majorities intact, unlike the Republican experience in most other Northern states in this period, were there also other dissimilarities? In Iowa did the GOP *not* relax its commitment to progressive reform, did the GOP *not* turn to business interests for its funding and to systematic use of the patronage for its power? Was the Liberal Republican movement *not* in Iowa a self-sacrifice by a disillusioned minority in reaction to corrupt machine politics?

With respect to a declension of progressive reform, the evidence is inconclusive. There seems indeed to have been some slowing of momentum in the area of social legislation; the provisions of Iowa's *Code of 1873* appear to have remained the basic statutes until at least the Progressive era.[55] But because progress often involved capital expenditures, some diminution of effort could only have been expected, given the long recession of 1873-97. In the realm of labor legislation, on the other hand, the 1880s was a particularly fruitful decade, a product, so we are told, of pressure from organized labor.[56]

There is no ambiguity, however, about the emergence of machine politics in Iowa. The political defeat of James Harlan in 1872 delivered the Republican Party of Iowa—and thus, practically speaking, Iowa herself—into the hands of a patronage machine of considerable power and longevity. In the 1870s, at least, its most influential leaders were three: Grenville Dodge, the famous western railroader and friend and adviser to Republican Presidents; James S. ("Ret") Clarkson, Des Moines postmaster and co-owner and until 1888 editor of the Des Moines *Register*, the state's leading newspaper, in later years also a minor power within the national Republican Party; and U.S. Senator William Boyd Allison, who would in time become, on the basis of tenure and personality, one of the most powerful and respected men on Capitol Hill.[57] It is convenient, and probably correct, to see in the Dodge-Clarkson-Allison triumvirate the origins of the political establishment that would dominate Iowa Republicanism until deposed by insurgent Progressives in 1908.

How much this machine's deference to railroads and other corporate interests may have represented a corrupt sellout is another question entirely. According to Edward Younger, who is pretty Beardian about all this, "Republican politics in Iowa had become in large measure the politics of railroads and other business." But Mildred Throne dissents, suggesting that "the traditional concept of the Dodge-Clarkson-Allison ring as dominated by the railroad interests is too simple an interpretation." She notes that when the clique's handpicked incumbent, Governor Carpenter, gave a speech that mentioned the ultimate necessity of a nationalized railway system, Ret Clarkson privately took mild exception, but printed the entire text in the *Register*. Carpenter subsequently won renomination and reelection. He then formally urged the 1874 General Assembly to pass what became the famous

Iowa Granger Law. But, it might be observed, so did the most recent campaign platform of the state's Republican Party.[58] Either the reigning establishment felt forced to coopt the regulation issue from those dissidents and Democrats organizing as Anti-Monopolists, or—more probably—its control simply did not extend to suppression of the widespread agitation for railroad legislation, whose adherents numbered not only insurgent agrarians but the business communities of Iowa's larger Mississippi River cities.[59] And like all successful establishments, the Dodge-Clarkson-Allison machine viewed itself as having not just one constituency but a number of them, with interests not always in singular harmony.

As for the Liberal Republican cause in Iowa, that is most appropriately seen as merely another congenial fusion by which the state's hopelessly backward political minority, the Democrats, sought to overcome its numerical handicap. Insofar as it involved real Republicans it apparently reflected only dissatisfaction with President Grant, with corruption in Washington, and with Congressional reconstruction. Its most important Republican leaders, ex-congressman J. B. Grinnell and General FitzHenry Warren, both were long-standing personal friends of the Liberal presidential candidate, Horace Greeley, neither was strongly radical, neither was particularly "in" with the state's establishment.[60] The only authentic disillusionment with the Iowa GOP on the part of either them or likeminded men was that it remained fiercely devoted to Grant, the great personification of national triumph in the Civil War, and to Reconstruction, the political effort to consolidate that triumph.

As a political effort itself, of course, the Liberal cause was a flop in Iowa. That very next year, however, the Anti-Monopolists cut heavily, if temporarily, into the Republican Party's customary legislative majority. The significant difference between the two movements is that while the first embraced an explicit criticism of Radical Republicanism, the second confined itself to economic issues, revealing again that same special sensitivity, a political conditioning by war and the memory of war, that helped win Iowans to the political equality of blacks.

NOTES

1. William Gillette, *The Right to Vote: Politics and the Passage of the Fifteenth Amendment* (Baltimore, 1965), pp. 26-27. In 1849 Wisconsin held a referendum on black suffrage, the negative result of which the state's supreme court reversed in 1866. See Leslie H. Fishel, Jr., "Wisconsin and Negro Suffrage," *Wisconsin Magazine of History* 46 (Spring 1963): 184-85, 195-96. It appears to me, if not to Fishel, that the framers of the 1849 referendum purposely burdened black suffrage with a handicap almost identical to that featured in the Iowa referendum of 1857, discussed below. Therefore, the court erred in reversing the outcome of the Wisconsin referendum, and it can by no means be considered an electoral victory, even retrospectively, for franchise extension.

2. James C. Mohr, *The Radical Republicans and Reform in New York during Reconstruction* (Ithaca, 1973), Chap. ix.

3. Leola Nelson Bergmann, "The Negro in Iowa," *Iowa Journal of History* 46 (January 1948):12-15.

4. Morton M. Rosenberg, *Iowa on the Eve of the Civil War: A Decade of Frontier Politics* (Norman, Oklahoma, 1972), Chap. iv.

5. Erling A. Erickson, *Banking in Frontier Iowa, 1836-1865* (Ames, Iowa, 1971), pp. 84-85.

6. Carl H. Erbe, "Constitutional Provisions for the Suffrage in Iowa," *Iowa Journal of History* 22 (April 1924): 185-207; Benjamin F. Shambaugh, *The Constitutions of Iowa* (Iowa City, 1934), pp. 236-50, 270, 305, 307-08, 314-15, 325.

7. Erbe, "Constitutional Provisions," pp. 201-03. Since all published references to this election apparently include an improper computation of the vote, it is worthwhile noting that "no" ballots cast in the referendum were to count for nothing; the true number in opposition to extending the franchise was to be calculated in a manner that can be expressed as

$$(C_f + C_a) - S_f = S_a$$

where C_f = number of votes cast for the new constitution
C_a = number of votes cast against the new constitution
S_f = number of votes cast for striking the word "white" from the suffrage article
S_a = total number against striking the word "white" from the suffrage article

To calculate the percentage in favor of black suffrage, then, for the entire state or any subdivision thereof, the formula is

$$\frac{S_f}{(C_f + C_a)}$$

The correct data source is Iowa Secretary of State, Election Records (microfilm copy, University of Iowa Library, Iowa City), reel 1. All Iowa voting proportions mentioned in the present article have been calculated from this official source.

8. This brief analysis differs from that included in Robert R. Dykstra and Harlan Hahn, "Northern Voters and Negro Suffrage: The Case of Iowa, 1868," *Public Opinion Quarterly* 32 (Summer 1968): 207, which is inaccurate in several respects. In fact, the senior author of that early essay (written in 1965) feels impelled to warn that it embraces a number of other errors of fact and interpretation. A list of smaller errata would be tedious. Its misstatements about the 1857 referendum and its improper grasp of the important black legislators question are corrected in the present discussion, while its seriously flawed analysis of disaggregated 1868 data, in part a methodological problem, will be remedied in new material I am preparing for publication.

9. Gillette, *Right to Vote*, p. 147.

10. V. Jacque Voegeli, *Free but Not Equal: The Midwest and the Negro during the Civil War* (Chicago, 1967), p. 127.

11. Leslie H. Fishel, Jr., "Northern Prejudice and Negro Suffrage, 1865-1870," *Journal of Negro History* 39 (January 1954): 24; Gillette, *Right to Vote*, pp. 26-28.

12. Harlan Hahn, *Urban-Rural Conflict: The Politics of Change* (Beverly Hills, Calif., 1971), p. 26.

13. Rankings calculated from William F. Fox, *Regimental Losses in the American Civil War, 1861-1865* (Albany, N.Y., 1889), pp. 532-33, and U.S. Bureau of the Census, *Historical Statistics of the United States: Colonial Times to 1957* (Washington, 1960), p. 13. Interestingly enough, the erroneous assessment of Iowa's relative manpower contribution was widely believed within the state in 1865 and was used as legitimation of black suffrage. For editorial examples see Eldora *Sentinel*, June 28, 1865; Independence *Guardian*, July 19, 1865.

14. Fox, *Regimental Losses*, pp. 534-35.

15. Column one figures taken from ibid., p. 535. Column two figures calculated from Svend Petersen, *A Statistical History of the American Presidential Elections* (New York, 1963), pp. 38, 40, and *The Tribune Almanac* (New York, 1862-64), passim. (For the off-year elections of 1861 through 1863 voting returns used were those reported in the *Almanac* for the top of the ticket. No returns at all were given for Illinois, Indiana, Michigan, and New Jersey in 1861, or for Indiana in 1863; the GOP averages for these states ignore missing data.) Column three figures calculated from U.S. Bureau of the Census, *Negro Population in the United States, 1790-1915* (Washington, 1918), p. 44, and *Historical Statistics*, p. 13. In columns two and three apparent ties actually have been resolved by carrying out the percentage computations to another decimal point.

16. Figures of columns one through three taken from Fox, *Regimental Losses*, pp. 526, 528. Column four figures calculated from ibid., pp. 526, 536.

17. G. Galin Berrier, "The Negro Suffrage Issue in Iowa–1865-1868," *Annals of Iowa*, 3rd Ser., 39 (Spring 1968): 244-45, 253; Des Moines *Weekly Register*, June 21, 1865.

18. J. C. Knapp to Laurel Summers, June 30, 1865, Summers Papers, Iowa Historical Museum and Archives, Des Moines; Davenport *Daily Democrat*, July 15, 1865; George Wallace Jones to Summers, August 30, 1865, Summers Papers.

19. For the situation in Wapello County, for instance, see Thomas C. Woodward to Samuel J. Kirkwood, July 25, 1865, Kirkwood Papers, Historical Museum and Archives; Ottumwa *Weekly Courier*, August 17, 24, 1865. According to Edward Russell this gambit failed miserably except in Davis County, "for long years bitterly Democratic and never more than barely carried by the Republicans." Davenport *Weekly Gazette*, September 6, 1865.

20. Berrier, "Negro Suffrage," pp. 247-49; Herbert S. Fairall, ed., *The Iowa City Republican Manual of Iowa Politics* (Iowa City, 1881), pp. 70-72.

21. Iowa Census Board, *Census Returns of the ... State of Iowa as Returned in the Year 1865* (Des Moines, 1865), pp. 118-21.

22. Both repositories are of course continually adding to their newspaper collections. I speak here of their holdings as of December 1973.

23. I am indebted to Lowell J. Soike for helping construct this scale and for completing the basic analysis of the material.

24. Anamosa *Eureka*, September 28, 1865.

25. Joshua Tracy to Kirkwood, October 4, 1865, Kirkwood Papers.

26. Des Moines *Weekly Register*, June 21, 1865; Eliphotel Price to Kirkwood, October 15, 1865, Kirkwood Papers; R. Noble to Kirkwood, November 9, 1865, ibid.

27. These conclusions are, of course, only tentative and may not survive sophisticated statistical inquiry employing county and township data. See Table 4 for estimates of nonvoters, 1864-67, which are in turn based on biennial tabulations of electors printed in Iowa Secretary of State, *Historical and Comparative Census of Iowa for 1880* (Des Moines, 1883), p. 228. Calculating total eligible voters would normally be a matter of straight-line interpolations between adjacent census counts, but in this instance more complexity is involved. Since actual enumerations of those entitled to vote were made in the spring of every other year, interpolations for annual fall elections are based on increments of 25 percent and 75 percent from each census figure. The 1864 and 1865 estimates presented a special problem, in that the 1863 and 1865 enumerations failed to include nonresident soldier voters. I have assumed that eligible soldiers voted in the same proportion as eligible civilians.

28. Sioux City *Journal*, October 28, 1865.

29. Benjamin F. Shambaugh, ed., *The Messages and Proclamations of the Governors of Iowa* (Iowa City, 1903-05), III: 84-87; *House Journal* (1866), pp. 644-45; *Senate Journal* (1866), pp. 574, 635-36. The party-identifications of assemblymen are given in Des Moines *Weekly Register*, January 10, 1866.

30. *House Journal* (1866), pp. 227, 545, 643, 645-46. Reps. Walden and Rogers were erroneously listed as voting.

31. The members' characteristics are given in Eleventh General Assembly of Iowa, *Rules and Statistics of the Senate and House of Representatives* (Des Moines, 1866), pp. 13-16. The roll calls used were (1) to postpone indefinitely HF 121, "A bill for an act to extend the elective franchise [to women]"; (2) to table HF 205, "A bill for an act to legalize and regulate the sale of intoxicating liquors"; and (3) to adopt SF 59, "A bill for an act to require owners of threshing machines to guard against accidents." *House Journal* (1866), pp. 273-74, 306, 719.

32. Des Moines *Weekly Register*, June 27, 1866; Fairall, *Manual of Politics*, pp. 72-73.

33. Davenport *Weekly Gazette,* June 20, 1866; Fishel, "Northern Prejudice," p. 17.

34. William Delbert Heinzig, "Iowa's Response to Reconstruction: 1865-1868" (master's thesis, Iowa State University, 1971), Chap. iii; Thomas H. Benton, Jr., to John F. Lacey, October 14, 1865, Lacey Papers, Historical Museum and Archives; Benjamin F. Gue, *History of Iowa* (Des Moines, 1903), III: 12-14; Fairall, *Manual of Politics*, pp. 75-76.

35. Gue, *History*, III:15; Fairall, *Manual of Politics,* pp. 77, 79; Davenport *Weekly Gazette*, June 26, 1867, May 13, 1868.

36. Edward Younger, *John A. Kasson: Politics and Diplomacy from Lincoln to McKinley* (Iowa City, 1955), Chap. xi. Once Kasson broke with the Radicals, of course, he was fair game for an opportunist with good credentials. But to call General Dodge's nomination over Kasson a victory of "personalities, not principles"—as does Stanley P. Hirshson, *Grenville M. Dodge: Soldier, Politician, Railraod Pioneer* (Bloomington, Ind., 1967), p. 135—is to obscure the real political issues.

37. Gue, *History*, III: 1-2; Charles E. Payne, *Josiah Bushnell Grinnell* (Iowa City, 1938), pp. 183-84. Leland L. Sage suggests that Grinnell, like Kasson, might have been purged for an insufficient display of Congressional Radicalism, but the acceptance speech of the man who defeated Grinnell for the GOP nomination, according to the local newspaper, "endorsed the course taken by Hon. J. B. Grinnell in Congress." Furthermore, a confidential report on the district convention at which Grinnell lost the nomination makes no mention of this being a factor. Mildred Throne, however, notes that Grinnell's negative stand on the Fourth Resolution might well have contributed to his failure to get the GOP gubernatorial nomination in 1867. Sage, *William Boyd Allison: A Study in Practical Politics* (Iowa City, 1956), p. 83; Des Moines *Weekly Register*, June 20, 1866; J. M. Hedrick to William Penn Clarke, June 25, 1866, Clarke Papers, Historical Museum and Archives; Throne, *Cyrus Clay Carpenter and Iowa Politics, 1854-1898* (Iowa City, 1974), p. 92.

38. William Salter, *The Life of James W. Grimes* (New York, 1876), pp. 280-82, 287.

39. L. W. Hart to Kirkwood, November 15, 1865, Kirkwood Papers; S. P. Adams to Kirkwood, November 20, 1865, ibid.; H. A. Wiltse to Kirkwood, January 13, 1866, ibid.; Kirkwood to Grenville M. Dodge, January 15, 1867, Dodge Papers, Historical Museum and Archives; Sage, *Allison*, p. 75.

40. J. H. Wallace to Summers, October -, 1866, Summers Papers; Fairall, *Manual of Politics*, pp. 77-78; Dan Elbert Clark, "The History of Liquor Legislation in Iowa, 1861-1878," *Iowa Journal of History* 6 (July 1908): 343-44.

41. Iowa Falls *Sentinel*, October 23, 1867; Charles Stanley to Lacey, January 22, 1868, Lacey Papers.

42. *House Journal* (1866), pp. 644-46; ibid. (1868), pp. 402, 514-15, 527, 566. The 1868 House actually held two roll calls on black suffrage, one approving the joint resolution embracing impartial suffrage and the five lesser amendments, the other being SF 186, which provided for submission of these six amendments to the people as referendum questions. The only apparent difference between the two roll calls are the names of those absent or not voting. I therefore considered a "yes" vote on either of these an approval of black suffrage, which allowed me to remove several names from the unclassifiable category. Two Republicans who served in both the 1866 and 1868 sessions, Charles Dudley and P. C. Wilcox, voted "yes" on the black legislators question in 1866, but failed to vote in 1868. I classified them as ultra radical in both sessions. Mathias J. Rohlfs served as a Republican member in 1866 and returned two years later as

a People's Party representative. He was ultra radical in 1866, and but for his party change would have been so designated in the second session. For 1868 party identifications see Davenport *Weekly Democrat*, October 31, 1867; Des Moines *Weekly Register*, January 15, 1868.

43. *Senate Journal* (1868), p. 385; Davenport *Weekly Gazette*, April 8, 1868.

44. Peter Melendy to "Dear Sir," August 12, 1868, Kirkwood Papers; John S. Runnels to William E. Chandler, September 14, 1868, Chandler Papers, Library of Congress, Washington; Melendy to Dodge, September 16, 1868, Dodge Papers.

45. Davenport *Western Soldier's Friend*, October 24, 1868.

46. Paraphrase of Grant's words in conversation with "one of the most prominent politicians of this state," in Des Moines *Weekly Register*, November 4, 1868.

47. According to my interpolation, only 13,013 Iowans entitled to vote failed to do so, yielding a turnout for the 1868 presidential contest of 93.7 percent. Exceptionally high turnouts for presidential elections continued to be the norm in late nineteenth-century Iowa. See Walter Dean Burnham, "The Changing Shape of the American Political Universe," *American Political Science Review* 59 (March 1965): 16n.

48. Technically, what is predicted is the variance in the support for the 1868 black suffrage referendum. The relative importance of the 1865 and 1857 votes is based on beta coefficients of .715 and .193, respectively. The Wright, Merrill, and Grant elections were not entered into the regression analysis because all intercorrelate with one another in excess of .70, aggravating the problem of multicollinearity to the point of making it impossible to distinguish between their individual effects on the 1868 referendum.

49. J. Van der Zee, "Proposed Constitutional Amendments in Iowa, 1857-1909," *Iowa Journal of History* 8 (April 1910), 92n.

50. Bergmann, *Negro in Iowa*, pp. 50, 53-54; Robert J. Kaczorowski to the author, December 6, 1973 (quoted by permission).

51. Johnson Brigham, *Iowa: Its History and Foremost Citizens* (Chicago, 1918), II:448. Brigham was state librarian in 1918.

52. Throne, *Carpenter*, p. 133.

53. E. H. Downey, *History of Labor Legislation in Iowa* (Iowa City, 1910), pp. 3, 9, 17, 35, 97, 111, 172.

54. John L. Gillin, *History of Poor Relief Legislation in Iowa* (Iowa City, 1914), pp. 92, 97-99, 118-19, 197-202, 233-34, 245, 267.

55. The first major innovation after the codification of 1873 was the establishment in 1898 of a board of control to supervise all charitable and correctional institutions. Gillin, *Poor Relief Legislation*, p. 181.

56. Downey, *Labor Legislation*, pp. 3-4.

57. This is the view, expressed independently in 1955 by both Mildred Throne and Edward Younger, now generally accepted by scholars of the era. See Throne, "The Liberal Republican Party in Iowa, 1872," *Iowa Journal of History* 53 (April 1955): 122; Younger, *Kasson*, pp. 240, 242, 277.

58. Ibid., p. 242; Throne, *Carpenter*, pp. 134, 159-60, 176-77; Fairall, *Manual of Politics*, p. 91.

59. George H. Miller, *Railroads and Granger Laws* (Madison, Wisc., 1971), Chap. v.

60. Throne, "Liberal Republican Party," pp. 122, 135-36; Payne, *Grinnell*, pp. 256-59; Brigham, *Iowa*, I:370-71. Both had unsuccessfully sought GOP gubernatorial nominations, Warren in 1863 and Grinnell in 1867.

HISTORIOGRAPHICAL NOTE
AND SUMMARY OF SOURCE MATERIALS

The essays in this volume serve at least three significant historiographical purposes. They broaden our understanding of the reconstruction era as a whole by revealing a good deal of what was going on among Republicans in the North; they offer an opportunity to assess in a new context many of the exciting theories advanced in recent years by reconstruction historians whose attention has been focused primarily upon Washington and the South; and, because of their state-level perspectives, they raise a number of new questions about political developments during the postwar period. Considering how appropriately these essays seem to fit into the larger patterns of reconstruction history, it is striking to realize that in most cases these essays are the only extant syntheses of the material they deal with and the only discussions in depth of the problems they confront. Why reconstruction historians for the last half century have devoted so little effort to understanding activity at the Northern state level is not an easy question to answer, especially since that was not always the case. Almost anyone who has investigated reconstruction historiography will know that William A. Dunning sent students to examine state politics in the South and that the studies they produced are still read, cited, evaluated, and reevaluated. Far fewer students of reconstruction, however, will remember that Dunning, one of the first historians to view as a whole both the reconstruction process and the reconstruction era, also sent students to investigate political developments in the Northern states as well. The books those students produced about the North were on balance less solid as historical monographs than the books that Dunning's students wrote about the South, largely owing to Dunning's own conceptualizations of the era and hence to what his students were looking for. But the limited value of those studies hardly explains why historians paid so little attention to the

Northern states for the next fifty years, notwithstanding the new perspectives and striking interpretive reversals that characterized the rest of the field.

One of the reasons why historical attention may have remained so fixed upon the national capital and upon the Southern states seems fairly obvious. Historians have always been drawn to a dramatic tale and seldom in our history have we had more drama than during the reconstruction years: a presidential impeachment, three momentous constitutional amendments, military rule, the impact of emancipation, and the struggles of a defeated society trying to reach some accommodation with the confusing edicts of the victors. But all of these great stories were breaking at Washington or in the South. By comparison, whatever was going on in the North probably seemed dull, even though, as these essays make clear, that was hardly the case.

A second reason may have stemmed from the fact that the few early scholars who did glance at the Northern states tended to emphasize the sordid aspects of what they saw rather than offer a balanced analysis. Textbooks created an impression that the only politicians in the North who were not bosses or the willing pawns of bosses were the Liberals, and they were fools. Even a very good student, when asked to name a politician at the state or local level in the North, would probably have known only William Marcy Tweed of New York and one or more of the spoilsmen who later rose to national prominence under President Ulysses S. Grant. The interpretations of reconstruction put forward by Charles A. Beard and Howard K. Beale linked the greedy Northern industrialist to the venal political hack and thus further solidified this stereotypical view of the postwar North. Except for the scholar with a peculiar fascination for American politics at their worst, in other words, the Northern states during the period of reconstruction did not appear to be a very attractive field for research.

A third reason for the long-term neglect of the Northern states may partly, perhaps, be related to shifts in the nature of the American political system itself. During the twentieth century generally, and especially during the last four decades, policy-making power in all fields has shifted quite rapidly away from the states to the federal government. The states, as a result, have more and more frequently looked like awkward vestiges of an earlier political structure, and it may have become either consciously or unconsciously more difficult for modern historians to take the states as seriously as historians in Dunning's day took them.

A fourth, and major, reason for the creation of an historiographical gap in our knowledge of the Northern states in the context of reconstruction lies in the nature of the questions that scholars asked about the period. Historians, as David Donald pointed out in *The Politics of Reconstruction, 1863-1867* (Baton Rouge, 1968), were for a long time involved in debates over whether Lincoln's plan for reconstruction should have been followed, whether black suffrage was ill advised, and whether the corrupt political practices of the Southern Radical state governments could ever be outweighed judgmentally by whatever positive actions those regimes either took or represented. In more recent years the role and the fate of black people as active historical agents has been a dominant theme in the literature of reconstruction. Though development of that theme was overdue, it, too, tended to keep the focus on Washington, where decisions about the freed people's status were made, and on the states of the South, where an overwhelming majority of black people lived. Only recently, as Richard Curry pointed out in his 1974 overview of Civil War and reconstruction historiography, "The Civil War and Reconstruction, 1861-1877: A Critical Overview of Recent Trends and Interpretations" *(Civil War History* 20 [September 1974]: 215-38), have historians begun to ask, or perhaps to frame in modern terms, the kinds of questions to which these essays address themselves both implicitly and explicitly.

A final probable reason for the relative neglect of political developments at the Northern state level is linked to the nature of most of the sources to which historians have ready access. A majority of published autobiographies, memoirs, letters and the like deal with figures of national, not state, prominence, and when a politician was prominent at both levels at various times in his career, as was frequently the case, information about the national phase of his life usually predominates. While the records of Congress for the reconstruction era are readily available to scholars all around the country, complete runs of state legislative journals and documents for the same period are surprisingly scarce. Recourse to a particular state's own library or to the Library of Congress was all too often necessary. Voting and census records at the county, ward, and precinct levels have only become available to scholars in a convenient form since the adoption of computer technology and the founding of central storage and service centers like the Inter-University Consortium for Political Research. Local newspapers are generally scattered all over a state and usually unmicrofilmed. In short, the sources readily available to historians of the reconstruction period have made it difficult to undertake the kind of study represented by the essays in this volume.

With this last point in mind, it seems appropriate to identify briefly the chief categories of material that students who wish to pursue some of the leads opened up by these essays or to write about related matters in other states will want to seek out. This volume is necessarily limited and by itself cannot fill the rather substantial historiographical gap that now exists in our knowledge of activity at the state level in the North. Indeed, one of the purposes of this volume is to stimulate further research and writing.

A sense of the general context of reconstruction helps tie events at the state and local level to the period's broadest trends. David Donald's compilation for the Goldentree series, *The Nation in Crisis, 1861-1877* (New York,

1969), is the best bibliography to consult for major studies published before the late 1960s. Most of the more important works that have appeared since then are cited and discussed in Richard Curry's "The Civil War and Reconstruction, 1861-1877: A Critical Overview of Recent Trends and Interpretations," (*Civil War History* 20 [September 1974]:215-38). Once beyond broad context, however, the student who wishes to pursue the kind of leads suggested by the essays in this volume must begin piecing together scattered bits of information from disparate sources.

One place to start is with the old standard multivolumed state histories, where they are available. Many of these are filiopietistic in the extreme, organized around implicit assumptions to which historians no longer subscribe and very revealing of their age. But they are not without value and can be mined for surprising amounts of solid data. The authors of the essays in this volume continued to find useful such venerable studies as William T. Davis, ed., *The New England States: Their Constitutional, Judicial, Educational, Commercial, Professional and Industrial History* (4 vols., Boston 1897); James Sullivan et al., eds, *History of New York State, 1523-1927* (5 vols., New York, 1927); Alexander C. Flick, ed., *History of the State of New York* (10 vols., New York, 1933-37); Clarence W. Alvord, ed., *The Centennial History of Illinois* (5 vols., Springfield, 1918-20); Alexander M. Thomson, *A Political History of Wisconsin* (Milwaukee, 1900); and Benjamin F. Gue, *History of Iowa* (4 vols., New York, 1903). There also exists for nearly every state at least one single-volume narrative history, often aimed at the required course market, which can be of some value in getting one's bearings in a state whose history is unfamiliar.

State histories can be supplemented with the histories of cities and counties. The half century beginning roughly in 1880 and ending roughly in 1930 was something of a golden age for local history writing, and much of the work produced then, though now somewhat quaint in tone, was especially rich in social and economic material. Two Connecticut studies, Richard C. Atwater, *History of the City of New Haven* (New York, 1887), and J. Hammond Trumbull, ed., *Memorial History of Hartford County, 1633-1884* (2 vols., Boston, 1886), are prime examples of this vast, underused body of literature. Others may be searched out in the notes to these essays and in card catalogues.

After state and local history, biography is another general category of material worth examination. Many of the political figures of mid-nineteenth-century American history have been the subject of biographies, including a certain number whose major activities took place in Northern statehouses. As pointed out earlier, biographies can be frustratingly skimpy on information of direct interest, but they can also add invaluable bits of detail. Many biographies are cited in the essays in this volume; students should refer to those notes not only to see which ones proved most helpful but also to see how the materials were used.

In addition to biographies, there are a number of useful autobiographies and political reminiscences. A. K. McClure's *Old Time Notes of Pennsylvania* (2 vols., Philadelphia, 1905) is but a single well-known example of this type of resource. Others are cited throughout this volume. All must be read, however, with a wide-eyed appreciation of the fact that the author will virtually always remember his own motives as pure, his own friends as statesmen, and his own stand on any controversy as the one that time has justified.

While there is a great deal of monographic literature that is tangentially related to this kind of research, only a few books, including Felice Bonadio's *North of Reconstruction: Ohio Politics, 1865-1870* (New York, 1970), and James Mohr's *The Radical Republicans and Reform in New York during Reconstruction* (Ithaca, 1973), address directly some of the kinds of questions raised in this volume. Edward C. Kirkland, *Men, Cities, and Transportation: A Study in New England History, 1820-1900* (2 vols., Cambridge, 1948); Horace S. Merrill, *Bourbon Democracy in the Middle West, 1865-1896* (Baton Rouge, 1953); Paul Kleppner, *The Cross of Culture: A Social Analysis of Midwestern Politics, 1850-1900* (New York, 1970); and George H. Miller, *Railroads and the Granger Laws* (Madison, 1971) are all examples of monographs that treat a subject relevant to these essays in either a geographically or a chronologically broadened context. Many such works could be listed and a large number of seminal monographs are cited in the notes to these essays. The most frequently referred to by the authors here are David Montgomery, *Beyond Equality: Labor and the Radical Republicans, 1862-1872* (New York, 1967), for an understanding of labor problems and their political implications during the era, and William Gillette, *The Right to Vote: Politics and the Passage of the Fifteenth Amendment* (Baltimore, 1965), for an interpretation of how the national problem of black suffrage was thrown into Northern state legislatures.

Two other types of secondary source material should not be neglected. One of these is the extensive article literature on these and related subjects. While Leslie Fishel's "Northern Prejudice and Negro Suffrage, 1865-1870" *(Journal of Negro History* 39 [1954]: 8-26) is important for its general perspective, articles more often afford an intensive examination of a closely defined subject. Searches through the annual indices of the state historical journals appropriate to a particular research project will generally be rewarded, as the notes to these essays attest. Second, students should not overlook unpublished dissertations. Many older ones, some of which are cited in this volume, can be borrowed on interlibrary loan. Most newer ones, like Phyllis Field's "The Struggle for Black Suffrage in New York State, 1846-1869" (Cornell University, 1974) and Joanna Cowden's "Civil War and Reconstruction Politics in Connecticut, 1863-1868" (University of Connecticut, 1975) are available on microfilm.

Although a great deal of information can be pieced together using the various categories of secondary information already suggested, the student will discover sooner rather than later that recourse to primary source material is essential to research on the kinds of questions raised in the essays in this volume. The three most important types of primary materials for these purposes are state records, extant newspapers, and personal manuscript collections.

The records of the states themselves, and of their various agencies, are invaluable and underexploited historical resources. Superintendents of public instruction, health departments, penitentiaries, asylums, secretaries of states, state treasurers, and many similar officers and agencies were required in most states to submit annual reports on the operations under their control. Usually published as legislative and/or executive documents, these reports are a nearly inexhaustible source of reasonably reliable evidence on a host of subjects. Messages of governors offer an annual overview, however slanted, of developments as viewed from the executive mansion. The debates of the many state constitutional conventions held during the reconstruction period provide some of the best data available on grass roots grappling over truly fundamental concerns. Obviously essential also, though sometimes disappointing, are the journals of the state legislatures themselves. Journals are occasionally very enlightening, but as a general rule they record little or no debate, sometimes omit divisions of a vote by individual members, and almost never reveal what went on in committees. Moreover, they are written, of course, without reference to political parties. For all of these reasons, it is highly desirable to supplement official state records with materials drawn from the second major category of primary source materials appropriate to this kind of research: extant newspapers.

Most newspapers of the reconstruction era were baldly partisan and must be read with that in mind. This characteristic does not necessarily make them undesirable, however, for the purposes of the modern historical researcher. Party positions are rarely veiled and party heroes are given detailed coverage, including occasional reprints of speeches and public letters on state affairs. In the absence of compelling knowledge to the contrary, students will generally find the best coverage of state level affairs in the newspapers published at the capital itself, though during the time legislatures were actually in session many out-of-town papers, including the more prominent urban dailies in any given state, usually sent reporters of their own to watch the statehouses. Local organs should not be overlooked, however, and the notes to these essays demonstrate how much can be done with the materials local papers contain. Robert Dykstra's analysis of Iowa press opinion is especially illustrative in this context. Students can check Winifred Gregory, ed., *American Newspapers, 1821-1936* (New York, 1937), and other similar reference publications to determine which of the newspapers that might be helpful for a particular project are available in his or her area either physically or on microfilm.

Manuscript collections constitute a third type of primary source material appropriate to research at the Northern state level during reconstruction. Personal papers, however, are not quite the stock-in-trade for the state historian that they are for the scholar whose focus is on national affairs. For one thing, the papers of people whose influence did not extend significantly beyond the borders of a single state tend not to have been saved or collected in the same systematic way that the papers of those who made it to Washington more frequently were. Moreover, even though many correspondents from back home wrote to nationally prominent figures, they generally tended to discuss how they felt about national issues rather than state ones; after all, that was probably the occasion for the letter. If a local chieftain wanted action at the state level he likely wrote his man in Springfield or Albany, not his United States Senator, and his letter never survived. Still, there are enough exceptions, such as the Henry Crapo and the Austin Blair collections for Michigan, to more than make the rule. Students could start with the collections cited in these essays and then try to widen their searches wherever possible.

While the categories commented upon in this note were the ones that proved most valuable to the authors of the essays in this volume, a large number of other sources can also be brought to bear imaginatively upon subjects like these. The field is remarkably open. It was hoped that these essays would fill at least a part of the historiographical gap which has arisen during the last half century. That gap is rather wide, however, and it was also hoped that this volume, by offering fresh perspectives and by suggesting some new questions, might encourage additional research.

THE JOHNS HOPKINS UNIVERSITY PRESS

This book was composed in Press Roman text
and Thunderbird display type by Naecker Brothers
Associates, Incorporated, from a design by
Patrick Turner, and printed on 55 lb. Old Forge Litho F paper.
It was printed and bound by
The Maple Press Company.

Library of Congress Cataloging in Publication Data

Main entry under title:

Radical Republicans in the North.

  Bibliography: pp. 194-200
  1. Republican Party—History. 2. State governments
—History. 3. United States—Politics and government—
1865-1877. I. Mohr, James C.
JK 2357 1865.R33   329.6'009   75-36939
ISBN 0-8018-1774-9